d20.
P3F

THE TEST OF TIME

THE BEST OF TIMES

THE TEST OF TIME

An Essay in Philosophical Aesthetics

Anthony Savile

CLARENDON PRESS · OXFORD
1982

Oxford University Press, Walton Street, Oxford OX2 6DP
London Glasgow New York Toronto
Delhi Bombay Calcutta Madras Karachi
Kuala Lumpur Singapore Hong Kong Tokyo
Nairobi Dar es Salaam Cape Town
Melbourne Auckland
and associates in
Beirut Berlin Ibadan Mexico City Nicosia

Published in the United States by
Oxford University Press, New York

British Library Cataloguing in Publication Data

Savile, Anthony
  The test of time.
  1. Aesthetics
  I. Title
  700'.1   BH39

  ISBN 0-19-824590-4

Library of Congress Cataloging in Publication Data

  Savile, Anthony.
  The test of time.
  1. Aesthetics. I. Title.
  BH39.S3   111'.85   81-18728
  ISBN 0-19-824590-4   AACR2

Typeset by Phoenix Photosetting, Chatham, Kent
Printed in Great Britain
at the University Press, Oxford
by Eric Buckley
Printer to the University

Acknowledgements

The author is grateful to the Editors of *The British Journal of Aesthetics*, *The Journal of Aesthetics and Art Criticism*, and *New Literary History* for permission to reprint material that originally appeared in these journals.

Analytical Table of Contents

Introduction

> To works of which the excellence is not absolute and definite, but gradual and comparative; to works not raised upon principles demonstrative and scientific, no other test can be applied than length of duration and continuance of esteem.
>
> Samuel Johnson; *Preface to Shakespeare.*

As long as the arts have attracted interpretation and criticism it has been common, though not universal, practice to appeal to the judgement of time in distinguishing accurate from inaccurate estimates, in buttressing authorial optimism against public scepticism, and in setting the individual artist in his rightful place in the pantheon of the great.[1] It is a practice that has received little reflective scrutiny, either being assumed to be obviously viable or else being dismissed as naïve and unimaginative. And this raises two questions in aesthetics, the provision of answers to which constitutes the main thread of this book. The first is how this device of criticism can have a reputable use at all, and the second is how far proper attachment to it may extend: whether, that is, it might be abandoned or whether it should be taken as an important, even fixed, element in our thought about the arts.

The position I advocate is straightforward. It is that if we are careful enough in our understanding of what it is for a work of art to withstand the test of time, and clear enough about what we claim for the work that does so, a sure legitimization of the practice may be found. Further I contend that unless we are prepared to trivialize our conception of art we have little choice but to endorse it as having a permanent position in art theory. In making out these claims I touch on many traditional themes of philosophical aesthetics, and the reader who decides that the general structure of my argument is excessively extended for the rewards it promises may want to concentrate on some of the more self-contained topics that I broach. I have therefore aimed to make what I say about the principles of critical interpretation, the nature of beauty and of depth, the ideas of excellence and stature, those of sentimentality and vulgarity, and the importance of the place that art may occupy in a man's life assessible quite independently of my guiding theme. On the other hand, because the views I develop on these subjects are often detachable from the over-all strategic end they serve, the reader's disagreement with me about the details need not always cast doubt on the validity of my central argument. That can be viewed as a structure that might stand even if some of the nuts and bolts that have gone into its making need replacing with better materials as our understanding of these various topics improves.

Lastly I should acknowledge that much of what follows is perforce concerned with questions of aesthetic value. To those acquainted with the drearier stretches of the subject this may come as an alarming admission: for with Nelson Goodman they may find that 'the emphasis on excellence in art has been partly to blame for the lack of excellence in aesthetics'.[2] But this truth—if it is one—cannot make that topic go away. At best it may put us on our guard against the ease with which it can be badly handled.

Chapter 1

The Test of Time

'His reforms in administration, judicial proceedings, financial and military organisation stood the test of time.' So speaks Rostovtzeff of the Emperor Diocletian.[1] But what exactly is meant by describing these reforms as having stood time's test? And what conclusions do we want to draw from their having done so? These two issues will occupy the present chapter. How we are to get to these conclusions from the simple-looking starting-point will take up most of those that follow.

I

The Premiss

Neither common parlance nor observation innocent of theory tells us more than a very little about what it might be for something to withstand time's test. We shall have to supplement that little dialectically, by choosing a description of the starting-point that looks as if it might justify kinds of inference we are inclined to base upon it. There will be nothing vicious about this procedure and there is no alternative to it. It leaves it entirely open whether such a derivation really can be effected. On the other hand it shows us a fair amount about what we must take ourselves to be talking about if the critical device I am concerned with is to be of any practical utility at all.

The first suggestion that comes to mind is that there is no more to passing the test than just surviving over a significant period. In their main lines Diocletian's reforms dominated the civilized world for several centuries and formed the basis on which the empire rested. Yet a moment's thought makes it clear that mere survival cannot be sufficient, and a second moment's reflection that when considered in relation to the arts it may not even be necessary either. I take sufficiency first.

In the case of Diocletian matters might have stood thus, though in fact they did not. After its original introduction the

administrative and military organization that he instituted
might have come to determine the structure of the empire in a
merely token way, much as the orders of precedence set out in
Burke and Debrett give one only a token picture of the organization of English society today. In reality the empire might
have been controlled by different factors altogether, and while
Diocletian's reforms could still have enjoyed a lingering survival they would not then have merited Rostovtzeff's warm
appraisal. We should not be able to say of them that they had
stood time's test because we should not be able to conclude
anything about their merits from such merely token persistence.

The same reflection will apply to art. Think of some long-
lived carving, say one of the red granite crocodiles of the
Ptolemaic period that inhabit the Capitoline museums. These
stone beasts may well survive for centuries without attracting
the notice of more than a few idle visitors, and their longevity
will do absolutely nothing to secure them a place in the halls of
artistic fame. So once again we shall not say they stand the test
of time. Indeed, if the sheer physical persistence of an object
were all that were relevant there would even be some reason to
think that the longer a work of art survives the *less* worthy it is of
our attention, and that would quite unfit our test for critical
employment. For consider works which we associate with particular physical objects: painting, carved statues, drawings,
and the like. The finer they are the more insistently we demand
to see and touch them. Hence the greater their exposure to wear
and tear, to accident and decay. The Limbourg brothers' *Très
riches heures du Duc de Berry* exemplify this well. Exquisitely
illuminated pages, they are in constant demand with the visiting public yet are extremely delicate. Were it not for the
museum's discreet substitution of copies in their place, exposure to natural light would soon wreak havoc with their limpid
colours. Only because this substitution is practised are they
safe from a risk of destruction lesser works do not run. It follows
that if survival alone were what mattered the verdict delivered
by time would too often be in favour of the mediocre and the
downright inferior and not of the genuinely great.

In the case of Diocletian's reforms it was obvious that what
mattered was less unqualified survival than *effective* survi-

val—that was what earned the historian's esteem. Correspondingly, in the arts what we care about is not survival *simpliciter* but effective survival's analogue, persistence of the work in our attention. This idea will receive some comment in a moment, but first we can reduce the theoretical importance of unqualified survival even further by making out that in the arts it is not even a necessary condition of a work's passing time's test, let alone a sufficient one.

Concentrating first on the autographic arts, by which I mean those whose individual works are constituted of matter, consider Leonardo's lost (probably destroyed) painting *Leda and the Swan*. Gone though the original canvas is we can still see Bugiardini's copy of it in the Borghese gallery, and while that is of little interest in its own right it does permit something of Leonardo's painting to survive. On its testimony, and on that of others—Raphael's drawing, the one in the Louvre, and the interpretation at Wilton—we can come to a tentative judgement of Leonardo's own work so that it may, despite its actual non-existence, still hold a place in our attention.

If another example is wanted imagine an exponent of auto-destructive art tracing his finest work upon the sands before the rising tide. The only record of his activity could well be photographic, and through this evidence we might reasonably aspire to sound judgement of his work. Maybe we would do better to confront the original and savour its passage (if only we could), but without that experience we are not at a total loss. Once more the work may survive in our attention without itself surviving.

In the allographic arts, where the existence and survival of the individual work is not tied to the persistence of any particular physical object, the case is parallel. A musical composition or a work of literature is extant as long as there remains available to us a causally appropriate method of constructing a true performance of it or of giving it a true reading. Here the rejected idea of simple survival has to be construed in terms of such persisting availability—already a large step away from any naïve suggestion about physical persistence—but it is still arguable that the loss of all means of reconstructing true performance or reading need be no bar to the work's passing time's test. Suppose for instance that some major composition of J. S.

Bach's had for some reason ceased to be available and was
therefore no longer extant. We need not also suppose that the
same holds true of some Busoni-like transcription of the work.
Nor must we suppose it impossible for a good musicologist to
get us to see what the original of Bach's would have been like
even though he could not reconstruct from the transcription an
accurate performance of the original. With his assistance, as
with that of Bugiardini, the no longer extant work might still
have some claim to survive in our attention.

Fanciful examples are of no importance in themselves, only
for what they show. And that, I take it, is a confirmation of my
assertion that the artistic analogue of the effective survival of
Diocletian's reforms is the work of art's survival in our attention. That, I claim, is a necessary element in the passage of
time's test, while survival strictly speaking is not, even though
for the most part only those things that do survive in the stricter
way survive time's test. None the less as far as logic goes that is
just a contingent matter.

Survival of art in our attention is an opaque notion about
which I shall not have much to say. Traditional discussion of it
as bearing on aesthetics has repeatedly insisted that there are
many reasons why a work of art may hold our attention and
that only some of them have any close connection with the
formation of reliable critical judgement. In particular our
attention must be 'aesthetic', given to the work 'disinterestedly', and 'for its own sake,' not for some extraneous reason. It
is, however, far easier to know what such terms as these exclude
than to give any positive and helpful characterization of them.
They would rule out attention given to a work solely on account
of its author's identity—say, to an obviously inferior Leonardo
or to an unrecognized masterpiece by Winston Churchill; they
would exclude vulgar curiosity about works which break price
records in the sale-room; also such interest in the monstrance of
Toledo Cathedral as is drummed up by the guides' revelation
that its surmounting cross is made of the first gold Columbus
sent back from the Indies. Only it is unclear what are the
principles one relies on to extend the list. Perhaps the most
satisfactory thing to say is that every ground of attention to an
object should be let in, as contributing to its 'effective survival',
that could pertinently bear on the formation of a critical estima-

tion of it as the work of art it is. That at any rate is how I shall take this notion here, and I shall pause over the stipulation only long enough to make four parenthetical comments.

(a) So glossed, the idea does not have the effect of allowing only those works of art to survive which are in fact correctly estimated or even enjoy high esteem. It is perfectly possible for our attention to be held for reasons which are relevant to the formation of critical estimation but for that estimate to be low or to be mistaken.

(b) The proposal guides us better than the negatively inspired examples in fixing the proper extension of the expression 'survives in our attention'. If we were ambitious and aimed at capturing its intension in this way too, then we should need to be confident that our ideas of the aesthetic as it applies to nature could be developed on a base that restricts itself to the arts. I myself do not find that an unattractive prospect and shall have something to say about one such derivation later on (Chapter 8 section VI).

(c) The suggestion also commits us to explaining what art itself is without reliance on an antecedently understood notion of the aesthetic. It is not evident that this is an impossibility. One might hope to introduce the two ideas simultaneously or else, more plausibly to my mind, proceed by first offering a recursive account of art and subsequently introducing the idea of the aesthetic on that base.[2] I shall have nothing to say about either project here.

(d) It is a welcome consequence of fixing the notion of the aesthetic in this way that it avoids any suggestion of formalism. The connection between our aesthetic interest in something and its involvement with matters of moral, emotional, and cognitive import may be as deep and inextricable as we like. This point is of much consequence and is extensively explored below. (See Chapter 5 *passim*, Chapter 7 section III, and Chapter 8 section VIII.)

To pass time's test, then, a work of art has to hold our attention for reasons that bear on its critical estimation as the work it is. To do this it must in particular hold our attention *under some interpretation*, and it seems clear that we have to say that the interpretation in point must be one that allows the work to be correctly perceived and understood. For supposing that we let in what we later come to recognize as a mistaken interpretation, since it could not found a justified estimation of the work the point of saying that under it the work had passed time's test would be nil. To the extent that we want survival *reliably* to underwrite evaluation we have to insist that the survival that counts must be under an interpretation that is appropriate to the work.

For the moment I shall attempt no greater precision than this. But it evidently gives rise to an issue that must occupy us deeply in due course. Can the interpretation that is allowed to be appropriate be one that varies over time? Shall we want to say, as many do, that at different times different ways of taking works of art may properly be recommended—perhaps as they accord better or worse with the cultural climate of the time—and consequently think that what survives for our purposes may have to take such changes into account? Or shall we say that proper interpretation is stable and liable to fade as time passes? The answers that we give to these questions are of the greatest importance, for not only do the alternative replies yield very different sets of works as withstanding time's test, they also force us to justify the inferences we hope to base on this premiss in different ways. Indeed it may turn out that on one of these alternatives justification of our critical practice is made impossible and has no worth. Such a consequence might itself have some weight in encouraging one choice here rather than another. (See Chapter 12 section I below.)

Description of the initial premiss cannot be left here. We know in advance that what survival must legitimize is an estimate of the surviving work as in some way exemplary; but, without further restrictions being imposed on what survival is, it will be easy to envisage situations in which a work of literature or music regularly attracts attention over a long period without our being in the least inclined to suppose it to be of high quality. This is far less bizarre than it sounds. Often we select a particular work for study because of the illumination it throws upon a different work, and we recognize that it is only by giving our attention (*aesthetic* attention) to the poorer piece that we come to form a just estimate of its successor's greatness. To take an example, we might agree with Auerbach that 'before Dante, vernacular literature—especially that of Christian inspiration—is on the whole rather naïve as far as questions of style are concerned, and that despite the influence of scholastic rhetoric'. But we also think that 'Dante, although he takes his material from the most living and sometimes from the humblest vernacular, has lost this naïve quality. He subdues every turn of expression to the gravity of his tone, and when he sings of the divine order of things, he solves his problem by using periodic articulations and devices of sentence structure which command gigantic masses of thought and concatenations of events; since antiquity nothing comparable had existed in literature.'[3] Now to make the truth of these sentences apparent to ourselves and others we may have to test what they say against early Christian vernacular literature, and then interesting though decidedly second-rate works may come to hold a place in our attention for their own sake which on their own they could scarcely justify.

To meet this difficulty we need only insist that the attention we give to the work that stands time's test be not only aesthetic attention but also be given to the work autonomously, in its own right, and not as a means to assist the evaluation and appreciation of other works. This clause has to be added because it cannot be assumed to be incorporated in the proper understanding of the aesthetic itself. For as we have just seen, the attention we give to the poorer work in learning to appreciate the greater must itself be acknowledged to be that; otherwise it could not serve its purpose. Hence even if some such phrase as 'disinterested' or 'for its own sake' should be useful to characterize that notion, we go further than this in requiring that the attention that the work receives be given to it in its own right as well.

One last preliminary matter calls for comment. I have spoken of survival without any attempt at quantifying it, and it would be natural to ask how much attention is going to be enough, and to inquire just whose attention is to count. To the former of these questions it ought to be apparent that there could be no determinate answer. Dr Johnson required the poet to have 'outlived his century, the term commonly fixed on as the test of literary merit'; Gustav Mahler apparently thought that fifty years would do when claiming that within that time his turn would come; Gertrud Schönberg is rather less commit-

tal, saying simply that posterity would best judge her hus-
band's work. ('When does posterity begin?', one might wonder.) The important things to note are that no one will be
impressed by a critic's reference to the passage of time unless he
sees the period during which the work has held our attention as
of considerable length, and that the critic will be wise not to
appeal to temporal considerations unless he thinks that his
reader will be struck by them. There would, after all, be no
point in making the claims we do in any other case. So it is
perfectly legitimate to leave this point vague. The work must
survive for a sufficient period. Nor should we forget that for the
most part our interest in time's test is not one that imposes a
yes/no answer to the question 'Does this work pass or fail?'
What we are usually concerned about is not what happens at
the margin, but how securely and how surely the work has
survived. At the back of our minds we have a belief that there is
a connection between the length of time over which the work
has held our attention and the degree of confidence we have in
our judgements of its merits, and this is one thing that has to be
explained.

This thought makes it easier than it would otherwise be to
say informatively who 'we' are whose attention to the work
determines the matter. As before there need be no precise
answer, but we know whose judgement, repeated or sustained
over time, we find to be significant. Our confidence in inferences that are based on survival will be greater according as the
work is widely appreciated over time by members of our common culture whom we recognize as artistically sensitive and
concerned with correct perception and judgement in the arts.
In particular we shall be impressed by the influence the work
has had on later artists and critics whose work we think important, and by the place the work holds throughout the community in its picture of its own culture and its own traditions.

Practising critics may be disturbed by the simplicity and
imprecision of these remarks. Such a reaction is not in point. In
the first place no question is yet begged about the uniform
accuracy of the perceptions that persons in this class make. For
it is the task of later theory to explain how we get from the
premiss that makes reference to this class of judgements to our
conclusions. Secondly there is nothing in what I have said that

denies that there may be much disagreement among members of the cultural core about the merits of any given work. Nothing said so far is incompatible with Schönberg's remark that 'I know after all, that the works which in every way arouse one's dislike are precisely those that the next generation will in every way like'[4] or with the common cynical view that the critic is often one whose responses to the arts are the bluntest. All that reference to a chosen class is meant to do is to point out that when we come to determine how well this work or that has stood the test we take into account the place that it holds in our culture, its degree of embeddedness, so to speak. Without reference to a core set of persons who give the culture its character, this notion of embeddedness would be empty.

The importance of the notion of degree of embeddedness that we attribute to the individual work will emerge later, especially when I discuss some corrupt forms of aesthetic judgement in Chapter 11. For the moment we may note its use in helping us to determine how well this work or that has survived the rigours of time, and make appeal to it in our final formulation of what it is for art to do so. In passing, we may also find it useful in disqualifying such things as many of the better-known and perennially enjoyed children's stories, or Nahum Tate's sugary version of *King Lear*, which practically replaced Shakespeare's version of the play in public consciousness for the best part of 150 years. It is only if we have a way of dealing with such cases as these, which might otherwise appear to be good candidates for secure passage of the test, that there is any hope of providing it with adequate legitimization. And what could we use to avoid these dangers other than a structured view of a culture, one in which some opinions carry greater weight than others? If there is no alternative to making this move, then we must expect it to surface in a decently articulated version of our starting-point.

The final formulation I propose then, is this. A well-chosen autographic or allographic work of art securely survives the test of time if over a sufficiently long period it survives in our attention under an appropriate interpretation in a sufficiently embedded way.[5] This condition will only be satisfied if the attention that the work is given is of a kind that generates experience relevant to its critical appreciation and attracts the

attention that is given to it in its own right. On the other hand, a
work of either sort will fail the test if, being sufficiently available, it does not fulfil these criteria. Note that these two alternatives, secure passage and sure failure, are not exhaustive. There
are many works of art which for one reason or another are never
even brought to the test. They are simply not available, being
lost or destroyed, damaged or obscured. With them I shall not
be concerned, nor for the most part shall I consider those works
we think of as failures. Accounting for the store we set by
success is taxing enough.

II

The Conclusions

In my introductory paragraphs I offered a rough and ready
description of the way we are inclined to use the information
that a poem or a painting 'lasts'. It helps us to sort out accurate
from inaccurate estimates of disputed works, and to assess their
stature. It assists us in buttressing our own assessment of works
we believe are not adequately understood and appreciated, and
to mitigate unfavourable criticism of them. That is a very
general way of putting it, and what is intended under such
heads can be more precisely put in terms of the conclusions we
draw from a work's success or its failure by our test, or from the
ways in which we compare one work against another in its
success or failure.

Success. (1) Where a work of art has securely passed time's test
we infer that it is a work of high quality. This vagueness in my
formulation is deliberate. There is no one scale of quality with
which we are concerned in our assessment of the arts, and
native intuition about the conclusions we draw from the fact
that a work has survived in our attention is not highly determinate. As before, precision can only come dialectically, with the
development of theory. However, while the phrasing I have
used in stating this first conclusion is pretty anodyne it is
certainly not empty. To be told that a painting or a poem is of
high quality or, as I shall sometimes say, is meritorious, is
clearly to be told something interesting about it. In the sequel it

is with the derivation of this conclusion that I shall primarily be concerned.

(2) Suppose a work of art that does pass time's test has at an early stage of its history been appreciated on the grounds that it displayed a particular aesthetic character, and that this is the reason traditionally advanced for thinking the work to be of merit. Then our inclination at a later time to appreciate the work for these same reasons will confirm the earlier judgements of the work. It is an inference of this sort that we use when, in a dispute about a work's aesthetically interesting features we say, in despair of present agreement: 'time will tell'. For here we assume that the same judgement made at a later date will show that our present opinion is well founded and is as objectively assertible as matters in this area can be.

(3) Closely related to (2) is the way in which we also use the judgement of a later time to disconfirm earlier opinions, and not simply to confirm them. When first heard, Beethoven's late quartets were assailed as unstructured and cacophonous. Later judgements insisting on their internal order and melody, and appealing to these features to support our own estimate of their merit, serve to show that the early views were mistaken. They point to a failing in the contemporary listener, and not in the composition. It is just such an inference as this that Hume uses in claiming that the reputation of a bad poet or orator will never be durable (see *Essay on the Standard of Taste*), for the assumption is that over time it is the correct judgement that becomes established. In this he is right, though not quite for the reasons that he gives.

Failure. If we contrast success in passing time's test with its contrary, failure, rather than its contradictory, lack of success, our conclusions are strictly parallel to those I claim we can draw from success.

(4) What fails the test of time we think of as lacking in some important dimension. This, like (1), is deliberately vague, and for exactly the same reason. The importance of (4) for the moment is just to remind us that we should beware of thinking that we may make an inference from failure to the absence of all merit in the work that fails. Often enough we come across forgotten works that are highly accomplished in their way, but

of which any claim to have been unfairly passed over would be ludicrous. So just as the first inference we made from success does not consist in attributing merit to a work in all dimensions, so failure does not comprehensively detract from it either.

(5) Earlier unfavourable criticism of a work may be confirmed by the failure of the work to pass time's test. The constancy with which particular criticisms are levelled against a piece of music or a poem may provide one with argument against the philistine objection that in these matters objectivity is not to be had. Failing the test is evidence, within the appropriate domain, that the work cannot but be seen in a certain dismal light.

(6) We may use failure as a corrective to earlier more favourable judgements. We may come to see our earlier enthusiasms as due to 'authority or prejudice', in Hume's phrase, and appeal to the effects of time to justify a change of view and protect it from any charge or caprice.

Comparisons. Two simple corollaries follow fairly naturally on these six points.

(7) If one work passes and another fails, and if there is any point to making comparisons between them—if they are not uninterestingly distant from one another—then we expect there to be a range of assessment within which it is informative to say that the first is a finer work than the second. It is sometimes suggested that such an inference is scarcely one of importance in aesthetics since that is above all the realm of non-practical choice, the realm in which we do not have to act. But this is misleading, since our preferences, and with them our choice of what we find it worthwhile giving our time to, cannot always be so easily be divorced from our more nearly practical choices about the light in which we regard important aspects of the world.

(8) Finally, when we know that a work of art has not securely passed time's test, then in the absence of any special explanation of why it has not done so, such as having been lost or having been available only to a very restricted group of people, we have some good ground for thinking that it is unlikely to be as worthy of our attention as those works which do have the stamp of time's approval. Unless there are special reasons for

not doing so, we should take non-passage of time's test as equivalent to failure, and in our reflections on it be guided by the inferences (4)–(7).

The effect of drawing these inferences is easily appreciable. First they enable us to test our critical opinions and assessments in a sure if not infallible way. Sure, because the inferences are supposed to be well-founded; but not infallible, because they are not conceived of as being other than defeasible in nature. Then also they have the effect of filtering out as accurately and definitively as may be the finer from the less fine, the greater from the less great, and in so doing reveal the true worth of the individual work. And they have, I claim, a large part to play in explaining why we think that the flow of time functions to secure some measure of objectivity in aesthetic judgement, an area in which it has often seemed notably difficult to come by.

If this line of thought is to impress as more than mere piety we shall have to meet sceptical challenges all along the way. We must rebut the Shavian contention that there is no more to be said on the subject than that 'one age's longing is another age's loathing' and that stabilities of taste occur only fortuitously. In particular the asymmetry of our preferring the later judgement over the earlier, on which appeal to 'the whirligig of time' rests, calls out for explanation and justification. Nevertheless it is heartening that the tradition of criticism in which we have all grown up places more stress on temporal considerations than we would expect if there were only a coincidental connection between value and survival. The very solidity of the tradition suggests that a preliminary readiness to take the verdicts of time seriously is not irrational. As Hume observed,

to say that an event is derived from chance, cuts short all farther inquiry concerning it, and leaves the writer in the same state of ignorance with the rest of mankind. But when the event is supposed to proceed from certain and stable causes, he may then display his ingenuity in assigning these causes; and as a man of any subtlety can never be at a loss in this particular, he has thereby an opportunity of swelling his volumes and discovering his profound knowledge, in observing what escapes the vulgar and ignorant.[6]

III

My description in section I of what it is to pass time's test
extended only to well-chosen standard examples of autographic and allographic art. It does not cover cases in which art
of either sort survives the passage of time without itself surviving, as may happen when what receives our attention is a copy,
or a colour print, or a plaster cast (as was the case with
Bugiardini's *Leda*, or the imaginary photograph of the equally
imaginary drawing by the Master of the Rising Tide). And
such cases are not just fanciful possibilities to which our sense of
intellectual neatness would like justifications of the inferences
to extend. In an age when, as never before, sensitivity to the
visual arts has come to depend so heavily on copies, colour
prints, and mechanical forms of restoration, it would be rash to
discuss the inferences without indicating how they might go
beyond the standard cases, for we can reliably surmise that
today, and progressively more so in the future, continued survival will often turn on the power of such intermediaries as
these at least as much as on that of the originals themselves.

A convenient way of finding a place for the non-standard
case is suggested by the way in which we tend to think about
restoration. Our usual rather simplistic way of viewing a
restored painting is to take it as a work whose visible surface has
deteriorated and which we save from further deterioration by
laying on more pigment. Much of the original often remains,
and restoration ideally takes the form of making good a certain
loss. Analogously in the case of a mosaic, a damaged pattern of
tesserae is restored to its pristine material and sensuous consistency by replacement of the missing stones. In these normal
cases it often happens that quite enough of the original remains
for us to have no hesitation at all about saying that the restored
work is the same one as that which was damaged. Yet not all
cases are normal and we must beware of refusing ever to think
of restoration in any other way, as we are reminded by Auguste
Proste's comment of the fate of Metz Cathedral: 'On voulait
réparer d'abord; on a été conduit ensuite à vouloir restaurer, et
aujourd'hui on démolit ce qui restait du viel édifice pour le
reconstruire entièrement.'[7]

Sometimes we cannot possibly say that restoration leaves us

with the work that existed before the repairs were carried out, and this is not only true of buildings that we view as works of architecture, but may hold of paintings or mosaic and of sculpture and carving as well. Think say of Leonardo's *Last Supper* in S. Maria delle Grazie. Practically nothing of the original surface has survived the ravages of creeping damp, and what we now see is almost entirely by later hands, largely those of the nineteenth-century restorers Cavenaghi and Silvestri (with more now to come). Or consider the restored mosaics of Galla Placidia in Ravenna, or S. Apollinare in Classe, where now probably no single original tessera remains. In neither case can we happily say that enough of the original still exists for us to view it. This being so, we need to treat these cases differently from those common ones of good restoration where the original work is indeed the work we admire.

In these abnormal cases, even though we do not want to say that the original survives we must admit that the restorer's labours permit it to survive time's test. In this respect such restorations are surely assimilable to Leonardo's *Leda* which survives through Bugiardini's copy. If possible it would be convenient to assimilate these cases to the standard allographic ones where in attending to one thing (a performance or a reading) we attend to another (to the work itself).[8] Then we should only need: (*a*) to specify what is to count as attending to the original (as we attend say to Mozart's *Don Giovanni* by attending to a performance of it), and (*b*) to say what objects will count as intermediaries of the right sort (akin to specifying what will and what will not count as a performance of the opera). Let us then consider the first of these demands.

It is clearly not necessary that the object we attend to should be a work of art in the same genre as that which survives, for my examples have shown already that sometimes in these cases what we attend to need not be a work of art at all. This might be said of the plaster cast and of the photograph. Yet what counts is not absolutely anything that conveys information relevant to the formation of crtical judgement of the original, for obviously we do not want to admit that the lost or destroyed works described by Vasari in his *Lives* survive time's test through his descriptions of them, or even that they might have done so in more florid and full Pateresque recreations. To let in photographs of paintings and rule out descriptions we might insist that we are only attending to the (autographic) original by attending to some distinct object which conveys its information about the former through the same sensory modality as that on which its master depends for its aesthetic effect.

Yet this provision is arguably overgenerous, for it would not exclude the following examples, any of which we might want to regard with suspicion: (i) Serlio's cut-away elevation of Bramante's *Tempietto*; (ii) Lord Burlington's and William Kent's reworking at Chiswick of Palladio's *Villa Capra*; (iii) interpretations of well-tried paintings as offered by Picasso in his version of *Las hilanderas* or by Degas's recreation in the Tours collection of Mantegna's Louvre *Crucifixion*; or (iv) (allographically) an English prose version of *Finnegans Wake*. Evidently further restrictions are needed.

One such narrowing of scope will be provided by insisting that there be sufficient structural affinity between master and mediating object. Thus it would always be a matter for discussion whether copy, or restoration, or photograph provided one with *enough* information of the right sort about the original to make it a good candidate. Nothing need be said about this use of 'enough' beyond what has already been said on a similar score before. What we are concerned with is how well the original would survive in such conditions, and accuracy and repleteness of the mediating object would certainly be relevant to the truth of the matter in individual cases, however puzzling it may be to judge it.

Further, it may be quite conceivable that one object should convey enough accurate information about another within the permitted sensory mode, yet not be suitable to afford us access to the original. This could happen where the structural affinities between the two are purely fortuitous. Then I doubt whether we should allow that the latter might survive through the former, and hence we might want to restrict the field still further by insisting that the intermediary be made either in the intention of conveying to us sufficient structurally relevant information about the master work (as in the case of a copy), or that it actually do so in part because of the causal role the original plays in its production (as in the case of photographs or plaster casts).

So it looks as if some sort of assimilation of non-standard autographic art to standard allographic cases might be viable. We have a fairly clear suggestion as to what kind of objects will do as intermediaries, and have allowed ourselves to say that it is by attending to them that we may count ourselves as attending to the original. Furthermore, we do not have in these cases any special difficulty about how it is that through our attention to Bugiardini's *Leda* Leonardo's work survives while Bugiardini's does not. For in that case our attention is not given to the copy autonomously and that, it will be recalled, was made a condition of the standardly-chosen work's passing time's test in the first place. Here we might say we attend to the original autonomously by attending to the copy with an eye to a reconstruction of the original, while the copy has little interest for us in its own right. But where master work and mediating object are both of sufficient stature then perhaps both might be viewed autonomously. Then both would survive in our attention given to the copy—but that is not a result that is always forced on us.

Nevertheless I doubt whether this approach is ultimately sustainable. It assumes too easily that we should accept that we are attending to the original in attending to the copy or the thoroughgoing restoration. And to many it will be clear that this is not true, for surely it is not to Leonardo's work that I attend when I look at Bugiardini's, even when I do so with an eye to forming an estimate of the original that inspired it. Similarly it seems hard to accept that in Ravenna I attend to the original mosaics when I study their laborious and accurate reconstructions. So for those who, like me, are unable to swallow this assumption another route must be found that bypasses this difficulty.

What we need to do is to acknowledge that there may be two ways in which a work of art may pass time's test. The first applies to standardly chosen autographic and allographic art as set out in section I. These works pass the test by surviving autonomously in our attention under an appropriate interpretation in a sufficiently embedded way. Secondly, if an autographic work is non-standard it may still survive, despite loss or destruction, by standing in the right relationship to a different object which satisfies the following five conditions:

  (i) it must provide us with experience in the same sensory mode as the original,

 (ii) it must provide us with sufficient structurally relevant information about the original to enable us to form a critical assessment of it,

(iii) it must be appropriately (intentionally or causally) related to the original through the history of its production,

(iv) it must receive such attention as generates autonomous interest in the original under its appropriately reconstructed interpretation,

 (v) through the satisfaction of condition (iv) it must enable our interest in the original to be sufficiently embedded in the sense previously explained.

While non-standard allographic survival is of far less importance than non-standard autographic survival we may note at least that a similar suggestion can be carried over to this sort of case too. My imaginary example of Bach's lost work could survive via the attention given to a series of performances of a different work (the transcription in my example) where the original's similarity of structure, suitably generated, is conveyed through the later work and to which we attend closely enough to say that we have an autonomous and sufficiently embedded interest in the original.

    The disadvantage of the proposal, even when refined and purified further than this, lies in its sheer clumsiness. Maybe the only thing to say about that is that non-standard cases are, though important, non-standard, and that it is no surprise that some more cumbersome explanation is needed to account for their capacity to pass time's test than is demanded by their more straightforward fellows. What matters is that we should have a workable way of allowing them to do so.

Chapter 2

Psychology, Progress, and Common Sense

In literature on art theory there is no shortage of attempts to span the gap between premiss and conclusion of the argument just set out. This chapter considers three of them, each of which is less than fully adequate to the demands of the problem. Recognition of their deficiencies should yield a clearer view than we yet have of what will count as a satisfactory treatment of the topic.

I

The crux of the issue lies in grounding the presumption that later well-entrenched evaluative judgements have a better claim on our acceptance than do earlier ones; and one common, and initially appealing, reaction to this thought takes the form of rejecting it outright. It declines the invitation to *ground* this presumption and undertakes instead to *explain* our willingness to make it. In effect it denies the legitimacy of our critical practice while stressing its practical inevitability.[1] Such a response is well discussed right at the start, because if correct it would dissuade us from giving ear to critical claims that invoke the test of time. We might, as it were, bow before time's verdict but be disinclined to see our doing so as more than a formal obeisance to the past. The test would then not be rationally justifiable, merely a convenient illusion.

How such a view can develop may be seen by reflecting on a remark by Reyner Banham about James Stirling's History Faculty Building in Cambridge: 'The sad thing is', he said, 'that Cambridge will eventually accept it as part of "the Cambridge tradition" and then no one will have the guts to pull it down when the useful life for which it was built has come to an end.'[2] To say why Cambridge will eventually accept the building as part of its tradition might involve either genuinely

aesthetic considerations or non-aesthetic ones. It would naturally best suit the purpose of someone intent on discrediting the
test of time to appeal to non-aesthetic matters here, and the best
device he is likely to find is one that is directly psychological in
cast. Thus he might argue that we simply get used to the
presence of salient buildings around us, that these buildings
have the forms they do for a host of different reasons, very few of
which are aesthetic, and that our habituation to them functions
by setting the standards we use in the formation of our consequent critical judgements about them. On this view, the later
judgement about a work of art is preferred to the earlier one
because over time we come to feel at ease with the works that
have contributed to the very formation of the standards by
which the later judgement is made.

I dare say that this view is sometimes accurate enough.
Undoubtedly our tastes are formed in part by acquaintance
with and habituation to what we have inherited from the past.
But as a general explanation it is inadequate because not all, or
even most, salient buildings are regarded with an equal measure of affection; and not every famous building has had a part to
play in the formation of our taste. Hence the psychology that
this explanation affects is far too undiscriminating to produce
the result we are promised.

None the less a refinement of what is essentially the same
idea is less open to this objection. It is a truism of popular
psychology that men attempt to establish a firm sense of themselves in relation to the rest of the world. In doing this the
individual attaches himself in his thought to one group of men
and distinguishes himself from others, and one important condition of achieving this attachment satisfactorily is that he
should establish himself as rooted on a past from which he can
see himself as having sprung and which he can view with some
affection and pride. Now one way in which we satisfy this
general need in a wider cultural setting than the local or
national one is through the arts. We are heirs to the renaissance, to the *âge de gloire* and the *siglo d'oro* and our confidence in
our present may be powerfully strengthened by seeing ourselves rooted in this past. Such an observation may be true
enough, but in the hands of someone who is sceptical about the
legitimacy of our critical inferences it can receive a curious

twist. He may say that far from it being a mere matter of good fortune that we can satisfy these psychological needs by appeal to some independently establishable excellence in the arts, it is the very force of the identity-supporting drive that provides us with what we deem excellent in works of art. We tend, that is, to select quite arbitrarily from what we inherit some salient works to exemplify the ideas of human excellence in which we wish vicariously to participate, and we then use these capriciously selected models to provide appropriate means of effecting our attachment to the past. What other explanation can be given for the astonishing fact that despite the ravages of wars, fires, economic catastrophes, bad quality materials and the like, we still retain masterpieces of the arts from almost every age? Surely it is not just that the masterpieces have survived, when had things been slightly different we might have lost them. Rather it must be that we shrewdly select as masterpieces works which are among those that have survived the vicissitudes of time, and which particular buildings, paintings, and statues these are is a matter for our decision and not in any way fixed by the past itself.

The upshot is twofold. First, we should not worry too much about the view that future generations will take of us. Their own need for psychological security will ensure that independently of aesthetic considerations they identify, in our legacy to them, masterpieces as great as Abbot Suger's cathedral at Saint Denis or Michelangelo's dome at St. Peter's—Stirling's History Faculty Building perhaps, or Centre Point, or the Centre Pompidou. Secondly, time's test reveals itself as an illusion, for the fact that certain objects hold a place in our esteem over time is now explained in purely psychological terms. Consequently the problem set out in the last chapter simply disappears: not solved, but dissolved. The passage of time does not select or help us to discern the best in an impartial way at all. Its judgement operates entirely by designating what is to count as a masterpiece, and fixes this up on an easy *ad hoc* basis. It may be convenient and psychologically inevitable that we do this but we cannot hope to justify the practice.

Although this model may enjoy some plausibility in accounting for our attachment to certain works of the past, it would be ridiculous to accept is as offering a general explanation of our artistic history. First, it suggests that no properly aesthetic reasons may be given in saying why those works which do funtion as our historical models should be the paradigms they are. Even if we were to allow that at some time in the past some buildings—the pyramids, say, or the Acropolis—have become fortuitously established as salient, the theory would still be unable to account for the necessity of referring later works to these models in order fully to account for the interest that the later monuments hold for us. A full acceptance of the psychological thesis would lead us to see the history of art as discontinuous, whereas what we in fact observe about it is its continuity. The development of architecture, painting, and sculpture becomes incomprehensible unless we see later works as referring in their aesthetic to earlier models, and this is something which the dissolutionist is forced to deny.

My criticism here is not that what we are invited to believe is inconceivable, but that the explanation it gives us of the known facts would in its own terms be less satisfactory than the explanation it invites us to reject. Once we understand the Vitruvian setting we can see why Bramante's architecture is so great an achievement, and once we set Borromini's building into the context that was formed by Bramante, we have no difficulty in saying why it should occupy the historical place it does. These references to tradition the dissolutionist asserts to be irrelevant, but all that he puts in their place is an arbitrary selection of paradigms, and an arbitrary selection with absolutely no explanatory power.

The force of this argument is even stronger when we recognize that it applies as much to startling innovation in the arts as it does to understood continuities. Take, for instance, the introduction of reinforced concrete into ecclesiastical architecture by Anatole de Baudot at St. Jean de Montmartre (rue des Abbesses). While not imitating Gothic church builders, Baudot none the less worked in his new material according to his understanding of their reasoning (as mediated by the perception of Viollet-le-Duc), and our judgement of St. Jean will be defective if it ignores this fact.[3] Similarly with novel work that explicitly aims at repudiating tradition. Only an understanding of what it is that is rejected can permit us to appreciate the work for what it is, and to explain and justify its place in art history. Psychologism must deny this fact.

Secondly, there is an evident submerged incoherence in the position just outlined which should undermine even the initial plausibility I granted it. The view undertakes to explain certain facts about the arts without any appeal to aesthetic thought itself. It simply assumes the untenability of such modes of thought. In making this assumption, though, it recognizes the existence of a social institution called 'art', yet subsequently it denies the coherence of the kind of consideration we shall need to rely on to explain what sort of institution this is. Thus acceptance of the psychological thesis threatens to deprive us of the very thing it sets out to illuminate.

Thirdly, if pursued fanatically and by itself the psychologistic suggestion is apt to make nonsense of our ways of thinking about artistic practice. Immediately we reflect on it, it must be apparent that the artist has to be thought of as critic, in the production of his own work. At each stage of his work he confronts and solves problems which prior choices in his work and its setting force upon him. His solutions cannot therefore be thought of as arbitrary, since they are arrived at in the light of internalized concerns and constraints derived largely from the tradition in which he works. If we fail to follow him in his thought our understanding of his work is thwarted. Yet development of the present thesis implies that as time passes the artist's own productions may justifiably come to be judged by different standards than those by which the work was made. About such an idea it has been justly said that 'a work of art would become utterly dependent for its sense on the traces of other [i.e. later] records of consciousness—a mere correlate',[4] and were such a view to become widely accepted it would be natural to expect the artist himself eventually to think of his engagement with his medium more as a kind of pointless shadow-boxing than as authentic struggle with the Muse. The intellectual labour of art is thus inevitably set at a discount, and the invitation that is offered is to abandon it altogether.

The practical consequences of accepting this invitation are, I believe, only too apparent in the work of those who have in fact embraced it. It may also be no idle fancy that sees its effects in the devastation we have so carelessly wrought on some of our loveliest cities. It is hard to deny that the London we know was a finer and more human city in the 1860s than it is today, and just as hard to deny that the wonderful Rome of the 1870s, the garden city of the Villas Ludovisi, Doria Pamphili, Medici, Spithover, and Borghese, was aesthetically superior to the spoliated town that now exists. One may wonder whether these sad changes could have come about except against the background of philistinism that set aesthetic concerns at nought, and thought of them either as quite vain or else as easily satisfied in the way it is here suggested they might be.

The view of time's test as some sort of confidence trick that we play on ourselves is untenable, then, and it challenges us to find a better. Although I have been harsh with a position that many readers will never have found even marginally plausible, it starts out from observations which we shall do well to bear in mind as we go along. They are that our sense of ourselves is connected with our past and with our attitudes to it, and further that there may well be elements of change at work in the formation of our standards of taste. Only, we should beware of constructing out of these truths an aesthetic that is arbitrary, or of deriving an art history that is discontinuous.

II

A second attempt on the problem appeals to the idea of progress in the development of the arts. While it has not recently enjoyed much favour, at times it has seemed so obvious a fact that the arts do progress that our subject cannot fully be treated without discussing it. Even if in the end we do not find the claim attractive, the question may still arise whether it is not an assumption of its reality that underlies our willingness to draw the inferences involving time that we do. If that were indeed so we should have both an explanation of these inferences and a way of judging with what little degree of seriousness they should be taken.[5]

Historically speaking, progress has been discerned in two apparently distinct areas, in the development of art itself and in the development of taste. Thus, concentrating on the artist and his work both Pliny and Vasari have drawn a picture of art history as a steady progression of the arts towards the fulfilment of a specific goal, a picture that might almost be epitomized in Leonardo's comment that 'it is a wretched pupil who does not surpass his master'. On the other hand, concentrating more on the spectator, Burke and Shaw assume a parallel development in public taste. Quite properly, though, these two areas are not kept sharply apart in their writings, and a brief argument will show how inseparable they are.

Consider a famous passage from Vasari:

Those masters whose Lives we have written in the second part made substantial additions to the arts of architecture, painting and sculpture, improving on those of the first part in rule, order, proportion, design, and style. If they were not altogether perfect they came so near to the truth that the third category, of whom we are now to speak, profited by the light they shed and attained the summit of perfection, producing the more valuable and renowned modern works.[6]

If we allow, with Vasari, that Masaccio's painting is more nearly perfect and more highly developed than Giotto's, we shall be unable to account for its greater value and renown unless we impute to Masaccio's public a superior taste to that which we attribute to Giotto's. For suppose there were no improvement in taste accompanying the alleged improvement in painting, then we would expect the public standards of taste which acclaimed Masaccio's work to have judged Giotto fairly harshly. But as we know this was not the case. Giotto's contemporaries judged his work as perfect as Masaccio's contemporaries judged his.[7] And if there had truly been no development of taste from the first period to the second, accompanying the progress of art itself, how could we explain the new work's establishing itself as more valuable and renowned than the old? By the old standards the new work could scarcely be even understood.

Conversely, we could not properly understand the idea of progress in taste without relying on the parallel idea of progress in the products of the arts themselves. In his Preface to *Three Plays for Puritans* Shaw wrote: 'I hate to think that Shakespear has lasted 300 years, though he has got no further than Kakoleth the Preacher, who died many centuries before him: or that Plato, more than 2000 years old, is still ahead of our culture. We must hurry on: we must get rid of reputations: they are weeds in the soil of ignorance! Cultivate that soil and they will flower more beautiful: but only as annuals.' Clearly he thought that we could develop taste ('cultivate the soil of ignorance') and thereby provide an impetus to actual artistic progress even though in the end its finest flowers are destined to fade. And it is hard to see how taste could improve in the absence of exemplars to give substance to its higher standards. For it is only by acquaintance with the finer work that our perception of the weaker work's defects takes firm root. In the abstract, judged against a standard of taste whose canons are only ideal, those very standards would have little chance of being recognized as genuinely progressive rather than merely aberrant.

So the development of taste and of the arts themselves must go hand in hand: 'as the arts advance towards their perfection, the science of criticism advances with equal pace',[8] and once this is acknowledged it may appear obvious that a later public will naturally be in a better position to make a sound judgement of the true worth of an early work than were its contemporary admirers. If it requires a more highly developed sensibility than was previously available to appreciate the full value of the modern work, how can we deny that a man possessed of such sensibility will make sounder judgements than his predecessors about earlier work? Also it may seem clear that works which have attracted the admiration both of earlier and of later generations are works of high quality, and that the more highly perfected our taste is at any time, the better able we shall be to guard against error in judging of our contemporaries. So it might initially be supposed.

The form of these condensed and rhetorical arguments must not be misunderstood. No claim is made that the arts have in fact progressed or that because they have done so we have an easy validation of the inferences we base on temporal considerations. It is rather that *if* we say with Pliny, Vasari, Burke, and Shaw that there has been progress in the arts, we shall easily find ourselves committed to a correlative progressive development of taste. Once this move is made, the attraction of time's test to men of sensibility is understandable enough.

It would be nice to evaluate this train of thought independently of the truth of its main assumption. For the best rebuttal of it takes the form not of denying that there is progress in the arts, but of insisting that even if there is it cannot be made use of in the way outlined. To mount such an argument, however, a clearer view is needed of what progress might amount to, and rather than attack head on I shall approach my target via two alternative conceptions of what progress might be, each one exemplified in famous anecdotes found in Book XXXV of the younger Pliny's *Natural History*. The first is contained in his story of Zeuxis' grapes and the birds:

It is recorded that Parrhasius entered into a competition with Zeuxis, who produced a picture of grapes so successfully represented that the birds flew up to the stage buildings; whereupon Parrhasius himself produced such a realistic picture of a curtain that Zeuxis, proud of the verdict of the birds, requested that the curtain should now be drawn and the picture displayed; and when he realised his mistake with a modesty that did him honour he yielded up the prize saying that whereas he had deceived birds, Parrhasius had deceived him, an artist. It is said that Zeuxis also subsequently painted a child carrying grapes, and when birds flew to the fruit with the same frankness as before, he strode up to the picture in anger with it and said 'I have painted the grapes better than the child, as if I had made a success of it as well, the birds would inevitably have been frightened off.'[9]

We may understand the idea of progress on which this tale turns to be that a picture is to count as more nearly perfect than another if it approximates more closely than its rival to a goal which is held invariant, and the achievement of which makes no appeal to psychology, or, to the extent that it does, to nothing in psychology that varies at different times. Thus a painting might be thought perfect if it presented us with a replica of natural appearances, where success is determined by some natural (psychologically neutral) test like avian behaviour, and progress is measured in terms of successive degrees of approximation to that goal.

On such an interpretation, appeal to a supposed progress in the arts could not sustain the various arguments I stated above. For even if we insist that psychology must not enter into the statement of the goal we cannot disregard the position of the critic who makes a judgement about the individual work's proximity to this ideal. For instance, when Vasari claims that he 'may safely say that art has done everything that is permitted to an imitator of nature, and that it has risen so high its decline must be feared rather then further progress expected',[10] he unjustifiably assumes that no theoretical difficulty besets his belief that he is in an adequate position to say that a perfect fit between representative painting and its objects has finally been achieved with the execution of Michelangelo's *ignudi*. But this assumption is quite unwarranted, as the following consideration shows.

We have already noted that Giotto's contemporaries judged his work to be a perfect exemplar of natural painting. Similarly with Masaccio's public, though we presume they may have noticed those defects in terms of which Giotto fell short of Masaccio. Vasari, likewise, sees Masaccio's shortcomings and judges them to be made good in the work of Michelangelo, Raphael, and Leonardo. Yet what Vasari cannot guard himself against is that his own taste might be superseded, and on the presumption that taste does in fact steadily progress he ought to admit that his own taste will probably be judged deficient by his successors—and rightly so judged. It is only if the judgement that the goal of perfection is achieved can be made from an atemporal vantage point that Vasari can found *in his own theory* the highest praise he bestows on his contemporaries. But it cannot, because Vasari, no less than the rest of us, is a creature of his own place and time.

This objection might be rebutted if there were any reason to think that the progress of the arts and taste would in fact terminate with Michelangelo, independently of the personal judgement of perfection that we are inclined to make. On the interpretation of the doctrine of progress I have given, however, there could be no available ground for such a supposition. In consequence the presumed fact of progress, so understood, could not underwrite the inferences it is supposed to. For even if such a conception of progress might sustain the thought that a later judgement is better placed than an earlier one to attain correct assessment of artistic merit, this is little consolation once it is realized that such assurance is only given subject to the reservation that we shall always be left in ignorance of how close the later assessment of the work actually comes to the truth, and that our present judgement of a work's excellence will possibly be overtaken by that of our successors.

Perhaps these obstacles to connecting the idea of time's test with that of progress arise simply from the naïve idea of progress I have picked on, and that a more sensible view—and one more faithful to those who have held a genuinely developmental view of art—would escape these strictures. Shortly before the story of the birds, Pliny introduces us to the unforgettable Crotonian maidens and in doing so makes use of quite a different paradigm of art:[11]

Zeuxis is criticised for making the heads and joints of his figures too large in proportion, albeit he was so scrupulously careful that when he was going to produce a picture for the city of Grigenti to dedicate at the public cost in the temple of Lacinian Hera he held an inspection of the maidens of the place paraded naked and chose five for the purpose of reproducing in the picture the most admirable points of each.[12]

What is notable here is that Zeuxis is no longer seen as aiming at an ideal which is imposed on him by a relentless Nature, but that he is shown as setting out to improve on what Nature presents him with. And clearly any improvement that he introduces into his art must be an improvement according to an ideal which it is up to him, Zeuxis, to choose. This thought was already present in Cicero's *De oratore*, and had taken firm hold in the literature by the time that Proclus came to comment on Plato (notably in *Comm. in Tim.*, II 81c). More recently it has received support from the great Austrian art historian Alois Riegl, who maintained that 'art never can be and never is intended as an imitation of Nature, but is a form of competition with her, that is aims at a representation of Nature. In art', he goes on, 'men reproduce nature as they would have her be, as she exists in their imagination. Now we can appreciate how it may be said that the art of mankind has always been ideal [*idealistisch*].'[13]

Now this change in the idea of what perfection in the arts might consist in clearly brings with it a different idea of what progress in the arts might be (though such a view does not, of course, have to be associated with a progressive view of the arts). No longer do we have to think of that in terms of a linear movement towards some goal whose achievement we can never be sure we have accomplished. Rather we may think of it as the gradual working out in the arts of a dominant ideal, an ideal which may change from time to time in the light of our recognition that the tasks it sets may have been fulfilled.

Thus, to follow an example that Vasari gives in the Preface to the *Lives*, if we think of classical Greek sculpture as setting itself the task of achieving a natural likeness of man, it makes perfectly good sense not only to say that Polyclitus improved on the rigid forms of archaic work, and that Praxiteles improved on the work of Polyclitus, and subsequently Lysippus on that of Praxiteles, but also that by the time Lysippus had died, that ideal had been achieved. We choose the ideal, and we are the only possible judges of when it has borne fruit: consequently we are not faced with the problem that I said would face Vasari on the earlier account of progress. Problems about making correct judgements are subject now only to the usual theoretically uninteresting difficulties and uncertainties that beset aesthetic assertions. They are not, as before, rendered irresoluble.

However, while concentration on the Crotonian maidens yields a more attractive view of possible artistic progress than does its counterpart, it is no better placed than the other to secure those inferences it hopes to base upon it. Before, they looked misleadingly easy to justify; now they do not even offer the illusion of being supported. The reason is simple. We have, for the sake of greater realism, moved away from a linear picture of progress to a pluralistic one. Progress is discerned at most in the development of an ideal, or in the working out of an ideal within a particular style. Yet what we saw in discussion of the idea of what it is to pass time's test was that a painting or a building is better placed to count as having withstood time securely in so far as our admiration for the work is deeply embedded. And the embeddedness of a work of art in our culture is something which depends on the work attracting our attention and admiration from a viewpoint that precisely *transcends* the dominant ideal or style of a period. Thus, while the works which are paradigmatic examples of our inferences are those which have spoken to men of all ages, progress in the arts and in taste seems now of necessity restricted to the growth of an art within an ideal and within a particular period. Thus the two do not meet; we cannot validate the former by appeal to the more restricted concepts which the latter makes available when once realistically construed.

III

The eighteenth century offered a number of related approaches to my question that can conveniently be taken together. In particular I have in mind the views of Lord Kames, Edmund Burke, David Hume, and Dr Johnson, with whose commitment to the test of time I began.

Believing men to have a common nature, Kames held that we respond to the same things in uniform ways. In his eyes uniformity of response, grounded in this common nature, must be the rock on which correctness of aesthetic judgement rests. 'This conviction of a common nature or standard and of its perfection accounts clearly for . . . the conception we have of a right and wrong sense or taste in the fine arts. A man who, avoiding objects generally agreeable, delights in objects generally disagreeable, is condemned as a monster; we disapprove his taste as bad or wrong because we have a clear conception he deviates from the common standard.'[14] Our own response to these assertions is unfavourable. We are too alert to the plurality of taste among men for them to strike us as remotely plausible. But it does no harm to remember that diversity of tastes was repeatedly remarked on by eighteenth-century thinkers of uniformitarian persuasion, and that they took themselves to have a satisfactory answer to what strikes us as refuting their belief.

What they tended to say was either that the significant theoretical uniformity on which sound taste is based is that found in polite society and among those who enjoy refinement of manners; or else that any failure of uniformity in aesthetic matters is ascribable to the working of certain common obstacles to natural response. In the former case, the natural response was presumed present and steady in the right circles; in the latter, the common nature to which the theory appeals is that which asserts itself quite generally once these obstacles have been removed and impartiality prevails. The less that is said about the first of these moves the better, since within the theory of common sense the appeal that was so often made to refinement is all too question-begging. In extending the metaphorical idea of refinement from the material world to the world of taste we cannot proceed without implicitly making use of aesthetic notions, and then we shall be hoping to identify the very uniformity that is supposed to underpin good taste in terms of good taste itself.

The second way of meeting the pluralist's objection does not commit this error. It also appears to show why we should want to use the test of time in criticism while at the same time offering a simple account of its working. Once we are receptive to the idea that our natural responses to particular works of art may be inhibited by factors which hinder our viewing them impartially, it may easily be supposed that these obstacles should, at the start of the community's acquaintance with a work, exert a force which as time goes by gets steadily weaker. So it seems that in the long run, as these obstacles to appreciation become ineffective, we shall see what the common response to the work truly is, and come to share it ourselves.

An instance of this train of thought is provided by Hume in the *Essay on the Standard of Taste*. Authority or prejudice, he writes,

> may give a temporary vogue to a bad poet or orator but this reputation will never be durable or general . . . A real genius, the longer his works endure and the more wide they are spread, the more sincere is the admiration he meets with. Envy and jealousy . . . and even familiar acquaintance may diminish the applause due to his performance: but when these obstructions are removed the beauties which are naturally fitting to arouse agreeable sentiments immediately display their energy; and while the work endures they maintain their authority over the minds of men.[15]

As Hume states the case it is notable that the obstacles he mentions are precisely such as to disincline us from saying that the attention the work receives while they operate is genuinely aesthetic attention at all, or that the judgement we make under their influence is properly grounded. As I put it in the last chapter, they are not grounds which could pertinently bear on the formation of a critical estimate of the work as the very work of art it is, and this fact cannot fail to be a damaging objection to the Humean account of time's test. For its effect is to bring to our attention that by Hume's way of reckoning that test runs from the original composition of the work to the time at which it does enjoy proper aesthetic scrutiny and universal appeal. Once that point is reached and the common sense supposedly asserts itself, the subsequent passage of time can bring no further benefit to the critic. Yet on our view of the matter the test does not even begin to operate until the attention the work receives is properly anchored. So the theory of obstacles steps in at the wrong juncture altogether.

The best known of eighteenth-century attempts on the problem is Johnson's. It was his contention that:

[w]hat mankind have long possessed they have often examined and compared and if they persist to value the possession it is because frequent comparisons have confirmed opinion in its favour. As among the works of nature no man can properly call a river deep or a mountain high without knowledge of many mountains and many rivers; so in the productions of genius, nothing can be styled excellent till it be compared with other works of the same kind. Demonstration immediately displays its power, and has nothing to hope or fear from the flux of years; but works tentative and experimental must be estimated by their proportion to the general and collective ability of man, as it is discovered in a long series of endeavours. Of the finest building that was raised it might with certainty be determined that it was round or square, but whether it was spacious or lofty must have been referred to time. . . . The reverence due to writings that have long subsisted is the consequence of acknowledged and indubitable positions, that what has been longest known has been most considered, and what is most considered is best understood.[16]

To make sense of this passage let us start with the crucial claim that 'no man can properly call a river deep or a mountain high, without the knowledge of many mountains and many rivers', and look for a way of taking it that makes it plausible. With this in hand we shall see how Johnson might have intended the rest of his argument to work.

I do not suppose that Johnson thought that no man may *truly* say a mountain is high without ever having seen one. That would be absurd, since the factual truth of what a man says is independent of evidence on which he says it. Nor should we saddle him with the view that no man can know that Everest is high if he has lived all his life in the plains. After all reputable authority transmits knowledge of the same quality as that attained through personal experience. On the other hand if we take him to be concerned with a man's desire to make sure judgements *on the basis of his own experience* there is some reason to believe that he must see many mountains before he may call one of them high. The source of this belief lies in the assumption I take Johnson to make that 'high' is an epithet that correctly attaches only to objects of a class which are high as members of the class go. Similarly in the case of a river that a man calls 'deep', and generally with other attributive adjectives that Johnson takes to involve covert comparisons. In the light of this presumption it is plain why a man should need experience to apply them: it is because to be sure that he is right in doing so he must have surveyed the class one of whose members he compares in these terms with the rest. If in calling a mountain 'high' I am implicitly saying that it is high as mountains go, then in order to be sure of what I say on the basis of my own experience I must naturally look many of them over.

From this it emerges why he should speak of the passage of time as he does. Clearly he assumes that the predicates we apply in discussion of the arts are in their grammar similar to his paradigms 'deep' and 'high'; hence if (as he should) a man seeks to make his aesthetic judgements on the basis of his own experience he will need to survey large classes of works of art in order to apply such terms as 'lofty', 'spacious', or 'excellent', (Johnson's own examples) with any certainty to the individual members. To do this takes time, and it takes time for two reasons. First, it is generally a long business for the individual to survey the relevant class of works of art with which the particular object is supposed to be compared, and secondly (more in point here), the comparison in question is with the members of an open class that only fills up slowly. So before effective comparison is even possible the community may often have to wait some generations for the class to be sufficiently replete to furnish the desired certainty of judgement. Once this is seen, the reason we think better of the later judgement than the earlier one is plain. It is that while the early judgement that a work has some feature may be true enough, our *belief* that it does will only be well grounded when based on evidence that may not have been available at the time. For only over a period will the relevant class be full enough to let us see if the judgement is a true one.

If this really is what lies at the heart of Johnson's argument it must be rejected. As I have put it, it rests on an untenable view about the main elements of the aesthetic vocabulary. In the first place it seems mistaken to think that the truth conditions of attributive words in general involve our treating them as covert assertions of straightforward comparison. A deep river is not necessarily a river that is deeper than many rivers are, nor is a spacious room one that is more spacious than many another. If these comparisons were involved in our use of the positive terms then it would turn out to be impossible for all rivers to be deep or all rooms to be spacious, or, to extend the thesis into the aesthetic dimension, for all men to be beautiful or all mountains to be sublime. Of course in actuality they aren't, but their not being so is scarcely something we can rule out in a simple a priori way.

This is not to say that no comparative account of these words can be explored. Only the way in which it might be done does not harmonize with Johnson's main idea. To get over the difficulty of the last paragraph he might suggest that we should not restrict ourselves to comparisons within the actual (past and present) extension of the terms in question, but look at their *possible* extensions too. So we might suppose something to be (attributively) F which is Fer than many examples selected widely over the range of possible F things. Then indeed every actual room could be spacious and every actual man beautiful; only quite independently of other difficulties to which the idea gives rise[17] it could scarcely give Johnson what he wants. For it is now far less clear than it was before how any waiting we might do to enlarge our view of the class's membership could be of any use. This is because nothing could give us any assurance that the actual growing membership of the class selects its new instances widely over the range of possibilities and thus *shows* us that the comparison works out as we say. To secure that we should need a bit of theory that stretches further than anything that observation over time could supply, and in the case of the arts it might well be that any such theory would encourage us to think that we know what the relevant possibilities are *well before* we wait for the class to fill out. Thus the very existence of an established institution of art supposes that we should only be able to aim at certain aesthetic effects if at the time we could be sure enough of recognizing ourselves to have achieved them when we do. This would then make it unnecessary for us to wait and see what happens before we apply the aesthetic vocabulary. And something like this seems to be correct; otherwise we find ourselves with an unduly narrow and unrealistic view of the possibility of a proper and defensible appreciation of any contemporary art that involves a significant measure of innovation.

Perhaps we should not make too much of these difficulties, for whatever ground Johnson himself might give for his initial claims, in the last sentence of the passage I quoted, he offers us something much more striking, and something that is utterly independent of any consideration of the nature of attributive adjectives. The assertion that 'what has been longest known has been most considered, and what is most considered is best understood' suggests that everything that is important turns on *understanding*. And it is here I think that the eighteenth-century reflection on this subject is most promising. Only in one respect was the eighteenth century ill-placed to appeal to the idea of understanding—and certainly this is true of some of the assertions that Johnson makes—for by their reckoning that had to be understood as a common response caused by perception of an object and as nothing more. And as we have already seen in discussion of Hume's theory of obstacles, that way of treating the matter does not serve us well. However, if instead we think of understanding in terms of a response to an object that is justified in terms of the details of the object itself, it becomes plausible to say that scrutiny of the object over time may well show whether earlier judgements were or were not correct. Continued attention is likely to test whether the object does sustain the judgements we make, down to the details, and over time we have ample opportunity of discovering whether anything turns up to cast in doubt our initial reactions to it. Such at least is a more hopeful account of Johnsonian claims, and one that has been recently revived in the following terms by F. N. Sibley:

[I]f aesthetic concepts are as I have pictured them to be, a proof that x *is* ø will consist in a convergence of judgements in this direction. But this may require time—to study the object, to acquire varied knowledge and experience etc.; time also over generations, so that detailed agreement emerges from the temporary variations we call fashions and fads . . .

... Possibility of error with a case that has elicited long lasting convergence decreases as the possible *explanations* of error become more obviously absurd; e.g. we could not sensibly reject a centuries-spanning consensus about *Oedipus* as being the result of personal bias, enthusiasm for a novel style, or passing fashion or fads . . . the long attested cases may virtually exclude the theoretical sceptic's doubt as absurd.[18]

We do not need to think that what we are here offered is in any way wrong in order to doubt whether it fully accounts for our readiness to make the inferences enumerated in the last chapter. On at least four counts some expansion and supplementation is called for, if what is presented as an explanation of the operation of time's test is to be a demonstration of its soundness rather than a mere reaffirmation of its efficacity.

(1) I have said that the major inference that we draw from survival in art is one that concludes something about the high quality of the lasting work. On the Johnsonian representation of the matter it would seem that for the most part what gets confirmed over time is the propriety of the various aesthetic descriptions we are inclined to give of the works we attend to. So if everything is to be provided by this version of the Johnsonian model, the element or critical appraisal would appear to be left in the air. Of course Johnson himself (and in his second paragraph Sibley too) suggests that evaluation falls within the scope of the convergence that passing time brings with it. Only, when we look at the account given in the last chapter of what it is for a work of art to pass time's test we see that it makes no reference to claims made about the quality of the art that engages our attention. Those are to be found only in the conclusions that we seek to justify.

(2) Although Johnson himself claims that length of consideration is effectively explanatory I doubt whether its importance really does appear from what either he or Sibley say. As I have represented it, the function of time is to allow the better view to emerge. Now we are almost bound to think that before convergence is achieved the estimations of those who from an earlier vantage point appreciate the works *we* attend to are themselves no very sure support for our later views. In some way that has to be explained they are of less interest and weight. But if one takes this far enough back one might doubt whether

they really add very much to the fact that over time we have come to a convergent position. In that case the fact that the work has *long* been admired cannot tell us very much—or indeed anything at all.

(3) If the Johnsonian explanation were all that there is to it, then, at least in the case of Diocletian's reforms and that of many artefacts, we should find quite different considerations at work. For their survival does not imply anything about their having been properly understood. In these cases we want to say that there is a direct connection between their survival and their excellence, and that it is direct because in some way the passage of time *tests* their capacities to survive. It would be strange at least if there were not something similar to be said in the case of the arts.

(4) Crucially, a work of art passes time's test by surviving when it is correctly understood (or when seen under an appropriate interpretation). However, as Johnson sees the matter, this supposes that there is nothing much left to explain. As he puts the case, it is simply that what is most considered is best understood: but to say that is to say little more than that the inferences are to be made. It does nothing to explain *why* we should hold by them or think that there is more to them than to a stampede of cattle that takes its time to gather momentum.

For these reasons we shall only make progress if we look beyond the spirit of the eighteenth-century arguments and supplement what the best of them offer. In the light of (3) above, I shall do this by trying to preserve a continuity with the kind of reflection which we might use outside the arts to explain the appropriateness, for instance, of what Rostovtzeff said about Diocletian's military and judicial reforms. But first we must clarify an issue which now starts to press. It is whether or not works of art will properly survive when they hold our attention under different interpretations at different times. According as we answer 'yes' or 'no', we shall see the class of test-passing works as bigger or smaller. So too we shall find it necessary to think about the validation of time's test in different ways.

Chapter 3

Autonomy of Interpretation

A widely held conception of what it is to understand art envisages the legitimacy of changing interpretations of its works over time. It consequently views stability of interpretation as unnecessary for art to survive, and supposes that we need to find a way of justifying our critical inferences for art which is taken in different ways during its career. I shall argue that this demand cannot be met and—pending final discussion of the issue in Chapter 12—conclude that this gives us ground for mistrusting any theory of art which sees its objects as autonomous and detachable from their historical origins.

I

'No poet, no artist of any art', wrote T. S. Eliot in 1919, 'has his complete meaning alone.' He went on:

His significance, his appreciation is the appreciation of his relation to the dead poets and artists. You cannot value him alone: you must set him for contrast and comparison among the dead. I mean this as a principle of aesthetic, not historical criticism. The necessity that he shall conform, that he shall cohere is not onesided: what happens when a new work of art is created is something that happens simultaneously to all the works of art that preceded it. The existing monuments form an ideal order among themselves which is modified by the introduction of the new (the really new) work of art among them. The existing order is complete before the new work arrives. For order to persist after the supervention of novelty, the whole existing order must be if ever so slightly altered; and so the relations, proportions, values of each work towards the whole are readjusted; and this is conformity between old and new. Whoever has approved this idea of order, of the form of European, of English literature will not find it preposterous that the past should be altered by the present as much as the present is directed by the past. And the poet who is aware of this will be aware of great difficulties and responsibilities.[1]

One way of taking Eliot's claim that no artist has his complete meaning alone is straightforward and unexciting. The significance we ascribe to a poet's words, to his tone and his choice of imagery, must obviously be grounded in a sensitivity to the way in which past writers have used those words, that tone, and those images. For the poet speaks to his contemporaries in a language that is shaped by past usage. It is that past usage, and in particular the literature of the past, which defines the area that is the common preserve of reader and writer and from which their communication must set out. In the absence of any such common preserve the writer could have nothing to communicate to the reader and would not merely fail to 'have his complete meaning alone' but fail to have any meaning at all.

This thought is unexciting as an elucidation of Eliot's opening sentence because it does less to explain why no poet has his meaning alone than to point out how he does just this. It points out that the resources of the past are available to the poet to draw upon and that, knowing what these resources are, he is in the best possible position to give his words a determinate stamp and weight of his own. Admittedly, the writer cannot be fully understood except in the light of a full understanding of the literary and linguistic tradition in which he writes, but, given this, what he says in making use of material that he inherits from the past *is* a matter for him alone. For the rest it is only a question of whether he has been properly understood.

I call this straightforward view *historicism*, a term whose other philosophical connotations are to be disregarded, and I leave detailed discussion of it to the next chapter. Although it is certain that Eliot was attached to this position and that we cannot make sense of the quoted passage without reference to it, it does not fully represent what he had in mind. For he explicitly stresses that the poet's works have to be understood as much in the light of *later* writing as of *earlier*. We have, that is, to think of the work of art as in some measure *autonomous*, as unconstrained by its history, and to accept this is to give quite a different flavour to the assertion that the poet does not have his meaning alone. The significance we ascribe to the poet's words, taken now autonomously, changes over time as the literature that post-dates the poet grows and develops, and these changes are not ones of which the poet can have foreknowledge in the composition of his work. In our ordinary way of talking, his meaning is not his alone because after he has laid down his pen his language takes on senses and shades of significance that he did not envisage at all. And the view espoused by Eliot, and after him by other theorists of the arts,[2] is that this too is a way of looking at tradition which we should regard as a necessary 'principle of aesthetic criticism'. We need to know what could force us to so strange a conclusion.

II

One argument for autonomy that is frequently offered sets out from commonplace observations concerning the psychology of perception. It is pointed out that the way in which we see and understand signs, and the interpretations we find them able to bear, depend on the mental set we bring to them. This set itself depends on the total set of beliefs and dispositions we happen to have at the time. Since these beliefs and dispositions are constantly changing, the mental set with which we confront a poem will also constantly change. Hence the judgements of appropriateness which we use in coming to interpret the poem, responsive as they are to the alternatives available at any particular time, will themselves change as those sets of alternatives change. So at different times we are bound to see the poetry of the past in different lights.

Note first how uneasily this ultimately psychological underpinning of the thesis of autonomy lies with that form of historicism that I have noted Eliot *also* wants to espouse. The upshot of the psychological defence is that the best available contemporary reading of a poem must after a while recede beyond the horizon of accessibility. This may be a natural occurrence, but if, as is suggested, it is inevitable, Eliot's insistence on the necessity of absorbing the pre-existing tradition appears to be self-defeating. Consider, for example, our understanding of the poetry of Milton or Spenser. The historicist insists that we can only come to a proper understanding of their work in the light of acquaintance with the tradition which they inherited. Now, except through literary study of their contemporaries, we have no access to that tradition. So to neglect this study will inevitably lead us to misunderstand these authors; yet in order not to misunderstand them we have to be able to perceive the pre-existing tradition accurately. It follows that we must resist the blandishments of whatever would make this impossible. Yet the psychological defence of the thesis of autonomy deprives us of a capacity to do so in so far as it makes us creatures of our *present* mental set. That is, it denies us access to the tradition in which Milton and Spenser wrote as it presented itself *to them*. So, defended from the standpoint of psychology, the thesis of autonomy invalidates the concern for tradition which initially seemed so obvious, and which Eliot wanted it to incorporate.

Happily, the psychological argument is not as powerful as I may have made it appear. We need to remind ourselves that its scope must be limited by a certain freedom we find ourselves to have. Interpretation of a poem or painting is, it is usually recognized, well thought of as a case of aspect-perception, of taking the signs in a particular way. And while the ways in which we can take the signs are indeed dependent on our mental sets, it is also true that we can ourselves do something by way of selecting or changing those sets. That is, we can contend against forces that make it natural for us to see things in one way, and try to see them in another way.[3] Of course, we cannot see anything in just any way we choose, but our will does have a certain empire over our perception. Knowledge that at a certain time a particular consideration could not have been relevant to contemporary understanding of a poem may, by a process of familiarization with the work and of imaginative effort, often bring us to discount that consideration. Knowledge that a poem could not but have been understood in a certain light by its contemporary readers may, with patience, often be incorporated into the way we *now* read it. That these too are observed facts of psychology weakens the power that psychology alone might have to secure the necessity of autonomous interpretation.

However, the thrust of the argument is not yet fully exhausted. For while we must indeed admit the existence of a degree of freedom in aspect-perception and thence in interpretation, it only becomes a weapon in the hands of Eliot's opponent if he knows how to use it. And Eliot, in defence of autonomy, may contend that this knowledge is unavailable, for to exercise our alleged freedom in a way he would think proper the historicist needs to know just how a poem's contemporary reading would have struck its audience; yet to come by this knowledge he cannot possibly make himself a part of the contemporary audience. He cannot go back to the past. All that he can do is to make the best he can of the literary evidence at present, or in the future, available to him, and this, Eliot may say, he has to understand in the light of his total set of present-day beliefs. Because this is so, the results of historical scholarship and textual criticism cannot but be conditioned (not immediately conditioned, maybe, but none the less conditioned at several removes) by factors that post-date the composition of the poem. Therefore we have ultimately to recognize that our hope of discovering the past as it was originally experienced is vain. Through our logical exclusion from return to the past we have an a priori guarantee that our understanding of the past must carry the present within it, and not one grounded in psychology alone.

For two reasons this riposte cannot however establish the case in Eliot's favour. In the first place, it seeks to infer from our reliance on our present-day understanding of literary evidence the inevitability of anachronistic infection of that understanding by our present-day beliefs. Such an inference is not valid. Maybe we are often so infected. Maybe there are inductive grounds for expecting it. But neither of these harmless concessions provides the warrant that is needed. The strongest claim that follows from the premises we are given is that we cannot ever *guarantee* that we have *not* been infected in the way suggested, but this is a long way from saying that such infection is inevitable. It is as far from proving this as is a proof that not-p is indemonstrable from proving p itself.

Secondly, when properly understood the argument does not encourage any particular scepticism about our ability to understand *the past*. It merely applies to the past a general argument about our understanding of others, the defence of which in its widest form would be foolhardy, if heroic. The thought is that if in interpreting someone else I start out from beliefs about the world that differ from his I shall at some point read my view of the world into my interpretation of his thought. Yet since I, being the particular individual I am, necessarily have some beliefs that he and other people do not, this argument would, if rigorously applied, condemn me to misunderstand everyone who seeks to communicate with me. This there is no reason to accept. In coming to understand another I can, on the evidence available to me, certainly locate beliefs of his which differ from mine, and so I can in theory avoid erroneously saddling him with my world view even when that is what dominates my understanding of the evidence I use to interpret him.[4] If I can do this in coming to understand my contemporary there is no reason to think I cannot also do it in coming to understand my antecedents, literary or other.[5]

A different and rather more specific way of grounding Eliot's claim would be to show that unless we adopt his position or one very similar to it we shall falsify our understanding of art in one or other of two distinct ways.[6] In the first place it could be supposed that we shall represent art to ourselves as transparent and contingent, whereas in fact it is not; or secondly that we shall unduly minimize the role of the spectator or the reader, and thereby make it impossible to explain the value of art. If either of these two charges can be sustained, Eliot's thesis of autonomy will be confirmed, even when the weak epistemological arguments just discussed are set aside.

Transparency. To view art as transparent is to view it as some sort of consumable. It is to think of it as essentially exhaustible and ultimately of a 'throw-away' nature. However, we know from experience that the finest works are inexhaustible and, it is claimed, the only way in which we can accommodate our experience to the theory of art is to acknowledge that the artist must relax his control of his work by putting its fruitful interpretation into the hands of an unpredictable future.

While the danger of exhaustibility may be bypassed if we do make the work hostage to the future, it is questionable whether we must succumb to it unless we do so. To see this, notice that the exhaustibility that is in point must be exhaustibility for the community rather than for the individual, because, life being short, the individual will rarely be able to avail himself of the supposedly beneficial changes in interpretation that the future may bring. But once we look at the community, there is no obvious reason why its members should find at a late period in history that they have exhausted a work under a stable historical interpretation simply because in that interpretation it has been loved, and maybe exhausted, by numbers of individuals among their predecessors. Hume once observed that 'a young man whose passions are warm, will be more sensibly touched with amorous and tender images than a man more advanced in years, who takes pleasure in wise, philosophical reflections, concerning the conduct of life and the moderation of the passions. At twenty Ovid may be the favourite author, Horace at forty and Tacitus at fifty';[7] and I doubt whether we could acknowledge the force of what he says if we thought that what men have enjoyed in the past and individually exhausted for themselves did not provide the same richness of experience for their successors as it once did for them.

Contingency. Even if stable interpretation does not force us to regard art as transparent in this way, it may none the less encourage us to view it as contingent in its value. By this I mean that we should regard the value of the individual work as contingent upon there being found no better way than it offers of transmitting the particular experience it does transmit. It is sometimes claimed that the value of art is not contingent in this way,[8] yet certain poets have themselves expressed the feeling that the value of their work *is* contingent in just such a way as this. Thus Rilke, writing to Stefan Zweig, says: 'It seems to me as if I had always one thing and again and again just this one thing to say, so that later these poems have simply been superseded by a better and more adequate expression, and they survive only as something like provisional statements set against what is now definitive.'[9] If this feeling were indeed common then the argument would turn on a dubious premiss.

Even when we discount such utterances, it is questionable whether a rejection of the doctrine of autonomy does lead to such a contingent view of art. The doctrine itself is supposed to avoid that consequence by holding out to us the prospect of a new experience of a work even when the old experiences have been superseded by the advent of better ways of transmitting them. This prospect will only impress us if we are convinced that such supersession of the old is actually likely on the historicist's view. But for two reasons I doubt whether it is. For one thing, it is common ground between the moderate and the radical thinker that our spiritual situation from which new art arises is in constant flux. Hence the impetus to transmit the same experience as has been well transmitted by our ancestors—even if it were possible—is unlikely to be very strong. In particular, this is so because the really remarkable artist—he who could succeed in this endeavour if anyone could—tends to be the man of genuine gifts, the man of originality, the man whose concern it is to offer us something new rather than to provide us with an improved version of something with which we are already familiar. He is not one to bother. Secondly, the very uniqueness of the powerful work—the particular way in which the experience is transmitted—is an important element in its value. But this is in no way endangered by the historicist's position. Aspects of the work may of course challenge successors in the tradition to emulate and to improve on what it offers, but the way in which such improvements are experienced is through their incorporation in different works of a later time, works which as a whole offer quite different experiences from those which furnished the model. Once this is recognized the original threat of contingency loses its power.

The only other argument for autonomy I find at all compelling is different from any of these, and rests on the thought that the spectator's role in the interchange between artist and spectator is improperly minimized unless Eliot's doctrine is accepted. The viewer of a picture or the reader of a poem, it is said, realizes the value of the work through coming to understand it, and understanding in the arts (or more specifically in those arts which have a subject-matter) is at least partly to be explained in terms of the reader or the spectator coming to see the material signs of the work as adequate to their referents. The more adequate the sign to its referent the fuller our experience of the work, and the fuller our experience, the more successful we shall be in doing what Richard Wollheim once called 'replacing association by understanding'. (See *Art and Its Objects*, §§ 39, 52.)

Given this view of aesthetic understanding it is easy to see why the radical picture presented by Eliot is so attractive. It appears evident from our very experience of the arts that posterior changes in our view of either the material signs or of their referents often enable our experience of some work to be more replete than was possible before they came about. So it may seem that unless we avail ourselves of these changes in our perception of the work we shall inevitably deprive ourselves of a richness of understanding which might otherwise be ours, and in terms of which we can best account for our concern for the arts.

The attractiveness of this view, with its double appeal to experience and to theory, is well displayed in its practical applications. In one way it is very responsive to changes in our perception of the material signs of the work, as Wollheim himself illustrates. Whatever else our predecessors made of Macbeth's disjointed syntax, they were scarcely able to see it as expressive of Macbeth's own inner turbulence. That perception only became natural to us through more recent critical writings. Or again, we should reflect that our ability to see the free brushwork of Titian or Velazquez as asserting simultaneously the 'sensibility of the artist and the materiality of the painting' (*Art and Its Objects*, § 39) depends on the development of painting after Manet, and was unavailable to Titian's or Velazquez's contemporaries. The later change in our way of seeing brings with it fuller understanding of the work.

Furthermore, this position is equally responsive to changes in the way in which the referents of the signs themselves are thought of. Thus changes in our philosophy, in our religious, and in our moral thinking, all bear upon the understanding of the topic to which the artist addresses himself; so again what is judged as an adequate or appropriate interpretation of the signs may be different at different times. We cannot today think of love quite as Dante did at the time of *La vita nuova*, nor of exploration and conquest as did Camoens when he wrote *Os Lusiadas*, hence our own reading of these two works will not now reflect that of their contemporary readers; not because we have lost a certain genius that they had, but because the world presents itself to us in such a different light from that in which it presented itself to them. Again, changes in our thought posterior to the work's composition invite us to make the work replete by incorporating them into our perception of it.

In either of these two ways then, through changes in the way we are able to regard the signs or, less directly, through changes in our understanding of the world itself, we are able to adjust our understanding of art to our own circumstances. And it is claimed we *have* to make such adjustments because unless we do so we shall find ourselves with interpretations of it that jar, or fail to incorporate what the work appears to offer us; or perhaps alternatively because we shall otherwise catch ourselves striving for a reading which is not naturally ours, which cannot be spontaneously experienced, and in which the signs are not optimally replete. So, given that we accept in advance that the great works of art of the past are of constant value to us, our ability to explain our willingness to cherish them as we do is dependent on recognizing that our view of them is subject to a perpetual *aggiornamento*.

This, I believe, is the strongest argument for autonomy, one which initially seems to have the support both of theory and of experience. Furthermore it is one that can accommodate something of the historicism Eliot desired in a way that does not seem open to those who set out from the epistemological arguments already discussed. This bonus is available because, granting the limited psychological empire of the will over aspect-perception already mentioned, we realize that we can come to a fully replete understanding of the signs only by *first* grasping their significance for the contemporary reader and then by amplifying this understanding in the light of later changes in the way in which we *now* most naturally see signs and referents.[10] In this way the moderate theory may be nested within the more radical one, whereas before it was carelessly edged out by the expansive intruder.

The nub of this argument must be the claim that by restricting ourselves to a merely moderate, historicist interpretation of the arts we should deprive ourselves of the opportunity that passing time gives us of making the signs fully replete, of replacing association by understanding. Is this correct?

I take it that the leading idea is *not* that at one time, say in the sixteenth century, the signs are seen in a way that is less than replete, and then at a later time, say in the twentieth century, finally come to full fruition. That cannot be the view, for it would saddle our ancestors with the unwarrantable charge that they were incapable of full appreciation of the arts of their own day. Rather, the argument must be that whereas in the sixteenth century the signs were seen as replete, the passage of time has threatened this repleteness by the introduction of stray elements into our perception of the works, and that the only proper way we can move is by incorporating these elements into our reading of the works by readjusting our interpretations. The passage of time, that is to say, introduces interpretative elements which threaten to be merely *associated* with the other signs of the work, and it is the spectator's task to find an interpretation which raises their status to that of elements which are fully understood.

If this is the correct representation of the view it is natural to ask whether it does full justice to the freedom already remarked upon in the matter of aspect-perception. Why is it that we have to make so much concession to those forces that tend to swamp the earlier interpretation? The answer, I think, is this. It is thought that the historically contrived interpretation, the interpretation which we reconstruct with difficulty, is unlikely to be sufficiently spontaneous. It is likely to be one which we do not experience with immediacy, one which we know rather by description than by acquaintance (to the extent that we know of it at all). And here, it will be claimed, experience *is* the ultimate arbiter, for it must be accepted that in the construction of aesthetic theory we are to acknowledge the claims both of the inexhaustibility of the really great work and also of the immediate nature of its appeal. And here it seems that the *historicist* account of the matter fails because it is caught in the dilemma of denying either the inexhaustibility of the work or the constancy of its immediate appeal to us.

If this is the way in which our freedom is to be discounted, the argument seems to me to be inconclusive, for it underplays what imaginative freedom we in fact have. If equates too easily our possession of that freedom with the possession of the *knowledge* (or the ability to come by the knowledge) of how the signs might have struck our predecessors, rather than with the ability to be struck by the signs as they were. And to put it like this is precisely *not* to accept that freedom as real. For that freedom consists in the possibility that I, the subject, should actually see—experience—these signs in a certain way, for instance as they struck my predecessors, and that I should be able to see them in that light for myself, to wit, immediately.

It is sometimes said, and not only by the philistine, that the desired immediacy of this experience is inevitably killed by the sheer weight of knowledge and analysis that is presupposed by the exercise of our freedom here.

> . . . and for the sage,
> Let spear-grass and the spiteful thistle wage
> War on his temples. Do not all charms fly
> At the mere touch of cold philosophy?[11]

wrote Keats, and he is certainly not alone in the thought that the delicacies of the poetic imagination cannot survive close analytical scrutiny.[12] Even such an eminent Warburg-style art-historian as Edgar Wind is open to Keats's suggestion, for after stressing the degree to which aesthetic perception may be quickened by knowledge, he goes on in Eliotic vein: 'While pleasing for a mode of vision which rests sense of form on sense of meaning, it is important not to forget that what quickens our vision can also clog it. . . . There is one, and only one, test for the artistic relevance of an interpretation: it must heighten our perception of the object and thereby increase our aesthetic delight.'[13] Yet it should now be plain that to insist, as Wind does here, on the *unique* importance of heightened delight is to abandon all theoretical or conceptual concern with meaning and sense whatsoever, and that simply assumes that the freedom of which I have spoken is unreal. To acknowledge, more realistically, that this freedom is not limitless and that sometimes we cannot revive the art of the past does not however argue for despising the labour of trying to acquire often inaccessible and recondite information in the light of which a given work may need to be understood.[14] It says merely that we may have to undertake that labour to understand the art of the past in the knowledge that on occasion the spontaneous response will have slipped from our grasp. This may be true, but it does not provide any independent argument for autonomy. Erudition, we should say, does not have to blinker the intellect or clog our vision, hence it need not inveriably live at odds with spontaneity.

Here the proponent of autonomy may well object that even if he tentatively allows this argument, it still remains to be explained what point there is in the cultivation of a view of the arts which is not naturally our own. We should be quick to answer him. As we shall see in some detail in later chapters, we have good reason to cultivate the historical standpoint if we can. For while the ways the signs are more *naturally* taken may indeed differ at different times, they were produced by an artist whose world is interesting because it was what it was, even though it may look different to earlier and later spectators. Both the artist and public of the sixteenth century and their present day counterparts must take the signs as directed at a world that is common to them, and because this is so the reconstruction of the so-called 'unnatural' experience of earlier viewers of the work may, if I can recapture it, be of concern to me now. For one thing, I may use this reconstructed experience to extend my awareness of how the world has seemed to others for another, it may help me to expunge corruption from my own more un-reflective responses to it.

III

These, then, are the strongest arguments currently advanced to justify a theoretical commitment to an autonomous conception of art. None of them, we have seen, is powerful enough posi-tively to force such a view on us, but of course it does not follow from this that the position is incoherent or untenable. And if this unproven view of our subject did allow us to account for the so far unsupported critical inferences of Chapter 1, then we would have some solid reason for adopting it. Should it further turn out impossible to justify these inferences in any other way, then the proponent of autonomy would have greater cause for optimism than anything yet advanced can legitimately afford him. So despite the largely negative results so far recorded it is still worth pursuing the attempt.

It should be evident that no account of time's test in the spirit of eighteenth-century ideas discussed at the end of the last chapter could be fashioned to the autonomous conception of interpretation. But recent critics, impressed by the power of one or other of the arguments just discussed, have thought it obvious that alternative explanations are available. Among them are Meyer Shapiro, Wellek and Warren, Stephen Pepper, George Boas, and the German philosopher Nicolai Hart-mann.[15] All of these thinkers adopt a more or less common approach to the topic, and the fact that they do so leads me to surmise that the view they propound, in slightly varying terms, is really the only serious candidate to rely explicitly on the autonomy here explored.

The central idea on which their common argument relies is that of the work of art's inexhaustibility. In its most ambitious form, that offered us implicitly by Shapiro, the excellent work of art is inexhaustible in that as time goes by it constantly acquires interpretations it never previously received, and presents its later audiences with an enriched view of it. With the assistance of sensitive critics, the audience may not only appreciate the traditional interpretations of the work, but may also ennest those traditional readings within a potentially developing set of enriching accretions. Shapiro writes: 'to see the work as it is, to know it in its fullness is the goal of collective criticism extending over generations. This task is sustained by new points of view that make possible the revelation of significant features over-looked by other observers'[16] and he obviously intends this collective goal to be satisfied only if what the later generations see when they observe a work takes in what their predecessors saw in it and does not abandon that in the light of their own later discoveries. This ideal clearly coincides with that of Eliot in both of its main contentions.

Taken strictly, this may not be a very happy way of saying that the traditional interpretation is ennested within the autonomous one, since the traditional view is precisely one that does *not* have any extraneous penumbra engrafted upon it, and what is here suggested is that the traditional view is *maintained* within the large perspective. Yet nothing should be made to turn on this stricture, since Shapiro would be quite content to allow the ennesting of the traditional interpretation within the fuller one by sufficient preservation of the original core. Accretion to this core may be thought of like those crystals that form on a twig cast into the underground saltlake at Hallein, which lend a glister and radiance to the twig's appearance that it did not originally possess.[17] We still have the body of the twig but it has been enriched by a patina that has later formed upon it; after the passage of time the twig is seen to greater effect.

As Shapiro puts his suggestion, however, it is ambiguous between two possible interpretations, one of which we must discount since it turns out not to be an autonomous view at all, but a historicist one. This is that what the later views do is not to *add* to the work at all, but simply discover what was in fact hidden from earlier eyes even though theoretically available to them. What truth there is in this view will emerge in the next chapter, but we should remember that if taken in this way the explanation of our inferences may come too close to that of Johnson and Hume for comfort. Anyway for the moment we can set this possibility aside.

By contrast, the properly autonomous reading of Shapiro's thought is that the collective criticism of generations takes in more than was ever even theoretically available to earlier readers, and that it does genuinely enrich the work. The poem or painting is brought to fullness over time, and we are invited to solve the problem of validation by reference to this process of growth. Thus, following Shapiro, we may say that it is only the later judge who is properly able to estimate the work, since only he has all the data before him on the basis of which fair estimation is possible. He is in a superior position *vis-à-vis* his predecessors, because in carrying over into his own reading of the work the splendours which they have enjoyed he is further able to see it as enhanced by the crystalline accretions with which time has endowed it. Moreover, since it is only the outstanding works of art which give rise to such a succession of satisfying readings, Shapiro's thesis also gives us a way of making manifest that connection between excellence and inexhaustibility that constitutes the essence of time's test.

For all its popularity this proposal is certainly unworkable. One difficulty it encounters is that it depends on denying to the work's contemporary anything approaching a full appreciation of the outstanding work, since full appreciation is only available to him who benefits from 'the collective criticism of generations'. And since it is generally the contemporary audience for which the work is prepared—who else, after all, is to encourage or act as patron to the artist?—we do right not to make it impossible for that audience to achieve this full understanding.[18] Another laming objection is that this theory can provide no way of selecting a point at which the process of crystallization or accretion is complete, or give us any reason to believe that the process should ever be completed. It is all very well to say that the goal of criticism is to bring the work to fullness, but if it is only then that the work may be properly judged (and this is what Shapiro must rely on to substantiate the claim that the later judgement is more firmly grounded than the earlier one) then we should always be in the position of one who thinks that there may well be reasons why he should suspend his judgement. The prospect of further accretion can never be ruled out, and because it cannot, the idea of collective criticism reaching its goal is unworkable.[19]

The moral to draw from these reflections is that if the autonomous account of art is to underwrite the inferences that the passage of time generates, it would be better able to do so if it freed itself from the obligation to carry along with it the benefits of traditional readings. For by doing this both objections may easily enough be avoided. We should give up Eliot's attachment to tradition and look at the matter in the more extreme way suggested by the writings of Wellek and Warren, Stephen Pepper, and George Boas.

Two brief quotations from these authors will make plain what this alternative is. In their *Theory of Literature*, Wellek and Warren write that a work of art 'has something which can be called a "life". It arises at a certain point of time, changes in the course of history, and may perish. . . . It has a development which can be described. This development is nothing but the series of concretizations of a given work of art in the course of history, which we may reconstruct. Our consciousness of earlier concretizations will affect our own experience.'[20] In a similar vein Pepper claims that '[i]f the art of an earlier age appeals to the later, it is often for other than the original reasons and . . . critics are required in each age to register the aesthetic judgements of that age.'[21] In neither passage do we hear any suggestion that over time there must be anything constant in our reading of a poem; rather, what is notable is that both authors ascribe importance to the very variety of interpretation to which we are liable to subject the work. And it is from this very degree of variation itself that these writers have been inclined to construct an answer to our problem, an answer which allows contemporaries of the work and its later admirers to appreciate it fully—though differently—on their own lines. Thus, adopting the stance to which Wellek and Warren and Pepper commit themselves, George Boas says that 'a given work of art may in different periods have an essentially different content—and therefore be admired for different, if not incompatible reasons. If this instance [i.e. *La Gioconda*] is typical it would appear that works of art which "withstand the test of time" change their nature as the times change. The work of art becomes the locus of a new set of values determined by the preoccupations and the predominant interests of the new critics or observers.'[22] What he intends us to believe is that a work of art withstands the test of time in so far as it has the capacity to satisfy us at different times when the work is seen under different interpretations, or to the extent that it displays what, in another place, he calls 'multivalence'. To justify the inferences we base upon a work displaying multivalence, Boas will say that the excellence and stature of the work is itself a function of its ability to enthrall us in several ways, and that its greatness 'cannot be divorced from the extraordinary fact that [great] works of art do have that "potency for life" in them which makes them of continual if of different interest to men.'[23] The passage of time then provides a test of the work's greatness in that it allows this potency to manifest itself, if it exists; and our judgement that, say, the *Mona Lisa* or *Hamlet* are works of the highest stature is a reflection of their ability to carry this force for continual life, or, to use a phrase of Eliot's, 'to carry the main current'. On this view, that a work of literature or a painting has passed the test of time is an indication that it does have a great 'potency for life' within it, and therefore that we are correct in believing it to be of outstanding merit. Here we have what is certainly a popular and apparently, for many people, a plausible way of settling our puzzles within the framework of the autonomous theory of art; moreover it is one which does not incur the strictures that I passed on Shapiro's idea.

Nevertheless the position is quite defenceless against a number of objections, the most telling of which are these three. First, our assessment of a work of art as great is directly connected with our *immediate* response to it; it is not properly founded on our knowledge (by description) that it *has* evoked a series of appropriate responses under various interpretations, most of which are beyond our own reach or, if within it, are of merely antiquarian interest. This is objectionable because it would make it possible for us to accept a work as a great one without believing ourselves to be touched by it at all.

Then, suppose we allow that the greatness of a work may be thought of as a measure of its 'potency for life', we are still left without an answer to the question why we should care for the preservation of what by this criterion turns out to be the finest art. We are considerably and rightly exercised that our successors and descendents should have an education that binds them personally and socially together with us and with each other, and this hope is one which we further by encouraging them to study great works of art and literature, works which, initially at least, they often find quite foreign to them. Yet the justification of this practice, were it to be given in terms of what they, our pupils and children, could make of these works *in their own terms,* could no longer rest at all on the cohesive force of a common transmittable culture that spanned any but the shortest of times.

Most serious of all, we shall on this view be at a loss to say why, in constructing an educational programme for ourselves or for others, we should make any reference to those works which *in the past* have exhibited that potency for life which on Boas's view makes them so great. As things in fact are, we know, more or less, what our successors will find worthy of their concentrated attention, and we know this because we know how our predecessors have responded to the art that was theirs. Yet on Boas's view the claim that a work of art has exhibited multivalence in the past does not explain why it will continue to do so in the future. That is, we have no reason at all to think that 'is multivalent' is a projectible predicate, and this most certainly introduces a deformity into our understanding of artistic greatness. The truth of the matter is that the expressions 'passes the test of time' or 'is a significant element in our tradition' are both projectible; we have good inductive grounds for thinking that if some work does satisfy them it will continue to do so. But the theory of multivalence cannot begin to explain why this should be so, and therefore cannot give an adequate theoretical account of the inferences we are able to draw from true sentences involving these claims.

From this I conclude that the hope of strengthening the otherwise weak arguments for the autonomous position in art theory by means of its success in accounting for the critical inferences is forlorn. If they are to be underpinned at all it is apparent that we shall have to develop an alternative way of narrowing down the range of legitimate interpretations of the art we know. To do this I shall suggest that we need to exploit more assiduously than is usual that freedom in the matter of aspect-perception on which I have already remarked. Even while we recognize that this freedom is limited we may still ask whether, within the limits that are imposed, we cannot find another way of making good the inferences which quite explicitly relies on the historicist position that Eliot and his followers found it so natural to reject. This is matter for the next chapter. Here I have argued only that the autonomous conception of the arts is undermotivated. Later (in Chapter 12), with this alternative in mind, I shall argue that it is fundamentally untenable.

Chapter 4

The Historicist Alternative

The purpose of history . . . is to show the past is not the same as the present. Contemporary standards do not give the right guidance to a past age; indeed, in most cases they are a positive hindrance. In decoding messages from the other side we get more meaningful results if we use their codes rather than ours.

John Shearman, *Mannerism*

I

To the undermotivated autonomous conception of art I have opposed the view I called 'historicist'. That I spoke of loosely in terms of the writer or painter drawing on the resources of the past that were available to him, and impressing on the signs he used a determinate stamp of his own. If all that we wanted was a conception that contrasts with this account of art, precision could be had simply enough by insisting that the canonical historical interpretation should not be allowed to vary over time and then leaving untouched the issue of how exactly it should be fixed. However, since my later argument will depend essentially on commitment to the historicist thesis, it is important to find a version of it that is both specific and attractive.

At first glance the task may seem forlorn, since the field from which a favoured candidate must emerge contains only four runners, none of which immediately inspires much confidence. (1) The canonical reading of a work might be taken to be that which is commonly accepted as the best *at some arbitrarily chosen time*—fifty years after its composition, say, or at the time of its author's death, or at the next coronation. (2) We could go for the best interpretation that the work *actually* received from its original public. (3) We might choose the interpretation which the author himself *intended* the work to receive. (4) We could endorse that understanding of the work which I shall for the moment simply call *the best available contemporary reading*.

Whichever of these candidates is chosen, the thesis of historicism is that a proper understanding and appreciation of a work of art at no matter what period must go through some canonical interpretation which does not change over time and which is determined in one or other of these four ways. Strictly speaking, historicism also claims that we cannot identify a work of art except in terms of a proper reading of it, since for something to be the particular work it is, it must be constituted of a set of material signs, the proper understanding of which is given by one of these four routes. If we left out any specification of how the signs were to be taken we should be leaving out something crucial to understanding of the object's own identity.

Of these four contenders however, the first two are quickly eliminated. Evidently we shall not want to have anything to do with (1). What counts against it is precisely what distinguishes it from the others, the very arbitrariness that lies at its heart. The choice of canonical interpretation that we come to make must depend on the strength that a candidate has in its own right, and an arbitrary choice of interpretation is precisely one that lacks all methodological strength. (2) fares no better. If we resolve that it is the best of the *realized* contemporary views of a work that we should aim to recapture, we preclude ourselves from criticizing that earlier view, from a distance, as being inadequate to the work. Yet it is our ability to do just this, from the vantage point that passing time gives us, that poses one of our initial problems, that of justifying our practice of controlling earlier interpretations by reference to the later and long-established view. Once we systematically identify correct interpretation in terms of some prior *actual* reading that the work received it becomes an impossible task to say what special advantage the passage of time might confer on a later public.[1]

The remaining two options may seem no better favoured. (3) seems plainly wrong, and (4) only escapes collapse into the autonomous position we are trying to avoid by presenting itself as a special case of (1). So it will seem at first sight.

What is initially so off-putting about (3) is that it offers to extend the power of the artist quite unrealistically over his material. If we take his intentions to be best evidenced here (as we do elsewhere) by his own avowals of intention, he would too easily be able to force onto us interpretations of his work that were in no way directly retrievable from it. And when we recall that the historicist expects to see the canonical understanding of the work turning up in the specification of its very identity, we see that the works themselves may become all too inaccessible to us. Consider for example North Italian quattrocento altar-pieces that depict a woman bearing a platter of severed breasts. Those we know to be representations of St Agnes. But we could easily envisage a painter employing the emblem to be muddled about its significance. He might believe that the saint it identifies is not Agnes but Lucy, and when he sets out to paint Lucy for some commission he does so by using this misleading emblem. On supposition (3), however, the picture is made incomprehensible. Not only can we not retrieve from the canvas the correct reading, since that does not reveal the intention to paint Lucy; even if we happen to know that it is Lucy that the artist meant to depict, we have no way of understanding what she might be doing with that platter whose contents have nothing to do with her.

This objection extends far beyond difficulties in identifying depicted personalities. It reaches to the descriptions under which particular figures are represented and to the expressive character of the works that are understood in this way. So a man may intend to represent a figure as being of a certain size and of a certain disposition but nevertheless fail to execute his purpose. On the current proposal it is unclear how that could happen. Similarly, he might intend his work to be expressive of a joy which we, his viewers, could not recognize in his work. Artistic success is not to be had so easily.

So we arrive by elimination at the last of the four alternatives, but even while we may agree that the best available interpretation is certainly something in which we have an interest, it may seem invidious to pick on the set of interpretations contemporaneous with the work's composition as delimiting our choice. Once intention has been removed from the scene, with the dismissal of (3), what motivation could we have for this restriction? With no answer forthcoming we should see that (4) turns into a special case of (1), for to insist on selecting the best interpretation from contemporaneously available alternatives is as arbitrary a restriction as it would be to select the best alternative from those available when the next monarch comes to the throne or fifty years after its composition. And at this point it may appear again that there is something more to be said in favour of the autonomous view that was overlooked in our discussion in the last chapter—to wit, that the alternatives to it are unacceptable. That at least would be the position if a better view of the matter did not offer a more rewarding understanding of what between them (3) and (4) may yield.

A truth about which there can be no serious dispute is that art is essentially a public matter. It could not exist for the artist by himself any more than it could exist without him. There are of necessity two partners involved, the artist and his audience, both of whose demands must find recognition. It is the indispensible place of the artist which dooms any version of historicism that abstracts from his intentions to inevitable failure; it is the importance of his public which makes unacceptable any stipulation of canonical interpretation that allows correct understanding to be only contingently retrievable from the text. And just as we can see what the publicity of art excludes, so too we should appreciate that it forces onto us a particular combination of doctrines (3) and (4) as the only defensible historicist position.

The effect on the artist of stressing the importance of the spectator should be to make him see that he can only hope to express his intentions in his art provided that he realizes them by a method that is fully accessible to his audience. If all parties are clear about their situation he will know this, his audience will know it, and each will know that the other knows it. In consequence, the artist will have to acknowledge that his work cannot properly be taken to have (and therefore have) the particular character he wants it to, unless the signs he lays down are interpretable, as giving the work that character, by a system of rules and conventions that both he and his audience can know him to be using. So in the case of Lucy and Agnes, we shall say that while the artist may well have intended the represented woman to be Lucy she could not have been Lucy because there was no way in which, *by a method mutually known to be relied on by himself and his audience,* his laying down the signs that he did lay down could have been taken to fulfil that intention.

Equally, constraints are placed on how the audience can take what the artist offers them. They recognize that they understand his work by retrieving his intentions from it. They know that they must use a method that makes those intentions extractable from the canvas or text. And to do this they must make the best sense they can of the canvas or text by a system they take the artist to have been using. Otherwise what they come up with by way of interpretation may well outrun anything that they might reasonably believe him to have intended them to understand. It is a consequence of this that we must understand the artist to be employing a system of communication that was *available to his contemporaries*. For what are the alternatives? Obviously we must not interpret him by a system that attributes knowledge to him of future modes of procedure, for he could not know what they might be, and therefore could not hope to express any determinate intention through their use. On the other hand we cannot take him to be using some past and now defunct system, for he could not then be sure that his contemporaries, the only audience he can knowingly work for, would not interpret that system according to their own lights, rather than those by which its own contemporaries might have understood it.

I conclude that the public nature of art involving the two distinct but essentially related parties forces the historicist to say that the canonical interpretation of the artist's signs must be that which yields the best available contemporary reading of them. He must also say that it is this reading which the artist must rely on in order to execute in his art what he intends. Further, we can note that this version of the historicist's position also makes it plain why, despite the rejection of intention as it first appeared in option (3), we can still think of critical activity as seeking to retrieve the author's intentions from his work. It is because that is where the artist himself must recognize it to be expressed if it is to find its way into his art at all. The discovery of the best contemporary reading is the discovery of what the artist must expect his intention to be taken to be. It is up to him to ensure that it really does correspond to his intention. Of course sometimes he may benefit from a mismatch; more commonly he will suffer. In either case he will have failed to achieve what he wants.

By way of corollary the proposal allows us to appreciate what truth there is in the popular dictum that art is a form of communication. The idea is liable to come out, in its crudest form, in the rather laughable manner of Sir Walter Scott's declaration that the painter, orator and poet each has the motive 'of exciting in the reader, hearer or spectator, a tone of feeling similar to that in which existed in his own bosom, ere it was bodied forth by his pencil, tongue or pen. It is the artist's object, in short, to communicate as well as colours and words can do the sublime sensations which dictated his own composition,'[2] and it is frequently observed how untenable this view is. In that sense of 'communication' the arts are not often communicative. But in a different way they are. They present to an audience through the artist's agency a thought or image which its creator desired should be entertained. And this desire, the desire that guides the construction of art, is only satisfiable if in the formation and combination of his signs the artist manipulates his material in accordance with rules and procedures that he knows his public will be able to follow. Take away the insistence that the painter or sculptor follows systems that are common property of himself and those for whom he paints or carves and we abandon the ability to assert in full seriousness that he paints or carves for anyone at all. That way lies aesthetic solipsism.

A second corollary of the position developed is that it alone allows us to acknowledge the importantly auto-critical nature of the artist's work. The painter or composer makes a start on the execution of some project, and controls what he does in its later stages, under the guidance of the stylistic canons he has adopted and the constraints that are forced on him by decisions that are already recorded in the material on which he works. Very often, of course, earlier stages may be readjusted and erased in the light of decisions the artist comes to later on (though in painting at least they may appear as *pentimenti*), and such alterations and adjustments must be alluded to in giving any account of the expression that the artist's mastery may find in his work. It is thus a precondition of our being able to talk of them as expressions of mastery that we think of them as governed by publicly known (or publicly discoverable) rules of propriety.[3] If we take away the publicity of the rule we deprive ourselves of what we need to talk of artistic mastery at all; take that away and we have taken away something that is fundamental to our conception of the arts in many of their various forms.

Finally, we may reflect that since both of these welcome conclusions depend on finding a satisfactory way of paying due honour to the artist's intention and on finding a place for it within the best interpretation that the signs yield, they could not be expected to flow from the opposing, autonomous, conception of the arts that jettisons all reference to intention altogether. That might make us suspect that it is not merely an undermotivated conception, as I have claimed, but, worse, quite unworkable. For the time being, however, I shall postpone this issue (to take it up again in Chapter 12), and look now at the favoured version of the historicist account of the interpretation in more detail.

II

In his monumental *Aesthetics* Hegel insisted that the arts always present something to the senses. Art for him was essentially the sensuous presentation of the Idea, and we may certainly follow him to the extent of saying that what we seek to interpret in the arts is always something that has a sensuous character: be it a material object, such as a pigmented surface or a block of marble, or something more abstract, such as a configuration of sounds, or a series of bodily movements, or a set of words.

For the sake of ease I shall allow myself to speak of the sensuous base of a work of art as the work's *text* or its *signs*, and I shall approach the topic of the work's canonical interpretation through the quite general question of how the individual set of signs that specifies the particular work is to be delimited. No progress can be made unless this is done, since without it we should have no way of knowing what it is that the canonical interpretation is supposed to interpret.

Where the spatial limits of a painting or a sculpture lie is usually easy to say. The painting is generally what the frame frames; the sculpture is what is mounted on the plinth, and so on. But we must not confuse our conventions for identifying the work with an adequate conceptual specification of the work's limits. When the frame does frame the complete painting that is a happy truth, but it is not always so. For instance, we know that the canvas framed in the Louvre as Leonardo's *Mona Lisa* is not the complete text of that work, since several centimetres of the picture were cut off from either edge in the last century, significantly changing the way in which we are now inclined to read the work; and no one would assert that the blocks of stone that are mounted on the façade of Wells Cathedral present the true text of the figures that were set there in the thirteenth century. They are far too weather-beaten for that.

Framing and mounting, then, to take just two examples, are no more than conventional ways of indicating that what is mounted and framed is the true text of the work, and this indication may often mislead us. To set the limits of the text we have to look elsewhere and insist that it be identified in terms of what the artist himself wanted the public to take as the basis of his work. We allow him the privilege of fixing what that text should be. Thus because what the Louvre frames does not coincide with what Leonardo intended, and because the decayed stones of Wells are now so little as the stonemasons intended them to be, we should deny that either present us with the full text of their respective works.

If it is the artist's privilege to specify the limits of his work, he has an obligation to make plain to his public where these limits lie, and it is the fulfilment of this duty that gives rise to the conventions we first noticed. This combination of intention and convention in the presentation of the text to the public is as it should be, for it and it alone does justice to the dual demand insisted on above that the work of art be the artist's work, and that the artist's work should exist in the public domain. These truths have played their part in the last section, and we must expect them to do so here too.

Too have spoken of the spatial (and temporal) limits of the text is to have said nothing of its *condition*, and it must be plain that even if the spatial limits of a picture were exactly as the artist wanted them to be, that would offer us no guarantee that we had before us the text which he wished us to see and understand. Over time the brightest paint will fade and perfect sandstone crumble. So in consistency with what is said about the limits of the text we should, in those arts where the consideration is relevant, also allow the artist's intention (suitably manifest) to determine the physical condition of the work that enters into the specification of the signs.

It might be thought that in making this move some inconsistency arises with our earlier decision to say that, on the historicist view, the canonical reading of the work is the best available *contemporary* reading, for may not the contemporary reading and the reading the artist wishes the material base of the work to yield be quite distinct? And if they are distinct, must not one of them give way to the other? To think this would be mistaken, however, for the contemporary reading of which I have spoken is of the *text as properly specified;* and if it should happen that the period at which the text is complete lies much later in time than the moment at which the artist laid down his palette, then the right reading of this text will still be one that is selected from those available when he has finished the work. Only it is not one which *could* then be given. When the text matures it must be interpreted according to the set of readings it could have received if only it had matured at the time it was done.

In speaking of one of his predominently white paintings, Malcolm Lowry has said: 'Give it time to yellow—to darken—to discolour—and then you will see what I mean—and what it is I want to show you', and Richard Wollheim has reminded us how we can only see the great nineteenth-century *cornicione* warehouses of Manchester properly when we see them with the patina of soot that passing time lays upon them.[4] Both cases are perpect examples of what I mean. The painter or builder finishes his work, then requires us to wait for the chemical changes he counts on to take place before he allows our judgement on the work to be correctly based; the builder brushes away the last crumbs of plaster and turns to another task. That does not mean that we are yet ideally placed to judge his work: time may be needed for it to mellow and blend into its surroundings. Yet still it is a contemporary way of viewing it that is the right one, only as it happened one that no contemporary was able to achieve.

Consequential on this fixing of the text in terms of the artist's intention three remarks are worth making. First, we shall refuse to take any condition we please of the work as that from which proper understanding must set out. However much we love the submarine goddess of the Louvre, we may have to reckon that Leonardo's intention as to the state of his painting was closer to Vasari's view of it than it is to ours. 'The nose, with its beautiful nostrils, rosy and tender, seemed to be alive. The opening of the mouth, united by the red of the lips to the flesh tones of the face, seemed not to be coloured but to be living flesh.'[5] So the historicist must stress the importance of resisting the temptation to hypostatize conditions of the work that we get used to. And this is no empty exhortation. Just as in regard to the stipulation of the spatial limits of the work, the artist's power to determine its relevant condition for understanding and judgement is something on which we rely to make that fundamental connection between art and artist on which an adequate theory of art must rest.[6]

Then, it may misleadingly appear to have restrictive implications for the size of the set of works that pass time's test. The set may seem curtailed because so few works remain in their preferred state for very long. We know, however, that physical survival itself it not a necessary condition of the work's surviving in the sense that concerns us. By parity of reasoning the same holds of the persistence of the work in its canonical state. We are often more interested to know how well a work has survived than whether it has done so or not, and the answer to the first of these questions may often be encouraging as long as changes that have come about to the text are not of a kind to make the best contemporary reading of it inaccessible to us. It has often been noticed that even severe damage may deprive us of surprisingly little of importance, and this thought can give us some reassurance in the face of what might otherwise appear to be a crippling constraint on the survival of the true text and of the works that are identified by reference to it.[7]

Thirdly, fixing the text by artist's intention allows a measure of indeterminacy into our understanding of the arts which many will welcome. For as long as the artist has in mind a *range* of physical conditions for his text which satisfy him and which lie within his vision there will be no very satisfactory ground on which we shall be able to select one state from the range rather than another as the proper base from which understanding should set out. Something of this recognition by the artist of the changing material nature of his work is heard in Stanley Spencer's injunction to 'let the work age gracefully',[8] but we should be careful in our general theory not to project his view of his own paintings onto that of other people haphazardly. Where one painter may tolerate indeterminacy of the signs another may not, and theory needs to be sensitive to variation among individuals' particular, publicly manifest conceptions of their art.

III

In place of the best contemporary *actual* reading of a text, I favoured the best reading that was *available*, and this idea of availability calls for comment. First, it can be seen that by appeal to it the obstacles which arose for option (2) of the first section are overcome. We can say of realized contemporary readings of some work that they were all defective in that they did not any of them make as much sense of it as they might have done. Furthermore, we can explain what it is that guides contemporarises in their interpretative endeavours as before we could not; it is the search for the best sense that they are able to give the work on the basis of common resources shared with the artist, and this guiding ideal has a clear place made for it in the form of historicism espoused here.

The notion of availability is also of crucial importance for us in explaining how it is possible for us consistently to say that some works are ahead of their time. For it appears that here we have works of art which the contemporary can make little sense of and which seem to require the passage of time before they are fully understood. The inability that we experience here is not explained by the initial unavailability of better interpretations that we later come to. Rather it is that we have not discovered what our resources actually consist of. For the artist asks us to take the signs he offers in a novel way that does make sense of them, and to follow him in extending ways of seeing and hearing, and he could only do this if, no matter how difficult, it is possible for us to do so. As in so many situations, we have to discover our own capacities, and the fact that it is easier for our successors to achieve what we found difficult—or even failed—to achieve in no way justifies the thought that the reading that we failed to find was one that was unavailable to us. Where we are concerned with real possibilities we can truly say in retrospect that the understanding that we missed was one we might have come to.[9]

Someone might object that by relying on such a notion of

availability we immediately make correct interpretation far less sure than it ought to be. How can we ever know that the interpretation contemporaries came to was the best that was available to them, in this rather speculative use of the word? To this question the reply is clear. There arises here no greater difficulty than when we seek to understand our *own* contemporaries, as in conversation we do all the time; for that involves making the best sense of them and of what they do, and we have no more certainty that our good hypotheses there are the best that could be made than we do when we look to the art of the past. This absence of any guarantee that we could do no better is no bar to our knowing that we understand one another in our own time well enough. So it cannot be made one when the same considerations are applied to the past. And this assertion may be defended even though in many cases we confess to doubt as to whether we have made the best of material that we have inherited. To expound the historicist's ideal in terms of a best available reading is not meant to assure us that we must always know what that reading is.

A more likely source of disquiet about my proposal comes with the suggestion of *uniqueness* of canonical interpretation that is implied by the presence of the definite article and the superlative in the phrase 'the best available contemporary reading'. Here we shall see that some marginal emendation is legitimately called for, though not just because it appears to conflict so grossly with the now fairly orthodox belief among theorists of the arts that there is and can be no uniquely right way of understanding paintings, poems, or other sorts of art.

Let us firmly set aside all objections based on the fact that what we take to be the obvious interpretation of a poem often is superseded by another which in its turn holds a seemingly secure place for a while. These matters are exclusively epistemological and do no more than make us aware of the difficulties involved in determining which interpretation is best. They do nothing to impugn the conceptual propriety of my reference to uniqueness.

A more interesting objection is that in the case of many works of art we frequently come upon alternative interpretations of which we are unable to say that one is better than another. In such cases we need to distinguish between alternatives which by their very presence enhance the work, because they are exploited, and those which do not.

In the first sort we must say that a failure to recognize the ambiguity of the work is a failure to recognize something which is important to its understanding, a failure to see something the exploitation of which is essential to the work's appreciation. Thus we treat so many of Escher's works, or the sixteenth-century Archimboldo's, and in our own day those of Salvador Dali.[10] Ambivalence in each of these cases in something that is traded on and enters into the best interpretation. So this sort of ambiguity, which falls within the range of artistry, is no threat to a thesis that commits itself to uniqueness in specifying canonical understanding. It is written into the way in which the work embodying it should best be understood—it is part of that very interpretation.

Not all ambiguity we encounter in the arts is of this kind, and because it is not a certain modification of the historicist position is called for. What is interesting, however, is less the fact that a concession has here to be made to those who see the historicist's concern with the uniqueness implied in concentrating on the best interpretation as a vulgarism,[11] than the less obvious truth that the concession is at most a marginal one, adding a refinement to the historicist's theory and not undermining it at all.

Consider a case of a poem or a play for which we possess a number of alternative interpretations, all available to contemporaries, lying within the set from which the canonical understanding is to be chosen. Let us further suppose that, by the standards of interpretation we are using, two of these alternatives are clearly preferable to all the others and that neither of them is preferable to the other. Suppose too that we do not feel that the work hovers between the two so that we see it as being either-A-or-B, but on the contrary think that it may be taken either in way A or in way B, but we cannot decide which. In such circumstances it seems that there is nothing else to say than that the work itself is indeterminate between the two possibilities and that either reading of it is as legitimate as the other. In such cases we have no a priori ground for saying that we must be able to choose between them (since the grounds on which a choice might be made are *ex hypothesi* removed), nor can we say that the ambiguity may be incorporated within the best reading as in the cases of exploitable ambiguity. The work is simply indeterminate in its canonical interpretation, and we should not be surprised that this may be so. For indeterminacy of this sort is no less real a fact about the arts than similar occasional indeterminacy in the sense of what a man says in everyday speech. Strictly speaking, then, the historicist's position should be put by saying that a chosen text's proper interpretation will be an *optimal* reading selected from possible readings available to contemporaries, where an optimal reading may often be unique, as in the ideal case it should be.

The extent of this retreat from the original position must not be exaggerated. (*a*) In the ideal case,[12] that around which the theory of art must be constructed, indeterminacy will not arise. Where it does, we shall always have to ask ourselves whether we can count it as something that makes for success in the work that displays it or not. If it is to, then it will do so by becoming exploitable indeterminacy and hence not of the sort we are concerned with. If not, there arises a dilemma. Either the indeterminacy lies within the artist's control or outside it. The only way it could lie outside his control would be as an indeterminacy between the theories which we use to interpret his work. Then, of course, the indeterminacy is not in the work, and need not disturb us. On the other hand, if it lies within his control, it must either allow of being rationalized as of aesthetic significance or not so allow. If the former, we have a case of exploitable indeterminacy again, which as we have said furnishes no counter-example. If the latter, it is non-exploitable, but by the argument used above it is not a suitable case to count as paradigmatic. It attempts to engraft upon the heart of the paradigm something to which mastery and artistry do not reach (since it has no aesthetic significance although it is also in the work). But in theoretically ideal cases the exercise of mastery is everywhere apparent.

(*b*) We must not conclude from the fact that we sometimes fail to find a uniquely best reading of a given text that the work in question is indeterminate between our best shots at it. For if we take fully seriously those mutually known principles of publicity that bind artist and audience together and which furnish the deepest theoretical support for the historicist's stance, we will recognize that we interpret what is before us with a view to locating that determinate thought which the artist had it in mind to put before us. And, given that we have to aim at finding a determinate thought (which may of course contain *exploitable* ambiguity within it), where we do not succeed in finding one we shall have good reason to pursue the search in preference to remaining content with what our theory tells us is a less satisfactory situation.

(c) Even when we reckon that further search will yield nothing, and we do determine that we have before us a genuinely indeterminate work, we must keep it sharply in mind that the indeterminacy can only lie between views of the text that were in fact historically available. We should not forget John Shearman's warning, quoted at the head of this chapter, that we need to understand messages from the other side by the use of their codes rather than our own. Much of the importance which indeterminacy of interpretation has attracted in this area stems from forgetting that the advent of novel interpretations on the scene to compete with those with which we are familiar depends on accepting not so much an historicist's view of interpretation as a view of the kind set aside in the last chapter.

(d) From the fact that the possibility of indeterminacy has to be left open it should not be concluded that we also have to extend consideration to those other alternatives which are less than optimal but none the less good ones in their way. We may, of course, have to survey them in coming to understand the work, and it is undoubtedly true that the journey of discovery would be less rich in its final achievement were we not to do so, but the statement of that journey's goal need make no recognition of the pathways towards it.

(e) Finally, the issue of indeterminacy is quite peripheral to our major task of setting up a legitimization of our initial inferences on the basis of a historical view of the work. Having noticed that the principles of publicity force on us the view that indeterminacy must be the exception rather than the rule, we can put to use the simple observation that those works which pass the test of time are to be expected to be central rather than peripheral, and conclude that prospects of indeterminacy are little likely to arise in the cases we want to study. How unlikely it is that a work of art should stand time's test on more counts than one (under alternative optimal contemporarily available interpretations). That it may occur I am happy to admit: but that it might occur as a typical case no one would want to assert.

IV

In speaking of an optimal available interpretation I have so far assumed that we are faced by no insurmountable difficulties in fixing what this should be. I have assumed that the standards for optimality that are in question may simply be referred to as those which in fact hold for the chosen audience. But this assumption may be challenged by a well-known argument that aims to persuade us that in the last resort we have to read *our* standards of 'best' here into our reading of earlier art. This challenge is a serious one since it threatens to destroy at its roots the historicist picture of the arts.

It ought to be common ground to everyone, whether of historicist inclination or not, that we can only make correct aesthetic judgements about works of art if we can say what category of art the individual work belongs to,[13] and then say what style it exemplifies. Unless, for example, we could say of an object that it was a *painting* rather than a thin three-dimensional work of a different kind, we could not begin to pick out those qualities relevant to thinking of it as a good work or a bad one. Similarly we have to know what stylistic conventions are in play in order properly to describe the content of the work and thus to ground evaluations of it.

No more should it be controversial that in identifying a work as being of a certain style we accept that it adopts a certain aesthetic. For instance we might say that abstract expressionism works in a style which emphasizes such qualities as strain, brutality, violence, and overt passion, and we could contrast this with the stylistic concerns of mannerism which we might list as those of effortlessness, sophistication, and courtly grace. And unless we understand that the work in front of us has adopted such concerns as these we shall not feel very confident in saying what its aesthetic features are. We need, that is, to identify the *primary aesthetic* of a work of art if we are to say in an interesting fashion what that work is like.

When we come to identify a work's primary aesthetic we may use a number of methods to do so. We may situate the work in its historical context, we may simply ask the artist to explain what he was trying to do and the conventions in which he was working, or we may read what later art-historians have written. All yield good evidence, though none of them will be criterial for identifying the right one. More to the point is to notice that each of them, in the end, will rely on certain methodological assumptions which we use to assign a work to one style rather than another. Thus we might find it plausible, given our understanding of the range of stylistic concerns that might be relevant to the understanding of a particular work, to say that that choice within the range is correct which (1) is best able comprehensively to accommodate the signs that constitute this work's text, (2) makes the production of the text explicable in the light of the tradition to which it belongs, (3) combines the virtue of comprehensiveness with a measure of simplicity, and (4) tempers these considerations by reference to the over-all unity of interpretation that the work permits, within the style that the work is tentatively assigned to by the preceding considerations.

It is not of great importance here to discuss the strengths and weaknesses of (1) to (4), since in detail they are of no interest to us for the present argument. What is important is that in appealing to them we are relying on *aesthetic* considerations in order to make a choice between various possible stylistic assignments. Furthermore we need to recognize that the same sorts of consideration will again be brought into play at a later stage, when, having made the stylistic assignments, we come to ask ourselves what the best available interpretation of the work is, within the style we have identified as being *its* style. These aesthetic considerations on which we of necessity rely in understanding works of art I shall call our *secondary aesthetic*. Using this expression we can summarize the purport of the last piece of the argument by saying that on the historicist view of the matter we rely on a secondary aesthetic both to identify the primary aesthetic of the work we appreciate and understand, and to determine which reading of the text within the primary aesthetic is to count as canonical. And it is at this point of the general discussion of the idea of canonical interpretation that the historicist thesis lays itself open to a charge of hermeneutic circularity. For, it will be said, although it has seemed easy enough to acknowledge that the primary aesthetic that is in vogue at one time is perceptibly different from that which dominates another period, what we fail to notice is that in trying to locate the canonical interpretation of work that belongs to the past we ought, if we identify that interpretation as the best available contemporary interpretation, to employ the *contemporary* secondary aesthetic in doing so rather than our own. Yet this is something to which we never give a moment's thought.

Put like this the objection may not seem very strong. It may seem to have no more force than a stern admonition. 'Don't forget', we might hear the objector saying, 'that if the best available interpretation of an undisputed text is to become one under which you view the work, you have to employ stylistic considerations which are those of contemporaries in coming to understand it, and that you cannot have any rational ground for thinking you have got these right unless you employ the contemporary secondary aesthetic rather than your own in coming first to recognize the relevant style and second to determine which interpretation (or interpretations) within this style is (or are) optimal.' But if this were all that was being said then as theorists we need not be very concerned. The correct response would be to take the admonition to heart and to recognize that the historical task may be much more difficult than it had previously seemed. None the less the difficulties would still appear to be of a practical kind, and not such as to cast in doubt the coherence of the historicist ideal. In so far as they appear to occasion any sceptical worries, we could be confident that they would respond to the well-understood therapy that general philosophy provides.

However, the barb of the objection has not yet been properly exposed, for what is suggested is that we really cannot shrug off the admonition as a merely practical one. It is no part of the objector's claim that we must just do more work than we think is ordinarily necessary to come to understand the art of the past. What he fears is that however much work we do we shall still not be able to avoid the imposition of our own secondary aesthetic on the earlier age, and that because we cannot avoid doing this our best-founded claims to have located the canonical reading are likely to be *rationally flawed*, even where as a matter of happy chance our secondary aesthetic and that of our predecessors coincide. The reasons why he has this fear may quickly enough be set out.

To identify another's primary aesthetic I have to know what his secondary aesthetic is. How am I to determine it? There seem to be two possible answers: if I am fortunate enough, I may have some written records from which I can extract some plausible hypothesis about what his standards were; alternatively, if I am less fortunate I may have to formulate my hypothesis on the basis of the art which he left to his descendants. Yet we can be happy with neither of these two alternatives. The second is obviously of little help to us; since we have already said we cannot understand another's art without knowing what his secondary aesthetic is. And clearly we could only make reasonable use of the art which we inherit from the past if we are in a position to understand it. So we are thrown back onto what he said his secondary aesthetic was, when he gave his thought to it. Yet we should beware of assuming too quickly that we understand what he tells us without having to interpret it. We have to translate what he says, and so we shall have to know that when he uses such words as 'comprehensive', 'unity', 'simplicity', etc., he does so in the same sense as we do, or know what else those expressions mean for him. Yet how can we decide this except by knowing which alternative stylistic assignments are the right ones for his works of art? And how can we know this without knowing what their canonical interpretations are; knowledge which we have just said is unavailable to us without antecedent knowledge of his secondary aesthetic?

The upshot is this. We could have no way of identifying another's secondary aesthetic if it differed from ours. Hence on the assumption that there is no more reason to think others have the same secondary aesthetic as we do than there is to think they have the same primary aesthetic, it will follow that we can never reasonably believe that we have correctly located the canonical interpretation of an earlier work of art, for at the heart of all our attributions of interpretation lies this apparently unwarrantable assumption. Hence, it may be said, historicism offers us an unrealizable programme. Furthermore, if this objection is correct we shall be unable to justify the claim that any art has passed time's test on the historicist interpretation of that phrase; in consequence, and because all alternatives have failed, we shall have no hope of rationally legitimizing any inferences about individual works that we are inclined to base upon it.

To this sort of objection there is fortunately a brief and devastating reply. It is that the argument rests on an assumption that there is a real possibility that our secondary aesthetic may differ from age to age, and this assumption is either innocuous or else false.

The first of these alternatives is simple enough. If we can have a ground for suspecting that the secondary aesthetic of one period is different from that of another, what gives us such a ground must also give us a ground for identifying it. Hence the difficulties are merely of a practical order and are not theoretically laming. On the other hand, if the argument is accepted that we could never identify a different secondary aesthetic from our own, then there will be no special reason to think that our predecessors had a different aesthetic of this order. What is needed by the objection is that we should be impressed by the possibility of there actually being a different aesthetic in force at a particular time, and one which we could not identify. Yet if it is admitted that we could not identify it under any circumstances, what clear sense could we give to the supposition that there is such a real possibility? If absolutely nothing will count as evidence for the supposition we have no reason to believe that a coherent supposition has been put forward, or that what we are invited to suppose has a clear sense.   So whichever way this argument is turned the historicist has a just response. Hermeneutic circularity, I conclude, poses no threat to his programme.

V

We can now set out in a preliminary way a different manner of justifying the critical inferences from any so far discussed, and one that is essentially based on the historicist conception of art here defended. All I shall do is to expound its bare bones. It will fall to succeeding chapters to put flesh on the skeleton now presented.

In Chapter 1 I cited Rostovtzeff's observation that Diocletian's reforms of administrative and judicial proceeding had stood the test of time. It is easy enough to see what makes his claim true, and easy enough also to see why this should have some bearing on our evaluative estimation of those reforms. What makes his claims true is that the reforms were robust and effective enough to last substantially unchanged for some hundreds of years. In saying that they stood the test of time, we are saying that they *withstood* that test, and that expression is the right one to use because the passage of time challenged Diocletian's institutions to resist pressures that inevitably built up over the years. The passage of time brings with it threats to the survival of the institutions, and the inference from the system's ability to resist these pressures to its excellence is clear: its excellence is the best explanation we can offer in the circumstances of the fact that those institutions did in fact survive.

What is important to the working of this schematic argument is that, unlike the various accounts discussed in Chapters 2 and 3, it relies on making essential reference to the passage of time as a corrosive force on a material or a structure which is dependent for its functional existence on maintaining its shape or effectiveness. The inference to the excellence of the tested object is grounded in the thought that only the better objects of the kind in question would be able to survive the pressures that the passage of time exerts on them. Moreover such a form of argument is quite general. It is not applicable only to constitutional reforms or to modes of judicial procedure; for the same argument applies to practically any artefact. And once we see this, we might suspect that there is some reason to think that it might apply to that artefact *par excellence*, art itself.

To see that the argument is of wide generality and also to see what has to be made out if it is to be as wide in its application as I suggest, let us state it again in greater detail and in connection with a more homely object than Diocletian's reforms. Take, say, a coat. We have no reason to think well of it simply on account of its lasting intact for a long period of years. So long as it hangs in the wardrobe and is protected against moth, it may be expected to do that. What impresses us is that the cloth and stitching resist the strong friction and strain that they are subjected to as the garment is worn. Although it is less obvious in the case of the coat than it would be with other artefacts like a motor car or a weapons system, we may also note that a factor which is relevant to our assessment of the garment is its ability to resist threats of obsolescence stemming from changes in the demands we make of the kind of thing a household garment is. If the needs we wanted our clothing to satisfy were more variable than they are then we might well insist that excellence in clothing had to incorporate a degree of flexibility in face of our changing needs, and take into account the ability of the design to meet this demand when we assess the garment's claims to have withstood time's test, or, as we more usually put it, to have worn well.

Our willingness to think well of the garment that meets these requirements is clear enough. As before, its excellence consists in its ability to meet the demands we naturally place upon it, and for the most part there is a sound inference—of a defeasible kind—from its not having yielded to time's pressures to its possession of virtues which we require of articles of its kind. So we may reasonably give someone to believe that, in the case of our jacket, the garment is a fine one when (a) it has worn well in the various ways outlined and (b) there is no special reason to think that its doing so is connected with qualities unrelated to those that determine excellence in clothing.

That this model applies straightforwardly to everyday artefacts may not be contentious. What is more so is that it might also serve in discussing the arts and that a sufficiently close analogy exists between artistic artefacts and others to warrant extension of the model in this direction. Can we take at all literally Théophile Gautier's quatrain on the subject?

> Tout passe.—L'art robuste
> Seul a l'éternité.
> Le buste
> Survit à la cité.[14]

The way the analogy will have to run if we are to do so is clear enough. We shall say that a work of art survives the test of time by having properties (e.g. *robuste*) which enable it to resist pressures on the hold it has over us in its canonical interpretation, and that in standard cases these properties will determine the merit of the work. What may be less clear is how complicated a matter it is to show that this analogy can be extended, or what has to be established before the simple-looking argument will have any sure application to the arts. At the very least the following contentions will have to be made good.

First, we have to be able to identify an analogue in the arts of the coat's ability to wear well. This, however, is one point that need not hold us up, since the answer is given in our account of what it is for a work of art to pass time's test in Chapter 1, specified in historicist terms as outlined here. Then, given the connection between excellence of the coat and its possession of properties which enable it to fulfil its function, we shall need to examine the idea of the aims of art, first to see whether there are any, and then to establish how their achievement is connected with artistic merit. Third, the analogy can only be sustained if in the case of the work of art we can locate pressures that the passage of time brings to bear on the ability of the canonical interpretation to hold our attention. Next, where the work does survive these pressures, we must make it plausible that it does so for reasons akin to the strength of the cloth or the firmness of stitching and adequacy of design. We must make out a case for claiming that the work is able to survive because it possesses virtues that are intimately connected with the ability of the work to achieve art's aims. Finally, if we are to have any confidence in our future use of the test of time and in its embeddedness in our critical practice, we must show, in addition to the above, both that the pressures that make for loss are likely to be constant, and that the sort of properties which might resist them will constantly count as virtues.

To explore and elaborate these several claims is the task of the chapters that follow. Prospectively, Chapter 5 seeks to identify some important aims of art and Chapter 6 is concerned with locating and describing the pressures that the passage of time gives rise to. The next two chapters argue that beauty and depth are instances of properties that may enable the works that possess them to resist these pressures. Chapter 9 then undertakes to make specific the conclusion we want to draw from survival which is rooted in these pressure-resisting properties. With all that in hand Chapter 10 seeks to find an argument which will take us from the one to the other. Only if everything goes well all along the line will we have made out the viability of the desired analogue of the artefact argument I have just sketched for the coat.

Even if all goes well so far it must be apparent how little of solidity will have been achieved. At most the conclusion will have been secured that if a work of art passes the test of time on account of either its beauty or its profundity, its doing so supports an inference to its high merit or, as I shall say, its greatness of stature. But what we are looking for is a generalized form of this statement, one which makes no mention of specific aesthetic features of the work such as its beauty or its depth. So the problem will have to be faced of broadening the argument and freeing it of dependence on special features of the concepts discussed in Chapters 7 and 8. This will be the topic of Chapter 11. And even then we shall not know whether the test of time is an indispensable element in the critic's arsenal. We shall still have to ask how sure we can be that it will be serviceable for future art whose character we now know very little about. It will be the aim of the last chapter to make a start on that remaining issue.

Appendix

Although critics have often been shy about setting out and defending in any detail what they take to be an acceptable version of historicism, it is interesting to note how often its truth is assumed to be self-evidently correct. Three examples from the literature are instructive reminders of this and should suffice to convince the doubter of the tenacity of this tradition.

In 1818 Hegel had no hesitation in writing:

The first requirement of the scholar is an exact acquaintance with the immeasurable extent of individual works of both ancient and modern times; works which have already become submerged in the present, which belong to distant lands or continents and which the misfortunes of fate have withdrawn from our gaze. And then too every work of art belongs *to its time, to its people*, to its own circumstances and is dependent on specific historical ideas and purposes, which is why erudition in the arts requires extensive and detailed historical knowledge, since the very individual nature of the work of art has to be understood and elucidated in terms of detailed and particular matters. This form of learning does not just require a fine memory for its store of knowledge (as does every other kind of theory)—it also requires a developed imaginative power to preserve all the various artistic representations according to their diverse features—particularly in comparing them with other works of art.[15]

Not long before this A. W. Schlegel had spoken of the spirit of true criticism as demanding a capacity 'to represent to oneself the characteristics of other peoples and other times, to feel one's way into their core and to come to the knowledge of everything that honours human nature, everything great and beautiful beneath the external adornment that it uses to give them body, indeed sometimes even to the extent to penetrating apparently off-putting disguise—and to do them just due.'[16]

And in our own day John Shearman introduces his book on Mannerism in these terms:

In my view the contradictions in contemporary meanings for the word 'mannerism' are to a great extent due to the fact that most of them are too contemporary and not sufficiently historical. In the attempt to rescue sixteenth-century art from the ill repute that much of it enjoyed in the nineteenth century, it has been endowed with virtues peculiar to our time—especially the virtues of aggression, anxiety and instability. These are so inappropriate to the works in question (the sixteenth-century view of works of art was admirably relaxed). My conviction is that Mannerist art is capable of standing on its own feet. It can and ought to be appreciated or rejected on its own terms, and according to its own virtues, not ours. This raises no particular difficulty unless we succumb to a certain aesthetic squeamishness, for some of the relevant virtues are unquestionably hard to accept today.[17]

These passages need no expository comment. What can be overlooked, though, is that each of these authors adopts the historicist stance from a fundamental desire to do justice to the reality of the world lying beyond the self and beyond that captivating temporal analogue of the self, the present moment. In each case we see the theory of art adopting the historicist position from a drive to engage with a suitably realistic view of the world. This is something which we can only applaud, and which may make the theoretical labours of the last sections more palatable than otherwise they might be. To give it up would be to take a step along the path of abandoning the reality of different times and of different people. To resist that temptation is to recognize that art is not just a mirror of the self, but also a glass through which we see the reality of alternative possibilities that are not our own.

Chapter 5

Understanding and Order

Not without justice does Stuart Hampshire complain that modern empiricist philosophies 'have detached aesthetics as an autonomous domain, only contingently connected with other interests . . . The enjoyment of art, and art itself, is trivialised, as a detached and peculiar pleasure, which leads to nothing else. Its part in the whole experience of man is then left unexplained.'[1]

One source of this modern distortion can be located in a once popular, and still influential attitude to understanding, typified in some versions of philosophical atomism. A second lies in the difficulty thinkers have experienced in avoiding a self-contained, so-called 'aesthetic', explanation of the interest we have in matters of form. Only when theory discovers a path around these snares will it be possible to combine those living truths about the arts that we know we must accept with a philosophy of art that makes it possible to do so. It is my aim here to describe what such a path might look like. In treading it we follow in the footsteps of too frequently neglected pioneers of aesthetics, that is, of Hegel and Schiller, and do something to satisfy the first of those demands set out above, that is, identify what we may reasonably take to be some of the central aims of art.

I

In Aristotle's *Poetics* we find an early attempt to make a direct connection between the literary and visual arts and understanding.

Imitation is natural to man from childhood: one of his advantages over lower creatures being this, that he is the most imitative creature in the world and learns at first by imitation. And it is also natural for all to delight in works of imitation . . . The explanation is to be found in a further fact: to be learning something is the greatest of pleasures, not only for the philosopher but also for the rest of mankind, however small their capacity for it; the reason of the delight in seeing the picture is that one is at the same time learning. (1448b.)

Reaction to this and similar passages has in the main been unenthusiastic. The retort that it has tended to provoke is that if it is understanding that is to be provided by the arts then we shall inevitably reduce them to the status of encyclopaedia articles or a medical handbook.[2] In the visual arts our paradigms will be such works as Leonardo's anatomical drawings or Shaw and Nodder's *Naturalist's Miscellany*, and fine though these undoubtedly are they can scarcely be what sustains art theory at its core. The value of art must lie elsewhere, and it is suggested, the Aristotelian insistence on understanding acquired through imitation is better abandoned than developed. This is one way in which the healthy theoretical connection between art and life is broken down, and the door left open for an aestheticism of the kind Hampshire deplores.

The most rewarding approach to anti-Aristotelian philistinism is to ask what conception of understanding could possibly make this kind of objection to Aristotle inviting, for it is only with an understanding of understanding that we get to the heart of the issue. Consider these four propositions from Wittgenstein's *Tractatus Logico-Philosophicus*:

1.1   The world is the totality of facts, not of things.

1.21   Each item can be the case or not the case, while everything else remains the same.

5.632 The subject does not belong to the world, rather it is a limit of the world.

6.52   We feel that even when all possible scientific questions have been answered the problems of life remain completely untouched. Of course then no questions are left, and this is the answer.

A non-solipsistic reading of these propositions suggests that to have an understanding of the world is to achieve an accurate and objective representation of the facts. Since each fact is independent of any other fact, our representations must in the last analysis be freed of all contamination from the subject's position in the world or the vantage point from which the world is represented. Otherwise objectivity would be lost and we should not be addressing ourselves to possible scientific questions. So what understanding seeks is a model of the world that makes no concession of an internal kind to our being part of it. Ultimately it presents the world from no viewpoint at all except that quite ubiquitous one which is God's.[3]

This stark and familiar view of understanding is of reputable antiquity and has long been fostered by that metaphor of the mind that presents it as a mirror or a block of wax correctly representing the world only when its images or imprints replicate the world itself without any distortion.[4] No wonder it should have appeared natural to explain the arts so baldly as mimetic, or to find the critic (Johnson) praising Shakespeare for holding up to view 'a faithful mirror of manners and life'. Yet even the metaphor of mind as mirror does not sustain the view it aims to illustrate. For a mirror surely can only be judged accurately to reflect the world according to certain rules for decoding its image; and this has long been recognized. Hence the idea of the perfect mirror that reflects the world as it is, without the assistance of any contribution from the mind in decoding that image, is a myth.

Questions of metaphor apart, it should at once strike us how narrow is the scope allowed to the understanding on the atomistic conception of it. Its domain is explicitly restricted, as indicated by 6.52, to the facts which the natural sciences may hope to discover, facts which we shall ultimately find described in a language cleansed of all trace of the subject's viewpoint, and answerable only to the world as it exists in isolation from the conscious mind. While such a description of the world is one that does indeed belong within the proper realm of the understanding, it is not one which we yet fully possess, nor is it one for the sake of which we could or should desert our other interests.

To see that the ideal of objectivity must be dissociated from that of a neutral, God's-eye, view, we need only notice that even a report on the secondary qualities of objects[5] — the timbre of a wooden flute, say, or the hue of the ink in which I write — cannot avoid the use of language which reports on the world in terms of the way it presents itself to me. Such reports are nothing if not factual, yet can only be made comprehensible if we explain them in terms of the way our perceptual organs allow things to appear to us.[6] And the moment we have allowed this dissociation in such a straightforward place in our account

of the world we shall, at no sure cost to objectivity, be willing to
let our understanding range over a number of further topics
which the atomistic thesis would declare out of bounds.

Take a small segment of our vocabulary of adjectives. Things
are malleable or stubborn, cumbersome or handy, awesome,
reassuring, alarming, and so on. When I am told about the
contents of the world in these terms, my understanding of it is
certainly extended even if these descriptions are only given to
me by one who knows my susceptibilities and sensitivities, or in
doing so reflects his own. So too when I list the contents of the
world under substantival heads. There are doors, gravestones,
chimney-pots, governesses, and over-garments; there are
poisons, glue, quagmires, and fertilizers, etc. Such lists remind
us that for many practical purposes we organize the world from
our own point of view. Not to understand it in terms which
reflect this is to fail to understand it—not to preserve understanding in a desirably sanitized form.[7]

Understanding, then, may retain objectivity without for-
swearing the human or personal viewpoint. What we frequently
want is to find a report on something from a point of view that is
ours or shared between us, and that report will remain objective if it is sensitive to argument, if it holds out a hope of our
coming to an agreement about the appropriate description to
apply, and if it is responsive to the evidence that counts for and
against it when that evidence arrives. This idea of 'objectivity'
is well-established and long familiar to aesthetics; prototypi-
cally, I think it is just what Kant meant by saying that judgements of taste have an *exemplary* necessity and universality.[8]

With these remarks made, there should be no difficulty in
allowing that the quest for objective understanding does not
come to an end with a true description of the world's contents
even when described from the human point of view. For as soon
as the point of view has been introduced it can itself become the
subject of thought, and in thinking about what point of view on
the world mine should be I take within the ambit of understanding the less than purely theoretical questions of how to see
myself and my own position within it. Understanding of the
world in human terms sooner or later leads to knowledge of and
questions about the self.

Even so the atomist may object that we have not got very far.

Perhaps the account he offered of the understanding was a depleted one, but that may be of no more than passing importance. Our elaboration of a view of the world from our own standpoint might after all be a mere ornament that serves to decorate the more rigorous, perspectivally neutral, understanding, an ornament that could, so to speak, be cast off at will. If this were so then nothing of the above makes the connection between the arts and life anything other than contingent, and it is this prospect of contingency that Hampshire makes plain we have to undercut.

To advance here will be to show that the perspectival view is really not an option at all, not an ornament but of the substance, and this is best done if we approach our theoretical understanding of the world obliquely through considerations that are intimately connected with our practical concerns. It is common ground between both parties to our dispute that they are persons, and we may take it for granted that they both recognize that to be a person involves self-consciousness, an ability to plan for the future, and the capacity to set about realizing the plans they form, through end-directed action. Only if the understanding we have of the world pulls its proper weight at each of these three points will it be possible for us coherently to see ourselves as persons. I shall suggest that this can only be done if we abandon the idea that perspectival understanding is no more than a dispensable luxury.

Not just any movement we make is an action. At the very least actions are only those movements that are undertaken for reasons. And the atomist will be inclined to describe reasons in terms of desires we have for the obtaining of neutrally described states of affairs. Backed by (neutral) beliefs about the world, these desires may be expected to promote our ends through movements which are actions. Thus we may scratch an itch because we desire to relieve the irritation and believe that scratching is an effective means to that end. In a more complicated case, we may prudently do the shopping in the morning in order that it be possible to satisfy our evening hunger when the time comes. In terms of such a conception of action, we must be able to plan our life and undertake rational action in fulfilment of our plans.

A number of absurdities infect this picture. The first is that it is in important respects untrue to the facts of experience. What it suggests is that all action is undertaken in response to some desire or other. But if we understand 'desire' in a properly non-vacuous way this is untrue. Often enough we undertake to do things that run quite contrary to our desires. Thus I may want to do nothing more than to abandon writing these pages. After having lived with them so long they bore me, I find the writing difficult, and the labour with the pen is physically too exhausting. However, setting store by their completion, I persevere and assert myself *against* my desires, not swimming along with them. Here we have nothing like the satisfaction of a desire to scratch.

To meet this objection some have been inclined (e.g. Spinoza, *Ethics*, Book V) to dream up a stronger counter-vailing desire with which I may combat the call to sloth. But this leaves the idea of resisting a temptation quite inexplicable. It seems that if the only motivation of action is desire and desires are only (neutrally) comparable in terms of their intensity, the only way I can resist one desire is by putting another in its place. But then we are at a loss to say what the temptation of sloth could have been. How can it be possible for me to find it tempting to satisfy a weaker desire than a stronger one when all that motivates rationalizes my action is orectic strength? Furthermore, how could we possibly justify thinking of temperance as a virtue? For in so far as it enables us to resist the strongest desire it cannot be a rationally admirable trait, and in so far as it works by the generation of desires of greater strength it can scarcely be a virtue.

A more fundamental difficulty in this scheme arises when we try to think about prudential action of the kind typified in the example of the shopping. There we act in the present for the sake of a desire that we do not yet have. I would probably far rather stay at home and finish my novel than bother with the butcher, yet none the less I put on my shoes and set off. How is this possible? Within the atomist's account of action there seem to be two alternatives that he could appeal to. The first is that I have a present desire that my expected future desires be satisfied when they arise, and that this present desire for my future outweighs my other present desire to stay at home and polish off the book. Or else he will argue that the future reality of my evening appetite is quite strong enough to transmit reasons for action into the present, where only present action will permit the satisfaction of my future want.

The first of these is open to the objection raised before. It does not seem that present strength of desires for the future is effective only if we are sufficiently weak-minded about our present selves. Moreover, if it were correct the following sort of situation would be incomprehensible. A boy of 15 thinks that he wants to be a milkman. That is how his desires for his future now strike him. To be a milkman he should leave school now and apply for a job at the dairy. If he stays at school he certainly won't get the job, since dairies always turn down over-qualified applicants for the jobs they offer. None the less he may stay at school despite having this desire and this knowledge, and quite without any clear view of what he will do with the qualifications he is likely to get. It is not irrational of him to do so. He may, if he is wise, say to himself that his staying at school will enable him to have desires in the future which he cannot now imagine himself as having, and that because this is so he should stay at school. This is perfectly rational, but its being so relies on an assumption that the atomist cannot make, namely that some desires are rationally preferable to others.

If the atomist turns to the second alternative he is in no better a position. Now he seeks to explain how a present desire and an expected, future desire may conflict, and how the expectation about the future may prove more powerful in motivating action than the actual desire he now feels upon him. The natural answer may be to say that this can happen just because he regards the future desire as more important than the present one, but the idea of importance, as we have just seen, is one to which he can not in all consistency appeal.

How crucial this last point is comes out when we review the idea of what I do when I make a plan for my future, or when I decide how to lead my life. On the atomist's picture, it seems that all I can do is to consult a good predictor as to what in the future my strongest desires will be, or else I must look into my own heart and see which desires are now the most intense when I contemplate alternative future possibilities. Yet neither alternative bears any resemblance to what goes on in realistic cases of practical deliberation, for each of them eschews all consideration of the worth of the various contemplated outcomes. This the atomist must neglect, for questions of worth cannot enter into his conception of neutral understanding. As the *Tractatus* puts it:

6.41 The sense of the world must lie outside the world. In the world everything is as it is, and everything happens as it does happen: in it no value exists—and if it did it would have no value.

The upshot of this is that our concept of a person cannot be constructed from such meagre material. In addition to thinking of ourselves as responding to our desires, we have also to see ourselves as recognizing what we desire as desirable or valuable.[9] Who first recognized this truth I do not know, but it does no harm to give some of the credit to William Hazlitt for pointing out that '[t]he idea that all pleasure and pain depend on association of ideas is manifestly absurd: there must be something in itself pleasurable or painful before it would be possible for feelings of pleasure or pain to be transferred from one object to another.'[10]

The importance of this thought for my purposes is this. It has turned out that we cannot give a coherent account of planning for the future unless we have available notions like 'desirable', 'valuable', or 'estimable'. These have no part to play in the atomist's description of the world, but they must have a part to play in ours. This can come about only if we find things in the world to be of value and to be worthy of our esteem, and that will happen only if we frame a vision of the world that sees it from a point of view that we share with others and that generates descriptions of it cast in terms of, and responsive to, our common interests. The language that I use in employing such concepts cannot be constructed out of (*a*) the attitudes I have to the world and (*b*) the bare facts of matter, for not only would I then be unable to come by any interesting attitudes, but I would not be able to rationalize holding one attitude rather than another. This in effect is just what Hazlitt is telling us.

The whole train of thought that I have been developing has a long history. It certainly goes back as far as Plotinus (see *Enneads*, IV. vi. 1–3), is found in the Cambridge Platonists, the Lake poets, and the thought of such German Romantics as Novalis.[11] It pervades the writing of the later Wittgenstein and is perhaps the most notable contribution to philosophy of writers of the phenomenological school.[12] As far as aesthetics goes the *locus classicus* of the anti-atomistic position is undoubtedly found in the Introduction to Hegel's *Lectures on Aesthetics*, and it is only proper here to allow Hegel to speak for himself, for he as much as anyone has a clear conception of its importance in our understanding of art.

The general and unconditioned need from which the arts spring has its origin in the fact that man is a *thinking* consciousness, that is one that constructs from within himself what he himself is and indeed whatever there may be. Natural objects exist in themselves [*unmittelbar*] and unreflectively [*einmal*]: man on the other hand in so far as he is a spiritual thing has a dual nature. First of all he exists as do the objects of nature, but then also he is something in his own eyes; he observes himself, imagines himself and is only a spiritual thing at all in so far as he is actively reflective in these ways.

Men come to this consciousness of themselves in two ways, first theoretically, in so far as they have to bring to their own consciousness whatever moves within the human breast, its darkness and its turbulence. Then too we have to represent to ourselves what thought discerns as our essence and to recognize ourselves in what we call forth from within ourselves as much as in what we receive from without.

Then secondly, man is realized for himself in practical activity, in as much as he has the impulse in the medium which is directly given to him to produce himself and thereby at the same time to recognize himself. This purpose he achieves by the modification of external things upon which he impresses the seal of his own inner being, and then finds repeated in them his own inner characteristics. Man does this in order as a free subject to strip the world of its stubborn foreignness, and to enjoy in the shape and fashion of things an external replication of himself. Even the child's first impulse involves this practical modification of external things. A boy throws stones into the river and then stands admiring the circles that trace themselves on the water as an effect in which he attains the sight of something of his own doing . . .

The universal need for art then is a rational one: the need a man has to raise his inner and his outer world to the level of consciousness in a form in which he can recognize himself. This need for spiritual freedom is satisfied on the one hand by his forging for himself an image of what exists and then by providing an externalization of this image. Through this duplication of himself he brings what is within himself to his own view and to that of others.[13]

Anyone who sympathizes with Hegel's thought is far better placed than the atomist to second Aristotle's connection between the arts and the understanding. In the light of the now acknowledged need to detach the idea of objectivity from that of the neutral standpoint, he will be able to accept that the mimesis of the arts—and not only that of the literary arts—is one from which we may learn in various ways, not all explicable in terms of the kind of instruction we receive from accurately illustrated handbooks of biology or medicine. We are thus liberated from taking as our literary and artistic paradigms those works which initially forced on us a rejection of the Aristotelian view. Safe from this objection we are also free to detail some of the ways in which understanding may be provided by the arts, and to record the special place the arts have in its acquisition.

II

The child who learns by imitating the world may do so not so much by copying people he sees in it as by trying out various ways of representing it, and by testing them against the constraints his imagination discovers. So too the writer may present us with a representation of the world as it might appear *from a certain point of view*; from reading what he writes, we come to see both how the world might be, even if it is not in fact like that, and also how it might be possible to regard familiar types of situation in new and enriching ways.

This way of taking Aristotle's 'mimesis', available to us with the rejection of atomism, brings with it notable benefits. First it permits us to reconcile the quoted passage of the *Poetics* with the later claim, at 1451a, that 'the poet's function is to describe not the thing that has happened but a kind of thing that might happen, i.e. what is possible, as being probable or necessary.' To portray how something might appear when seen from a certain point of view is to do just what Aristotle demands. The probability or necessity of which he speaks does not characterize events that actually take place, but our way of taking the represented world. It is in the light of this thought that the earlier passage should be read, and only the non-atomistic Hegelian account of understanding allows us to make such sense of Aristotle's work.

Another advantage it has is to enable us to see what goes wrong in the thought of Romantic writings on art which present the poet as aspiring to a higher truth than that to which his more earth-bound fellows might attain.[14] This was the line adopted by thinkers such as Schelling or Solger, whose view was that 'the form of art must be the form of things as they are in the Absolute',[15] or that 'art is the Being and presence and reality of the eternal essence of all that is'.[16] Anything else, I suspect, struck them as too coarse, precisely because they thought it lacked the purity of neutral objectivity, or because it threatened to take them back to the workaday handbooks of the naturalist or the student of medicine. Only by inflating and eternalizing the truths of nature could they to their mind secure what they wanted, since they had no proper theoretical estimation of the instructive powers of a knowledge of possibilities. The assumption they were inclined to make was that we could only learn something worthwhile from a representation if we carry away from it a generalization that holds universally and of necessity. Hence their constant references to the Divine. This we can say is false, and proper awareness of the interest of possibility—be it of possible real alternatives or alternative possible views—enables us to avoid Romantic excess.

Of all writers on this subject none is more acute than Friedrich Schiller. In an important passage in the *Letters on the Aesthetic Education of Man* he is anxious to warn us against 'the nefarious influence exerted upon our knowledge and upon our conduct by an undue preponderance of rationality', where by 'rationality' he has in mind, among other things, just the kind of *Ideenwahn* that beset the German Idealists. To listen to Schiller is to appreciate just why the representation of the 'kind of thing that might happen' should be of such interest to us. First he tells us that '[h]owever strong and however varied the impact made upon our organs by nature, all her manifold variety is then entirely lost upon us, because we are seeking nothing in her but what we have put into her; because instead of letting her come *in upon* us, we are thrusting ourselves *out upon her* with all the impatient anticipation of our reason.'[17] We are inclined to understand the world from the point of view of the assumptions we bring to it, and because these assumptions are frequently unreliable, we are often as likely to misperceive the world as to perceive it accurately. To present to ourselves, in the arts, alternatives to the ways in which we are accustomed to believe events are guided enables us to detach ourselves from our assumptions—enables us to acquire an innocent eye in a way that few other activities can do.

Then too he is keenly aware of how our affective responses to others become ossified through the too rigid application of schemes of thought that we have elaborated to fit all possible practical circumstances, and which are far too insensitive to the realities of life and the subtleties of feeling to serve as more than fetters on our humanity.

It would be . . . difficult to determine which does more to impede the practice of brotherly love: the violence of our passions, which disturbs it, or the rigidity of our principles, which chills it—the egotism of our senses or the egotism of our reason. If we are to become compassionate, helpful, effective human beings, feeling and character must unite, even as wide-open senses must combine with wide-open intellect if we are to acquire experience. How can we, however laudable our precepts, be just, kindly and human towards others, if we lack the power of receiving into ourselves, faithfully and truly, natures unlike ours, of feeling our way into the situation of others, of making other people's feelings our own?[18]

About this Schiller is surely right, and we shall find no remedy to help us to an appreciation of the complexity of other people and of their legitimate demands on us without imaginative enquiry as to how things might be for them. The only alternative, and one against which Schiller inveighs, is blind appeal to principles by which we often only project our own preferences on the rest of the world. Their chilling attraction is unlikely to survive the recognition that the world does not have to present itself to others as it presents itself to me. The man of practical affairs, Schiller wrote, 'often has a narrow heart, since his imagination, imprisoned within the unvarying confines of his own calling, is incapable of extending itself to appreciate other ways of seeing and knowing.'[19] Aristotle, we may be sure, knew that it was not only the man of practical affairs who lies open to the dangers of narrow-heartedness. Knowledge of possibilities provides one key to the closed portals of the heart.

Both of these points can be formulated by concentrating on cases of coming to see how things might be without at the same time coming to develop alternative possible ways of viewing or responding to the world. From the position in which I now am it is easy enough for me to say something about how things might otherwise have been without my having to adopt a new perspective on the world myself. But only sometimes. Often I need to envisage and develop for myself new forms of affective response, and it is quite proper for us to incorporate into our notion of extended understanding this development of feeling. To come by new modes of feeling is to understand the world in new ways, and this we have seen stressed by Hegel when he speaks of the arts' capacity to awaken and form our affective life. Sometimes, it is true, he speaks as if our feelings, ready formed, await only the occasion of their evocation in the arts before they display themselves, and this way of talking invites dismissal on the ground that the evocative nature of the arts is scarcely of fundamental importance in our understanding of them. But when he is more precise Hegel does make it plain that the evocation in question need not be thought of except as a calling forth from us of a certain possibility of response, by means of fashioning for us new ways of thinking about the world: by developing a vocabulary in which the emotion or response can get expressed and hence can exist at all. As he also saw, in providing us with a vocabulary in which to think about possible situations, and therefore a way of feeling ourselves sympathetically into alternative ways of seeing things, the artist may enrich our ways of thinking about ourselves. Our interest is not perhaps in ourselves initially, it is in the characters and the situations portrayed, but as Aristotle pointed out (*Poetics* 1451b), 'poetry is something more philosophic and of graver import than history, since its statements are of the nature rather of universals, whereas those of history are singular,' and we can consequently understand defects and limitations in our own and others' ways of seeing things through being shown articulate and compelling accounts of how others have done so. Poetry is of wider range than history in that the primary intention of the historian's reader is fulfilled with the recognition of what happened, while the interest of the reader of poetry is not so focused.

One illustration of the position of art as one among other institutions for the provision of alternative perspectives on the world is furnished by the popularity in the late seventeenth and early eighteenth centuries of that ingenious device, the camera obscura. It has been said that its widespread use among artists and public in those days not only brought to the eye a new layer of reality, but also influenced well-established ways of thinking about the world through its dynamics, its colours, and its very naturalness. And it is plain that this invention contributed in a familiar way to the breaking up of habitual and lazy thought patterns, and enjoyed the popularity it did, just because it did for a time seem to strip the world of a veil that stifled the freshness of its appearance.[20]

But undoubtedly the arts have a special place in this domain that strengthens their claim on our attention, and justifies our seeing their capacity to act in this way as one important source of our attachment to them. How special this place is will be apparent on at least three counts. First, the artist in the construction of his work, and the spectator in his appreciation of it, both enjoy the benefit of standing back from the immediate business of life. They have the advantages of reflection that the practically-engaged man does not, and this is one fundamental source of the arts' ability to abstract from our everyday presumptions. This ability the artist shares with the operator of the camera obscura, when we concentrate on a purely depersonalized view of the natural world; but of course the artist enjoys the benefits of imagination and selective attention to his subject that quite transcend the narrower limits of the machine. It is through the distancing effect of selective illustration that the anatomical drawing succeeds where the photograph or real life example is prone to repel. The learned amateur, Hazlitt says,

is struck with the beauty of the coats of the stomach laid bare, or contemplates with eager curiosity the transverse section of the brain divided on the new Sturzheim principles. It is here, then, the number of the parts, their distinctions, connections, structure, uses; in short an entire new set of ideas which occupies the mind of the student and overcomes the sense of pain and repugnance which is the only feeling that the sight of a dead and mangled body presents to ordinary men.[21]

How much more powerful in this way are the arts as we move away from what *can* be mechanically reproduced and turn to the realm of the inner self and its affective grappling with its world.[22]

Secondly, the very publicity of the arts marks for them a special place. For their publicity and the continuous availability of the individual work makes them especially fit to supply the paradigms of understanding that more private discoveries and ways of thought do not enjoy. Take away the public paradigm, and the sense of what binds people together, their common concerns and the feelings of shared interest based on a common way of seeing the world, is itself loosened. Not for nothing do we so easily associate the idea of the arts with that of a culture; and evidently the inventive capacity of the individual comes to fruition only on the basis of what he has inherited from others and not had to construct laboriously for himself.

Finally, a point which Hegel makes with vigour if not always with approval, the arts' sensuous base gives them an immediacy of appeal which it is easy for discursive understanding to lack. Their sensuous base forces the artist to present the general idea through the particular image, and we need have no fear of allowing this particularity of the arts to be one of their strengths. For discursive understanding has to be tested against what is to be met with in experience, and the capacity of the arts to articulate and test our experience through their particular representations is one we have every reason to set store by.

III

So far I have argued that once we free ourselves of a certain misconception about the understanding we are better able than we would otherwise be to respond to the demand that the connection between art and life should be non-contingent. So much for the first source of theoretical distortion of the arts. In addition to this, however, I claimed that the atomistic depreciation of the understanding tends to bring with it an insistance on the formal aspects of art, and that a consequence of empiricist aesthetics has been to detach these too from their connections with our extra-artistic concerns. This is a debilitating error, and one which we again find Schiller showing us how to avoid, through his perception of the unbreakable link between our sense of form and the promotion of goods from which we cannot even in imagination detach ourselves.

To talk usefully about form we need to distinguish between those things that are ordered and those that are merely related. Let us say that x and y are related in a respect R simply if they satisfy the open sentence $\zeta R \xi$. In contrast I shall say that x is ordered in respect of y if the state of x is dependent on that of y, or if their states are to be explained in terms of some goal they both subserve. So, for instance, the bits and pieces lying scattered before me on the table are merely related as they lie there, whereas the parts of the typewriter at which I work are ordered—ordered in that their relations are explicable by reference to the place they have in a system that they help realize. Order thus implies relatedness, but not vice versa.

On this view, order may be found in the natural world as well as in the world of artefacts, and in the natural world in both animate and inanimate varieties. The planets are ordered in the solar system, their positions being functionally interdependent; so too are the parts of my body, for they are as they are because of the contribution they make to the persistance of this living human organism. Overriding all these matters, though, is the fact that as well as obtaining independently of us, as in these various examples, order may be something which we find in the world *because we perceive it in ordered terms*. Thus objects may seem to hang together in a systematic way when we see them as contributing to a unitary *Gestalt* or *Ganzheit*. In such cases we *may* do no more than see the world as displaying an order which it has independently of us; but just as often we cannot say that the order we see in the world is so independent; it is our seeing it that encourages us to say (truly enough) that it is ordered, and our doing so is a prime example of the way in which we describe the world objectively in terms of our interests in it. So, for example, we may see a group of mountains as grouped together even though their having the configuration they do is not geologically determined but politically.[23] The geological accident does not impugn our description of them as ordered as we see them. Order may appear in the world as dependent on our appreciation of it.[24]

Few today are likely to underestimate the contribution of our view of the world that this capacity for perceiving things as ordered makes. In the *Critique of Teleological Judgement*, Kant goes so far as to argue that its extensive use is an a priori condition of the possibility of experience itself; but for my more modest purposes it will suffice to remind ourselves of how deeply this capacity is rooted in the psychology of perception and of the self. We know that for creatures like ourselves, the capacity to order the contents of our visual and other sensory fields is a prerequisite of perception proper. Without the help of ordering schemata we could barely even recognize temporally distinct experiences as experiences of the same thing. For to regard myself as perceiving the same thing on different occasions I have to be able to classify different-looking views of it under the same heading, and this would not be possible unless, independently of the immediate phenomenal content of my experience, I had available to me a model in terms of which to order that content.

Similarly, it is a psychological truism that, without the firm struts provided by my ordering of events and objects into larger wholes, I am more likely to forget what my past contains than if I can make use of them. Such powers of thought as I have that depend on the development of memory are therefore also dependent on my powers of ordered perception. Hence a restricted ability in this sphere will have the more obvious sorry consequences for my ability to satisfy relatively simple, memory-related desires, and thus for the formation and satisfaction of more complex ones.

These claims are commonplaces of human psychology, and I do not offer them as anything more. However, in the *Aesthetic Letters* Schiller declares the sense of form (order) to reach deeper into the soul than these psychological remarks might lead one to suppose, and in now expounding some of the claims he makes I hope to do all that is philosophically necessary to warrant the thought that as persons we are not merely psychologically attached to things that depend on this power of order, but that we have a non-contingent interest in its development.

'The drive to form derives from the absolute being of man, or from his rational nature, and strives to set him in freedom, to bring harmony to the variety of his experience and to affirm himself against the vicissitudes of circumstance.' Thus Letter XIII. Here, as elsewhere, Schiller's main concern is with the connection he discerns between form and freedom, and which he derives historically from Kant. Within Kant's aesthetics the judgement that something is beautiful is an expression of our pleasure in finding that an object or a group of objects sustain a certain formal way of viewing it or them. The ordering that the elements before us sustain is a manifestation of our capacity to exert ourselves freely in the phenomenal world, which otherwise would be given over to the ineluctable causality of the natural realm. How the elements of intuition are arranged is very much up to the subject, and not imposed upon him by the nature of the objects judged—though of course they impose restrictions on him—nor, apparently, by the causally bound empirical self. The ability to see things as ordered is thus for Kant what provides the noumenal self with access to the world of phenomena.

Although a proper commentary on Schiller must acknowledge his close dependence on Kant, the link he asserts between freedom and form can be registered sympathetically enough without appeal to his Kantian metaphysic. What an admirer of Schiller may well insist is that, in a world dominated by causal forces, our experience of freedom is only as full as our ability to direct ourselves in accordance with desires which we see entering into patterns of which we make sense, and from which we do not feel ourselves to be persistently and unremittingly alien. If this is the kind of liberty which we both desire and know ourselves to have—rather than one which seeks blindly to except us from the causal forces to which everything in the world is subject—then its realization depends *inter alia* on our having developed a power of seeing the elements that make up our lives as hanging together in coherent ways. Furthermore, the extent of this freedom, happy or not, is potentially greater as that power is itself more flexible and more highly developed.

A man goes to a concert because he has a ticket and longs to hear the announced performance of a loved sonata. We expect there to be a causal explanation of his desiring to hear the work, but that tells us nothing about whether the man records himself as having gone freely to that concert. That will depend, we feel, on whether his desire to go and his going strike him as emerging from and fitting in with other things he thinks of as constituting his immediate past and his own personality. It will depend on whether the present desire is one he can integrate into the resultant picture he has of himself. This integrative capacity cannot be detached from his ability to order the elements of his life into something approaching a whole, a capacity to say with supporting reasons that one element has the place it has because others are as they are. Remove this ordering ability and we remove one thing that is presupposed in our calling our lives our own. On this score Schiller need not be gainsaid.

Of course it is not enough to secure Schillerian liberty that we have and exercise this capacity to order. We know too well that there are many people who do just this and still feel themselves excluded from the world that they construct. Both the schizophrenic and the paranoid have an organized world, but in the former case the ordered elements fragment and do not hold, and in the latter, the rigid structure that is erected is precisely one which excludes the subject and is experienced as being organized against him, hostile and thwarting. So the order a man *constructs* is not guaranteed against being his prison simply on the ground that it is *his* construction.

This is no criticism of Schiller. We need understand him to be saying no more than that a developed sense of order is a *sine qua non* of experienced freedom. Similarly the search for harmony, Schiller's second concern, can only be conducted through the development of an ability to attach ourselves with *pleasure* to the relationships we discern between ourselves and the natural world, and between ourselves and other people.[25] Thus we may say, with Schiller, that given that we experience a need to find a coherent pattern in our lives, and to strive after experienced harmony between ourselves and our surroundings, we should not be surprised to think that our capacity for perception of order is one to expand. Success in the greater enterprise must in some measure depend on the talent we have in the construction of patterns we do not feel are imposed on us from without, and which we do not seek to repel.

This material alone will explain the propriety of Schiller's speaking in the same breath of form and of the affirmation of the self against circumstance. For one thing, the exercise of perceptual ordering protects us against what would otherwise appear as uncontrolled chaos, and the recognition of recurrent forms in the world gives us a sense of security against the background of which we are able to plan for ourselves and our future. It is also true that in making strong and diverse attachments to the world we can protect ourselves against some of the defeats by which we are recurrently threatened and which Schiller would certainly allow to fall within the scope of 'circumstance'. A developed sense of order exerts itself in a multitude of ways, and with luck will allow the extension of our attachments in sufficient measure to make for the persistance of Schillerian harmony even when circumstance makes some of the orderings around which we have built our lives untenable. Order affirms that the self by providing sufficient pattern to a life to secure it against breakdowns that do occur.

None of this, of course, says anything about the ability of the *arts* to further recognized goods through the promotion and extension of this prized sense. It restricts itself entirely to the claim that a developed sense of order in our perception and understanding of the world is an important component in the achievement of humanly important aims and desires. However, I indicated before that it would be a travesty of Schiller's thought to represent him as anything other than eager to apply to the arts these reflections about the 'drive to form', and in a number of ways it is perfectly proper for him to do so.

The most general and obvious way is, for my purposes, the least helpful; but it must at least be mentioned. It observes that the development of the power of order is brought about in general through our contact with the arts, much in the way that a child might cut its teeth on an ivory ring, or a pilot learn his flying skills on an earthbound simulator. We might acquire the skill in recognizing complex patterns of one sort or another in the arts and then come to employ them for ourselves elsewhere. Something of this thought is what Schiller has in mind in assimilating art to play, and it is also something which we can see both Aristotle and Hegel alluding to in their remarks about children. However, this idea cannot help us here, not because it is false (which I doubt), but because in its application we are most unlikely to have any reason to think that we can identify the contribution of the *particular* work to this very general extension of our powers. While the truth of this suggestion may indeed tell us something about the over-all place of aesthetic experience in our lives, it contributes nothing to our understanding of the assessments we make of the individual work.

A more helpful thought is that just as the acquisition of a novel understanding may involve us in coming to see things in a very different light, and therefore in coming to pattern things in new ways, so too the provision of such an understanding through the arts may be achieved by their showing us a particular novel ordering of things, showing us how the world may appear when ordered in that way. We expect to apply to the arts for this service because our powers of invention and imagination and those of perception and understanding lie so often poles apart. Too frequently we only come to understand and adopt new ways of thinking if they are executed for us before our eyes, when we see how they appear when they are actually employed. So it is in this case. Our understanding can be hampered by constraints that work against our exercise of the imagination, and the scope the arts have for the exercise of imaginative freedom is reasonably relied on to make good our own limitations.

Thinkers struggling with the idea of form in the arts, and intent on describing its excellence, have repeatedly been struck by the thought that formal excellence appears to us harmoniously to reconcile the tensions of multiplicity within a unity. Suppose that this is right. Can we make any connection between our aesthetic interest in this phenomenon and the extra-artistic interests of life? Certainly we must not hope simply to project harmony onto the world that surrounds us in the vague way suggested in Lamartine's *Voyage en orient* (1835): 'Chaque pensée a son reflet dans un objet visible qui la répète comme un écho, la réflechit comme un miroir, et la rend perceptible de deux manières: aux sens par l'image, à la pensée par la pensée.' That sort of projection would be too crude. None the less there is a connection with the extra-artistic judgement of a kind which is traditionally recognized (e.g. by Kant) in the account of beauty that views it as a form which produces pleasure and whose value cannot be detached from the ways in which the world strikes us when we are within the power of the beautiful thing—its power being reckoned to endure longer than the perception itself through the way in which it tempers and conditions succeeding thought.

Talking of his early life, Edwin Muir recalls the oppression caused him by a daily journey through the slums of Glasgow: 'These journeys filled me with a sense of degradation: the crumbling houses, the twisted faces . . . filled me with an immense blind dejection.'[26] Such reports bring home sharply the spiritual effect of close association with the ugly and brutal. In contrast, Muir speaks of the liberating joy that the beauties of Prague afforded him, and there too we see the formal values of architecture carrying over into our appreciation of life itself. What we observe in such examples is the fact that achievement of formal excellence in our own creations spreads its effect wider than the mere pleasure in its perception. If we omit all mention of this real though little-understood connection of our aesthetic satisfaction with the non-aesthetic life, we shall naturally leave ourselves with a depleted account of the worth we find in the arts. There is no reason at all not to see in the sort of mechanism that Muir illustrates something of what Schiller aimed at when talking of the affirmation of the self against circumstance, for at their best they temper benignly our vision of other things too, and we need to advert to this power in a full explanation of our estimation of their finest products.

To speak of these things is to speak, if obliquely, of the expressive powers of the arts and of their formal qualities. I do not propose to say anything more directly on this topic. Suffice it to note that any analysis is defective if it does not allow that, in expressing values to which we are attached independently of the arts, the arts affirm and strengthen those values. Hume writes that 'it is a rule of architecture that the top of a pillar should be more slender than its base',[27] and that because such a figure conveys to us an idea of security it is pleasant. Now we do not have to be associationists of a Humean stamp to allow something of this to be true. We come to see the slender-topped pillar as secure, and seeing it as secure and pleasing touches the way we think about security itself. The process is naturally enough a two-way matter: our prior attachment to security makes it easy for us to embrace the forms of art which we come to see and describe in such terms; then also our appreciation of the variety of forms in the arts allows us to extend our vision and estimation of the world beyond them by reinforcing the values we recognize them to embody, and which we there experience with pleasure.[28]

Chapter 6

The Pressures of Time

The immortal puts on mortality when great conceptions are clothed in the only garment ever possible—in terms whose import and associations are fixed by the form and pressure of an inexorably passing time. And that is the situation we have to face.

J. L. Lowes, *Chaucer*.

Two steps forward have now been taken. As an analogue of the artefact's wearing well I said that the poem, the statue, and the building are durable provided that they survive in our attention long enough, and in a well enough embedded way, under a canonical interpretation. Then I identified some aims that the arts espouse and whose fulfilment we may expect to bear on our critical assessment of the individual work. We need next to specify strains and pressures that beset the arts over time and which correspond to the forces of friction and obsolescence that test a car or a coat over the years, as they are driven or worn.

The area in which to look for these pressures is indicated by a number of constraints that the foregoing argument imposes. First, it is plain that the forces involved do not so much physically wear away the work as dislodge it from our attention. Because the durability of the arts is defined in terms of their ability to retain our gaze, what makes them fade must act by lessening the power of the individual work long to maintain whatever place it ultimately establishes for itself.

Second, whatever makes for this detachment of interest must be presumed to work in the same way and with the same force against *any* candidate for survival. This is required because if we are to uphold the view that the works of art that survive do so by resisting these pressures, they must bear on those works that withstand them as much as on those that yield.

Third, in locating these forces we must respect the demand that, among the works on which they bear, the analogues we find of friction and obsolescence be temporally as well as culturally impartial. They must not be open to the suspicion of being likely to apply only at some times and not at others; for then the survival of works of art over periods in which these pressures were presumed *not* to operate would be of no evaluative significance. Pretheoretically, we are little inclined to think that this very often happens.[1]

Consistent with these three constraints and with our also retaining an interest in the arts at all, there are two notable ways in which the place held by an individual work conceived of in historicist terms may be undermined. We may find that our attention comes to be removed from that work and to be fixed elsewhere in preference, so that we no longer readily return to it and find less call than once we did to occupy ourselves with it. As individuals we often find this happening as our taste matures—recall Hume's reflection on the natural development of taste from Ovid via Homer to Tacitus—only now we are not so much concerned with the individual as with the group, and here too the same thing happens: works of art that engaged our predecessors no longer speak to us with the same insistence as once they did. Such, surely, is the fate that has overtaken the work of Guido Reni, say, or much of Tennyson's poetry. Other evident examples abound.

Let us call this sort of loss 'loss by *displacement*', attention here being displaced from its original object and removed to others instead. With it we may contrast the loss that occurs when the way in which one and the same work engrosses us changes over time, when we come to be held by an interpretation that involves us adopting a reading of it which is non-canonical and which has displaced a reading that was at some earlier time well established. This second type of loss we may call 'loss by *disturbance*', it remaining true that our attention returns over time to the same work, but only in a disturbed fashion.

To say that disturbance and displacement are distinct forms of loss carries a commitment about the identity of works of art. It is that when we come to give identity-criteria, be the works in question particulars (buildings, paintings, carvings, etc.) or universals (poems, sonatas, operas, etc.), we shall have to make reference to their proper interpretation. For if instead we were to allow them an identity that floats free of interpretation, as was envisaged in Chapter 3, it would turn out that disturbance was not a form of loss at all, and hence not a distinct form of loss from its counterpart.

To the unwary it may seem that even if we do specify identity criteria as I propose we shall still be precluded from making the distinction. To take one example, suppose we cease to regard Donatello's statue from Orsanmichele as representing St. George and erroneously come to view it as of St. Michael; apparently that is a case of disturbance; but shall we not then see that statue as a different work—not as *St. George* but instead as *St. Michael*? And then how should we resist thinking of the loss as an instance of displacement rather than of disturbance? Again the two seem to collapse into one another. However, this line of thought is mistaken. We need only notice that if the work to which our attention is directed is specified in terms of its canonical reading, here as a representation of St. George, it is to *that* work, to Donatello's *St. George*, that we attend even when we take it as representing St. Michael. So a disturbed reading and an undisturbed reading of *St. George* are readings of the same work, whereas displacement of our attention from Donatello's *St. George* to someone else's *St. Michael* would genuinely be a case of loss of attention by one work in favour of attachment by another. The two cases cannot be assimilated.

Confirmation of this view is provided by three further considerations in favour of building the canonical reading into the criterion of identity: (i) it makes it possible to speak of our *mis*understanding a work of art, which the rival view finds a difficult matter; (ii) it gives us a way of recognizing that Donatello's statue is *necessarily* of St. George—which is intuitively appealing, and (iii) it allows us to distinguish between that statue and the actual piece of marble which constitutes it. For we can now say that that very piece of marble—even shaped just as it is—might have represented St. Michael, though the work of art we know has to be *St. George*.[2]

Just as displacement and disturbance are thus distinguished for arts whose works are particulars, so too when we extend consideration to those that are universals. For there clearly remains available to us the difference between giving our attention to a piece of music under an interpretation which the canonical understanding of it would exclude, and giving our attention to another piece of music altogether. Similarly with the literary arts. The distinction is thus quite general. Furthermore there is no reason to believe that the pressures that make for either kind of loss should attach more to one art than to another, or that some of the arts are preferentially exempt from either of them. So we may ask quite unrestrictedly why we expect pressures of either sort to emerge with time. Having an answer to this question we shall then be justified in thinking that when these pressures do not make themselves felt some explanation of their failure to do so is called for.

Consider first loss by displacement. A work of art enjoys favour for a time and is then found to have moved towards the periphery of our cultural consciousness. One obvious explanation of such a shift points to the power exerted on established models by engrossing novelties. Formally speaking, of course, there is no incompatibility between our being attached to old and well-tried forms and our being engaged by what is new, but because there are limits to the art that can have a significant life in a community at any one time it is only natural to expect innovatory forms, attractive for whatever reason, to displace established ones. In practice, the novel can only work its way into our consciousness at the expense of something already in possession, and while the determination of what it is that eventually yields its place to the successful newcomer is a complex matter, we can consistently admit that the threat posed to the established order by novelty is one which is quite impartial in its operation.

To complain that a thirst for novelty is too weak a force for change for us to take all that seriously would be misplaced. For one thing, it does no harm to remember that even if the mere novelty of experience is not of itself a great recommendation for it, its power need not be exhausted by those claims on us which we can justify. Coolly to recognize that the novel has no rational claim on us as such will not prevent it from exercising the *de facto* power it has. Secondly, the novel exerts pressure not just by being new, but because it introduces enriching experience of kinds to which we are unaccustomed. It is a version of just this latter thought, rather than the former, that must underlie Plato's reflections in the *Republic*, 424–5, on Homer's line:

> For men more praise
> That which is newest of the minstrel's lays.[3]

There he makes it plain that he would, in his ideal state, have nothing against novel songs as long as they are constructed in established and accredited moulds, but that once the poet strays outside known forms he threatens us with 'the alteration of the most fundamental laws of the state', and must therefore be repressed. If Plato were setting himself against novelty as such, the distinction between novelty within established forms and novel forms themselves would be pointless. But he sees that the attraction of the novel forms is indivisible from the appeal of new ways of thinking, and that our interest in them is propelled by forces that find their satisfaction outside the reach of the well-tried and the mansuete. That he fears.

Not altogether sharing Plato's timidity about social change, and having a different conception than he of the proper relation between individual and state, we see no need systematically to fear the changes that new articulations of our relationship with the world inevitably impose on our organization of the heritage we receive from the past. To the extent that we are not politically repressed and not incurably self-alienated, we like to welcome the goods that novelty can bring, and our openness to this thought itself does something to increase the stress on what we do know from the side of what we do not.

Secondly, just as, apart from its other merits, novelty has some attractions of its own, so the established work carries with it a burden in virtue of its very familiarity, a burden which is quite independent of any particular artistic defects from which it may suffer. The individual of course often responds to familiarity with tedium, but such a notion is no help when we are concerned with the community whose composition is constantly changing. None the less a social analogue of the individual's tedium may be found in the feeling that what the past offers us no longer impinges very directly on our own present concerns—a feeling encapsulated in Oscar Wilde's shot at the naturalistic novel: 'M. Zola sits down to give us a picture of the Second Empire. Who cares for the Second Empire now? It is out of date.'[4]

This claim must not be misunderstood. It is not that the interests we have in working out and externalizing the modes of conduct and social realities of our own time do, or should, occupy the centre of our attention, or that it is a proper demand on the artist that he devote himself to the issues of his day.

Indeed, I wholeheartedly concur with Hampshire in finding it

a depressing error of social realists to suppose that 'important' themes are important, and that an art naïvely relevant to 'contemporary realities' is the relevant art of the time. We look to literature and the visual arts for significant redefinition of reality beyond the categories of journalism, 'significant' in pointing to unnoticed experience and in suggesting possibilities within us which have been excluded by social arrangements. We commonly find these definitions in original poems, fiction and paintings which disturb the sense of an imposed social congruence and which are animated by a hatred, expressed or unexpressed, of the losses in individual energy that are entailed.[5]

With all of this we can agree, but still insist that we display a tendency to direct our attention away from what is well known to us and away from what, because of its very familiarity, seems not to bear directly on us as at any moment we understand ourselves to be. This fact of psychology plays its role in accounting for displacement within the received order of art, and is untouched by quite proper strictures on fashionable or politically expedient ideals of social relevance.

As I have offered this point, it has been entirely general; and in the history of aesthetics there is at least one strand of thought which has sought to resist it. I have in mind the brand of formalism advocated in this country by Clive Bell, and before him in Italy by Francesco de Sanctis, and possibly before him in Germany by Kant. What these thinkers would have said about Wilde's remark is that it is directed at the wholly transient content of Zola's work and that that content is ill fitted to be the locus of our aesthetic interest. As a criticism of Zola, they would say, Wilde's observation may be pertinent enough, but with works of art that are properly engaged with issues of form, the power of familiarity must strengthen the hold on us of what is well-established rather than weaken it. So, for instance, in the *Nuovi saggi critici*, de Sanctis writes: 'Homer's gods are dead. The Iliad remains. Italy may die, and with her all memory of the Guelphs and Ghibellines: the Divine Comedy will live. Content is subject to all the vicissitudes of history, it is born and dies: form is immortal.'[6] Now it is of course all too easy to criticize the tradition in which de Sanctis writes, easy to dismiss the thought he offers us as trading on an untenable distinction between form and content and assuming an indefensible account of the aesthetically interesting. None the less something of what he tells us does make sense and needs to be preserved, and only when we see what it is can we be sure of the correctness of my claim about familiarity. One harmless way of putting the formalist's point is to say that whereas the ostensible subject-matter of a work of art may cease to have any independent and general interest for us, as, say, the Second Empire, the treatment of it that is offered in the arts is not subject to the same attrition. As Wilde himself puts it, 'What does subject matter signify? Treatment is the test',[7] and the reason why this is so has little to do with the interest that the subject-matter itself may or may not have for us. It resides in the fact that so many of the judgements we make of the treatment of the subject are framed in terms which we adopt in coming to understand the work in the first place, and are more or less independent of what it is that is treated. And it is for this reason that successes of treatment strike us as more telling rather than less as the conventions within which the aesthetic judgement is made become more firmly rooted. So, to give an example bearing explicitly on the theme of displacement, Charles Rosen has said that

there is a belief that . . . the dramatic qualities of Haydn, Mozart and Beethoven are due to their violation of the patterns to which the public was conditioned by their contemporaries. If this were true the dramatic surprises in Haydn, for example, should become less effective as we grow familiar with them. But every music-lover has found exactly the contrary. Haydn's jokes are wittier each time they are played . . . This is because our expectations do not come from outside the work, but are implicit in it: a work of music sets its own terms.[8]

How does this way of putting the matter affect the issue of familiarity and the formalist's objection to my appeal to it? Not surprisingly, the answer must be that things remain as they were. For the survival of Haydn's dramatic qualities, or of the *Divine Comedy*, or of the *Iliad*, evidently provides us with cases of successful resistance to the pressures to which they are subject. They provide no reason at all to think that the handling of the themes they treat may not itself be liable to be taken for granted as we come to find it immediately expressive. It remains true that for this very reason familiarity encourages us to make inaccurate perceptions—even of matters that the formalist admits as genuinely *formal* matters—and finally induces failure of appreciation and consequent detachment of attention. This is a perfectly normal sequence of events, and is in no way incompatible with the acceptance of the part of de Sanctis's thesis that commands our sympathy. So familiarity remains an agent of displacement.

A third, equally important, source of strain derives from what I shall call the failure of naturalness. Over time established forms, familiar though they be, cease to be ones in which we naturally express ourselves or to which we find ourselves spontaneously attuned. This can happen because they cease to articulate values that are potent within our lives. Then we are likely to find that the strangeness of the represented order distances us from it and promotes further shifts of attention away from the images of the past. Provided only that we have some reason to expect the passage of time to bring about such unnaturalness, this force too will satisfy the constraints noted above; and this expectation can be made good by pointing to the tides of cultural change that wash our history and alter the way we intuitively look at the arts of the past as well as any other surviving traditions that come down to us. From a changed conception of ourselves and our world, however brought about, earlier views familiar though they be cannot but strike us as alien, and the view that has become alien undoubtedly has a harder task in holding its place than it had when it was naturally assumed.

It may seem paradoxical to claim that the failure of naturalness and increase of familiarity both contribute to the dislodgement of established art. Is it not rather that when the still familiar work becomes unnatural these two forces cancel each other out, and that when the unnatural work has lost its familiarity then it stands to benefit from precisely the novelty I have said attracts us? The paradox is at most a seeming one. In the one case it suffices to notice that familiarity and unnaturalness are not incompatible. Hence they need not—though I dare say they sometimes may—work in opposite directions. On the other hand, where what we experience as unnatural has ceased to be familiar it may still not strike us as interestingly *new*. Its age will be apparent and then it will scarcely benefit from the promise that novelty holds out. Strangeness and novelty are distinct concepts, and must not be confused.

The strains on the established order stemming from the advent of novelty, from growing familiarity, and from increasing unnaturalness, come as close as any to providing plausible analogical images of friction. We may now look at the other head of displacement I mentioned, obsolescence. The most widely canvassed idea in this area is that after a time particular artistic themes become exhausted, and that when they do we turn elsewhere for sustenance. Whatever truth there is in this observation, we must be cautious in its deployment; for the minerological metaphor of 'exhaustion' warns us that the theme in question is not primarily one which is exclusive to the individual work of art, but one which is shared by a number of works having a theme in common. Because this is so, the talk of exhaustion threatens to move us away from our present concerns, more in the direction of style than of the individual work executed within it.

None the less the metaphor can be applied to the individual painting or poem when the perceptions that they offer us eventually work their way into the view of the world that familiarity with them helps us to achieve and to establish. With the passage of time the arts mediate the change between one conception of the world and another, and as the newer views become firmly rooted so we stand in less need of that assistance in their maintenance that mediating works of art provide. The force of the striking painting or poem may be diminished as what it shows us becomes something that we internalize. Since almost any successful work of art has something of this effect on us, the threat of exhaustion when understood in this way is a perfectly real one. Nor should concern with the individual work of art lead us to imagine that exhaustion of a style is quite irrelevant to us here. For when the style in which an individual masterpiece is cast is felt to have worn itself out, new works in the style are less frequently met with than was once the case, and the style itself loses its direct appeal. This has its effect, naturally enough, on our perception of individual works to which the style has given birth: as the style yields to one in which we more naturally express ourselves so its exemplars themselves come to impress themselves upon us with increasing reticence.

So at least we may suppose—if only we have a plausible model for the exhaustion of the style itself. For without such a model my reference to a style's becoming worn out is quite question-begging. Clearly enough, the picture of a style with just so many possible works available to the artist, which become used up as he goes on, is nonsensical; and the popular vegetable analogy of growth and decay is hardly more attractive. Nor shall we want to look to the vagaries of Riegl's *Kunstwollen* or the endogenous dialectic of Wölfflin's *Kunstgeschichtliche Grundbegriffe*, since they lack that theoretical independence of the historical facts they are used to explain which any truly explanatory concept must possess.

An alternative to any of these limping makeshifts is hinted at by Dante in Canto XI of *Purgatorio*. There Oderisi da Gubbio warns the poet:

> La vostra nominanza è color d'erba
> che viene e va, e quei la discolora
> per cui ella esce della terra acerba (115–17.)

—the same sun that brings on the green shoots of repute also causes them to wither; and the literally-minded reader is prompted to ask what constant force for change the sun ('quei . . . per cui') might here symbolize. The best choice seems to be that it represents one of a number of ideals espoused by the art of a given style towards the realization of which the artist strives. As we become acquainted with one response to such an ideal, so we acquire a glimpse of what alterations to our achievement may promote a more adequate response, and this perception, grounded in our first efforts, makes for a closer match the next time round between aim and execution. So, for example, Dante understands the relationship between Cimabue and Giotto,[9] and so we may see developments of quattrocento art where what was at stake was reputation[10] and where 'the establishment of classics naturally provoked the ambitious to seek yet higher peaks'.[11] So also we see the development from the rigidity of archaic Greek sculpture to the realistic work of Lysippus.[12] In these cases it is the same, or a recognizably similar, ideal which produces both the primitive work and the mature one that displaces it, exactly as Dante suggests.

This model of limited, problem-relative, intra-stylistic, artistic advance—as opposed to the problem-neutral, trans-epochal progress criticized before—has been very familiar since the publication of *Art and Illusion*, for it does no more than generalize the mechanism of 'schema and correction', or 'making and matching', to which Ernst Gombrich there drew attention. And clearly it is some mechanism such as this that we must understand Dante to have in mind if we are fully to appreciate the encounter with Oderisi, and make the necessary distinction between the quoted tercet and the earlier lines that present an entirely capricious picture of artistic change:[13]

> Non è il mondan romore altro che un
>   fiato di vento ch'or vien quinci e or vien quindi
>   e muta nome perchè muta lato. (100–2.)

I am encouraged to conclude then that exhaustion operates in two ways against the survival of the individual painting, piece of music, or poem, by making them seem dated. It makes itself felt either by adding weight to the already recognized forces of familiarity or unnaturalness, or alternatively through those ways in which strain is predictably imposed on the individual work when the styles and artistic ideals that imbue it develop as a result of reflection on earlier achievement. In both cases the idea of obsolescence may be appropriately enough transferred from its primary application to the simple artefact and find its station in our account of displacements which we observe in the domain of art.

So much for the idea of displacement. Its complement, disturbance, is more quickly dealt with, and can be seen to come about in two ways. Something of the preferred understanding of the work may get *eroded* as time passes, or else something may be superadded to the original by a kind of cultural *accretion*. It would be of course a simplification of the facts to say that we should expect some works to be disturbed by one force and others by the other. That is not what typically happens. More often what we find is that both processes are at work at the same time and in a cumulative fashion: erosion makes for disturbance both by eroding aspects of the preferred understanding of the work, and also by changing the shape that earlier accretions to that reading have given it; accretion makes itself felt by adding interpretative material to both the model and also to those versions of it that are left when already active erosive forces have eaten away at it; crystals form on Stendhal's twigs both on the twig itself and on previously formed layers of salt.

To bring together the scattered material we have already come across, let us recall a number of sources from which erosion stems. It is indisputable that with the passage of time we find that visual and literary allusion on which the proper understanding of so much art depends may easily get lost. This quite general phenomenon is perhaps most obvious and most effective in the case of architecture, for often the understanding of how a building is to be seen depends on our having access to *other* buildings to which allusion is made and on the knowledge of which we are dependent for making appropriate aesthetic judgement of the edifice before our eyes. Necessarily the allusively indicated building is older than that which alludes to it. It has therefore been exposed to the risk of physical destruction and natural deterioration. Furthermore, since that building itself may need to be understood in terms of allusion to yet others, even if it stands in pristine glory we may find it difficult to understand allusion to it by later works, because by the time we come to regard them the material we would need to comprehend the allusion is lost.

It is not only material changes in our environment that bring about this kind of loss. Changes in the patterns of education, for instance, make it hard for later generations to respond to the intended significance of certain signs in a composition and to recognize the importance of ways of speech which our ancestors would have regarded as second nature. To take one blatant example, a man who knows no Latin and who has no acquaintance with the *Aeneid* will not make much headway with *Paradise Lost*, at least when he comes to attempt reconstruction of that epic rather than a modern-dress version of it. If, with Richard Wollheim, we describe the struggle to acquire appreciation as the struggle to replace association by understanding, it is evident that the occurrence of erosive change in our perception constitutes a powerful threat that original understanding should be replaced by random assocation. It is also evident how pervasive such changes in fact are.

More subtle than these two sources of loss is a third, at least as wide-ranging in its effects as either of them. Any artistic work of significance assumes the general currency of ethical, religious, or metaphysical presumptions against the background of which it has to be understood. As time passes we expect these presumptions themselves to change, and because they change something of an obscuring veil is cast over artistic utterances produced against this background. Furthermore, we know that just as these very broad assumptions have been unstable in the past, so they are unlikely to achieve a permanent stability in the future. So however cautious we are about the preservation of our physical environment, or however conservative we are in our conscious choices about the education of future generations, we cannot preserve ourselves from the effects of change in the framework of our thought.

It is for reasons such as these that we are likely to sympathize with a thought James Dewey expresses in *Art as Experience*: 'It is simply an impossibility that anyone today would experience the Parthenon as the devout Athenian contemporary citizen experienced it, any more than the religious statuary of the twelfth century can mean, even to a good Catholic today, just what it meant to the worshippers of the old period. The "works" that fail to become *new* are not those which are universal but those which are *dated*.'[14]

To sympathize, but not wholeheartedly to agree. For what Dewey supposes, and what my last reflection has suggested—namely that we have to *share* those ethical, religious, and metaphysical attitudes in order to respond to the work that is informed by them—is in its full generalization surely false. Earlier on I insisted on the importance of imagination in our coming to understand what the past has handed down to us, and we have met no argument yet that shows that its exercise cannot make possible what Dewey thinks is beyond us. Properly understood, what his observation has to teach us is that a historical understanding of any art is likely to become more difficult as time passes, and 'that is the situation we have to face'. Changes in our framework of beliefs contribute to this difficulty and play their part in hastening erosion of understanding; but this does not mean that we are powerless to resist it, or that what erosion does occur always occurs at the same rate or in the same places. Even where it cannot be resisted it can be recognized, and at those points we may confront the past with a sharp sense of loss. We must not conclude that this loss dominates all the past. Just as sometimes the search for time lost is vain, sometimes what it yields is time regained.

The truth of these generalities is hard to assess except when faced with persuasive instances. Dewey of course offers his, and they need to be matched by others that point in the opposite direction. Here is one: the appeal of the cancan in the later years of the last century and the early decades of this depended very largely on its being experienced as engagingly *risqué*. Without its naughtiness it would have been nothing. Since those times our sensibility to the shocking has changed almost beyond recognition, so much, one feels at times, that the idea of what is shocking is almost lost. In these circumstances we should, following Dewey, expect the dance could only be found ridiculous today and certainly hardly exciting. Yet this is not, I think, correct. For what one notices with surprise is that when well staged and the context properly prepared—when our mental set is suitably reorganized—much of the original *frisson* may be recaptured. And if it can be done here, then why not elsewhere where the gains are so much greater?

Disturbance by erosion has its counterpart in disturbance by accretion. Earlier discussion of the theme in Chapter 3 indicated as its sources changes in critical practice, in artistic practice, and in the general cultural climate of the time, and nothing else need be said to amplify this list. My earlier appeals to such changes took it for granted, though, that these are *inevitable* concomitants of passing time, and we may want to be assured that this is indeed so.

Without espousing any indefensible claims about social determinism, it is easy enough to agree that static models for society are self-defeating. The picture of itself that a culture offers, and uses in the deliberation about its aims and achievements, is the product of many adaptations of the patterns of men's desires to their conception of what is desirable. The recognition that something is desirable is possible only in so far as we come to regard it as attainable (or at least think that it is feasible that it should be attained). And as we achieve greater mastery of the natural world, making use of the discoveries of the past in doing so, so we prepare for developments in what we see as desirable and thus make way for pressures on the inherited cultural climate. So even when we make no references at all to the arts, we may allow that it is a moral certainty that our ways of thinking about ourselves are liable to change. Furthermore, we know that this instability is increased when the products of the arts are regarded, as they must be, as contributing to the intellectual and cultural climate in which we live. For in the arts we find the sharpest public presentations of particular modes of understanding and patterns of order, and hence the most potent determination of adjustment and change to ways of understanding we have come to accept as natural. Once we take the arts seriously, we cannot avoid thinking of them as making for changes in our world view: and then as calling forth new articulations of those changes within their own domain. An instability in the cultural climate that can be predicted without any reference to the arts gives rise to the expectation of change in the arts themselves the moment they are admitted as participants in the cultural patterns that make up our lives. From this undetermined dynamic of change we can conclude that the way we see the past, and therefore also see the arts of the past, will almost unnoticeably incorporate accretions which are due to changes in the web of our thought that have come about since the occurrence of the events we seek to understand, or since the construction of the art of the past that we admire in the present.

Only examples can bring home how precarious understanding is, once we adopt the historicist standpoint that is a precondition of the possibility of legitimizing the critical inferences. So to close this discussion of disturbance I offer one instance of the effects of both erosion and accretion as they work together, and to illustrate the subtlety with which they impinge on works of art which we think intuitively we have little difficulty in understanding aright.

In the chancel apse of Sant'Andrea della Valle we see Matteo Preti's *Crucifixion of St. Andrew*. Our proper response to that fresco, set as it is behind the high altar, must be in some sense devotional, and to understand it in any other way must be to misunderstand it. Yet to succeed in responding devotionally depends on our being able to set ourselves imaginatively within the field of the picture, to think of ourselves, the viewers of the fresco, within its pictorial space and present at the scene of the martyrdom. Not to think of ourselves like this is to force onto ourselves a non-devotional stance and to see the work exclusively as an exercise of a painterly virtuosity that combines ill with its devotional intent.

Preti's fresco dates from 1650 or 1651, and at that time scenes of public violence, even in the form of public execution, were more commonplace, and experienced as less repulsive, than they are today.[15] Acceptance of public violence may very well have protected the seventeenth-century Roman churchgoer from offence and made the devotional spirit of the painting accessible to him. For us, however, things are different. Perhaps it may not be necessary to be wholeheartedly Christian to respond to the work's devotional intent, but undoubtedly our twentieth-century resistance to witnessing violence makes the imagined transposition of ourselves into the pictorial field much more difficult than it would once have been. The imagination that we are witnessing the martyrdom (definitionally an *unjust* execution) is difficult to tolerate today, and this contributes either to our finding the work repellent or to our falsifying it by distancing ourselves and then seeing it as little more than a vulgar showpiece.

Here the devotional response is eroded over time by a change in public sensibility that has accompanied changes in philosophical and emotional estimates of the value of human life; and if we do achieve the imaginative leap that is required of us by the demand for devotion, our response is threatened by accretion, in the form of repulsion or disgust which close imaginative attention to the picture makes difficult for us to avoid. At one and the same time the historical reading of the work that we aim for is threatened from both quarters.

If the justice of this diagnosis is recognized, someone might be led to ask whether it does not forcefully bring out the self-defeating nature of the historical approach I have recommended. The question is very natural; and it must be answered. This we may do by recognizing that the force of disturbance is limited. Very seldom do we find disturbance to be total; it reaches in different ways into different works, and in different degrees of depth. To have lost *some* of the sense of the original is not to have lost it *all*. As my remarks about the identity criteria of works of art make plain, even a major misunderstanding of the work is not a threat to the *work*, but only to our understanding of it. Understanding is always a matter of degree. If this is not recognized all hope of legitimizing the critical inferences is lost.

Even so, an opponent will say, does not the discussion of Preti's *St. Andrew* show how very easily an adequate understanding of the arts may become lost to us? And if the canonical understanding can so easily be lost, as here it is, is not the pursuit of that elusive goal (even if theoretically desirable) practically pointless? To this suggestion my response will be plain: something has been forgotten; the very fact that Preti's *St. Andrew* is a mediocre work that has no great claim to have withstood time's test.

To remember this and to understand why it is so is to accept no more than any rational historicist must: that the future becomes present only at some cost to the present reality of the past.

Chapter 7

Depth*

It was not however the freedom from false taste . . . which made so unusual an impression on my feelings immediately, and subsequently on my judgement. It was the union of deep feeling with profound thought.

Coleridge, *Biographia Literaria*.

Not all understanding displayed in the arts retains our attention over time, but some sorts do so better than others. This is particularly true of that art which, on account of some understanding it makes available to us, we call profound. Why this is so, in contrast, say, with what is merely clever, assertive, or intellectual, should emerge from an account of what depth of understanding is and a description of how if finds artistic embodiment. Here most of my discussion will assume a literary paradigm, but its extension to other non-abstract arts should in the end look natural enough.

I

In abstraction from all artistic matters I begin by asking when understanding evinces depth, and do so at first in terms of understanding that is austerely theoretical. About that, a number of truisms spring to mind that any elucidation of the idea will want to respect.

(i) A thought is shallow or deep only in relation to a topic. Unless we assign it to a subject-matter we can make no defensible judgement of its profundity. Where several topics are in question the judgement will be indeterminate until the relevant one is specified.

(ii) Depth of theoretical understanding must standardly be

---

*The reader anxious to pursue the main line of the argument without delay may like now to pass directly to Chapter 9. He should be willing to take with him the additional premiss argued for here and in Chapter 8 that depth and beauty in art provide two examples of qualities which we can standardly expect will enable the art possessing them to resist those pressures on its survival which were described in the last chapter.

expressible in the form of a proposition. Otherwise we could not say it had a content, and it then would risk ineffability.

(iii) Third, we expect the profound to enjoy a constancy to which the superficial lays no claim.

(iv) Last, we incline to assume that depth and truth are intimately linked.

Of these four it is the last that most urgently needs some argumentative support. One thinker ready to dispute it was Nietzsche, who held that 'a feeling is accounted deep because we esteem the accompanying thought for deep. But a deep thought may lie very far from the truth—as for example any metaphysical one.'[1] If he is right here, depth and truth are at best contingently related, but it is hard to believe that he was not confusing a use of 'deep' encased in scare-quotes with its more standard usage. After all, no one was more vigorous in pointing out how much of what passed for depth was really idle mystification; and few have been better able to see that such 'deep' thoughts are rarely true. Hence the jibe at contemporary metaphysics. But if this is what Nietzsche had in mind it would throw no doubt on the link there is between depth and truth, for while 'deep' thoughts may not be true they are not deep either, so their falsity shows nothing to the point.

It is open to the Nietzschean here to say that there is a better way of understanding him. A deep thought is simply one that holds a key position in a structure of beliefs, a thought on which others are taken to depend. Metaphysical thoughts are deep because, in philosophy, they do hold such a position. None the less they need not be true. This is so because a structural position in a set of beliefs (which may itself contain much false-hood) is quite independent of truth. So the dependence of other beliefs on some keystone belief is independent of that belief's truth. Depth and truth are thus unrelated.

This argument is unattractive. For one thing it is incompatible with our withdrawing the qualification 'deep' from a belief that we reject as false. But not only do we *now* say that the thought is not a deep one, but we also say that previously we were mistaken in taking it to be so. The mistake we recognize ourselves to have made need not, however, be to have thought that that belief had some particular structural role to play in our understanding of its subject-matter. About that we may well have made no mistake at all. Rather our mistake lay in thinking that it was true.

Secondly, the structural thesis makes it difficult to account for our interest in the discovery of depth. On that view a profound discovery will be something that organizes and adds cohesion to a set of beliefs about a subject-matter; yet merely to have this power is not enough, since independently of the belief that the new cohesive element is true it has no claim on my acceptance. Hence independently of my belief in its truth it has no great claim to my interest. And if depth is unrelated to truth, neither has it.

Thirdly, the structural proposal undermines the contrast noted at (iii) between the constancy of the profound and the shifting nature of the superficial. It would readily hold that a belief that is profound in one man's understanding of a subject may not be so in the understanding of another or in the same man's understanding at a later date. One and the same belief may consequently be superficial and profound at different times, and what beliefs are profound are not of necessity constantly so. So the contrast disappears. (Of course it would none the less be a constant truth that a belief is, if profound, constantly so, relative to a particular ordered set of beliefs that it organizes. But then, *mutatis mutandis*, the same would be true also of the superficial beliefs of such an ordered set, and the familiar contrast would still elude us.)

None of these difficulties arises if we retain the connection with truth. If a belief is false then its very falsity will prevent what it records from organizing the subject-matter in the way we thought it did. Our mere *use* of the belief to organize the world does not enable it genuinely to do so. Secondly, because our interest is in *true* theory and is guided by our concern for knowledge, profundity of understanding must be of more than mere architectonic interest. Lastly we expect the constancy of the deep truths of a theory to be explained in terms of their constantly holding; peripheral matters are thought to be more fluid in character. The traditional contrast between depth and surface remains available.

What sometimes makes people unwilling to take this step, and encourages them to embrace the purely structural position, is the thought that we often refuse to abandon a claim that a man's understanding of a subject was profound even when we knew that strictly speaking what he said was false. Newton's mechanics involved universal claims which today we know to be untrue, yet this does not seem to impugn the depth of his discoveries. But all that I have urged is that truth and depth are intimately linked, not that the former is entailed by the latter, and sufficient linkage may well be maintained by insisting that it is *approximate truth* that is in question rather than its absolute ideal. Newton, we think, nearly got things right, and it is only if we come to abandon this belief that we call the profundity of his mechanics in question. Once we relax our demand for truth to this extent, the residual attraction of the exclusively structual thesis disappears.

This does not mean that structure is irrelevant; on the contrary it is fundamental, for unless we manage accurately to say what is the structural role of the profound truths of a theory we shall not easily get beyond the rather watery metaphor of surface and bottom on which common ways of talking rely. In the literature the only writer I know of explicitly to accept this challenge is Hazlitt, and dissolution of the metaphor best proceeds from what he offers. Depth, he wrote, 'consists in tracing any number of particular effects to a general principle, or in distinguishing an unknown cause in varying circumstances with which it is implicated and under which it lurks unsuspected. It is in fact resolving the concrete into the abstract.'[2] Rather than just seeing here a cursory assemblage of unrelated ideas, let us take the last sentence as a distillation of Hazlitt's thought, and treat the preceding disjunction as illustrating different ways in which the concrete may be resolved into the abstract. The resolution that is offered is not of course a *reduction* of the particular facts and events (the concrete) to abstract general truths; rather the latter *explain* the former, and the resolution is entirely explanatory: effected, Hazlitt thinks, in either of two main ways. First, and here I enlarge, we can appeal to general truths in describing the structure and function of systems in which particular effects occur. These latter can be explained in terms of their place in the system, and then the general truths are not causally involved in the production of the effects. Thus the circulation of the blood is explained, thought not causally, by reference to the body's need for oxygen and the function of heart and lungs in satisfying that need. Alternatively, as for example in the explanation of rule-governed intentional behaviour, we may find general principles underlying diverse observed phenomena that are causally involved in the production of the effects. So we might explain a variety of grammatical sentences in terms of the same underlying rule, and be forced to make reference to that rule in the causal explanation of the particular utterances; otherwise that would not be the rule that was there being followed.[3]

Details aside, such a reading of Hazlitt suggests that there is a good prospect of illuminating the metaphor of depth, at least where systematic theoretical understanding is involved, in terms of true explanatory generalizations of one sort or another. But for our purposes this can only be a start, since obviously not all such generalizations about the observed nature of some subject are deep ones. Many explanations we propose and accept remain superficial despite their truth, and nothing that Hazlitt has to offer indicates how to accommodate this fact. But it is not hard to see in outline how he might quite consistently have gone on.

Where we desire to advance explanation of some matter beyond the superficial we often do so by incorporating it within a wider-ranging explanation, so that the initial explanation becomes redundant and is subsumed under the broader principle. That is one way forward. Sometimes by contrast we retain our original explanation as non-redundant, but come to see that its own applicability to the particular case is determined by further wider-ranging principles of the same theory. That is another way. What each procedure suggests is that we count an explanation as deep only as we approach the limit of a series of such subsumptions and supplementations. The limit is located at that point beyond which no further explanations are to be found.

This I think is correct, but with one reservation. It is that the identity of such an explanatory series must be bounded by a particular theoretical vocabulary. Unless this were so the prospect of indefinite progress in science would deter us from characterizing any of the explanations we give of natural phenomena as deep, since we may have little reason to think ultimate any terminus of explanation that we actually come to.

For all that, the popular programme of eventually explaining the facts of psychology in terms of neuro-physiology, and those of neurophysiology in terms of those of chemistry and physics, in no way stops us from believing that there are deep truths of psychology and deep truths of neurophysiology. And this is just as it should be, because having noted at the start that a deep truth is always a truth of a certain subject-matter or topic, we should not be surprised that the limiting explanation that qualifies as deep for the subject should be cast in a vocabulary that is appropriate to our initial ways of introducing it. Hence we should have no qualms about filling out the lacuna in Hazlitt's treatment of depth in this way. Nor should we hesitate on account of any uncertainties that might show up in our decisions about what properly belongs to the theoretical vocabulary of a given subject-matter, since however vague this notion may be its very vagueness will be matched by the security or hesitancy with which we make judgements of depth in the area. To be uncertain about the boundaries of the subject naturally brings with it uncertainty about what we should count as its profundities. As long as these two uncertainties march together no disquiet need arise.

The emended version of Hazlitt's proposal then is this: a truth about a certain subject-matter offers us a profound understanding of that matter as it approximates to the limit of a series of wider-ranging explanations of its topic, where the limit in question is fixed in terms of an appropriately chosen theoretical vocabulary fitting what we set out to explain. The undoubted attractions of this view will be enhanced when three of its natural corollaries are noticed.

First, it enables us to see why we easily think of depth as being abstruse. It is not simply, as Hazlitt observes, that the 'general principles lurk unsuspected beneath the varying circumstances with which they are implicated'; at least as important is the fact that to find the true common principles we often need to forge a theoretical vocabulary whose adequacy to its task depends for its deployment on our having a range of knowledge that usually takes us well beyond the natural subject with which we are concerned. The difficulties of profound understanding often stem as much from this as they do from the labour we have to tease it out.

Secondly, we can now state more accurately than before the truistic contrast between the constancy of the profound and the variability of the superficial. In any science of nature the laws to which we ultimately appeal are thought of as unvarying and holding for all time. Once we come across generalities which we fancy change over time we start to hunt for further constantly applicable explanations for the supposed variations. So we naturally expect terminal explanations to display stability. Failure of stability is itself an incentive to seek deeper underlying truth. On the other hand, what lie at the start of a series, the superficial facts and events that get explained, are frequently unstable in that the forms they take on and the ways in which they present themselves to us are, as Hazlitt says, the result of 'varying circumstance'. Different forces come together and work themselves out in particular cases in different ways. What are shifting and inconstant are the manifestations of forces that are themselves unchanging.

Lastly, Hazlitt's proposal tells us why we find the theoretically profound a source of interest and a goal of discovery. Once we come to possess the deepest understanding of some topic we have as much knowledge of it as may be achieved within the body of some theory. And that is a matter of interest to the intellectually curious creatures that we are. Furthermore, it is true that in that fortunate position we shall be well provided with the theoretical knowledge that we need to connect our understanding properly with successful practical thought. This prospect plainly gives us additional cause to concern ourselves with depth in our theoretical understanding of the world.

II

The more willing the reader is to follow Hazlitt, in the last section, the more puzzled he may be about applying his suggestions to literature, or indeed to any of the arts. It is bound to seem at first that because of our concentration on the general and the abstract we shall be forced into the absurd position of Schopenhauer, for whom it was the task of the finest artist (typically the musician) to reveal 'the inmost essence of the world and utter the profoundest wisdom in a language which his reason does not understand'.[4]

Apart from the special difficulties of applying such a dictum to music, what is estranging about it is the assimilation it encourages of artist and natural scientist, combined with a high-minded contempt for the discoveries that the natural scientist himself makes. This contempt is manifest in the suppositon that there exists a deeper level of reality to which the understanding of the scientist cannot reach, and one which only the intuition of artistic genius can penetrate. From my general line of argument it should appear that neither assumption can be welcomed.

As for the latter of them, it follows from my analysis of theoretical depth that one truth will only count as deeper than another if the first explains at least as much as the second. If what the artist of genius discovers about 'the inmost essence of the world' really is to count as the profoundest (theoretical) wisdom then it must tell us at least as much as the best theory for the relevant topic. Hence it should be judged by the same standards as are applied to the assessment of scientific theory. To suggest that this holds in any of the arts will appeal to no one.

The former supposition, that the tasks of the natural scientist and the artist run together, must also be treated with suspicion, as we saw in Chapter 5, and most certainly when it is taken in its grossest and least developed form. Preoccupation with the formulation of theoretical generalities as one of its proper and major concerns is not a pronounced feature of the artistic mind. Much more typical is the kind of sentiment expressed by Proust in his preface to *Contre Sainte-Beuve* when he claims that it is only by abandoning intelligence and concern with the abstract that the writer can recreate anything of our impressions and thus realize in his work anything of himself— 'la seule matière de l'art'.[5]

But even when we are struck by this thought and impressed by Proust's insistence on the presentation of particular appearances, the reconstruction of particular images and the recreation of particular feelings, we need not on that account abandon all thought that artist and scientist have common interests, and need not on that account alone despair of treating profundity in art along Hazlittian lines. For there is at least one way in which it has seemed possible to reconcile the generalities of deep theoretical explanation with the artistic concern for particularity, one which is set out with great clarity in a passage of *Wilhelm Meisters Lehrjahre*. At the point in question Meister is outlining the grounds of his new-found enthusiasm for Shakespearian drama, after a long period of immersion in the French classics, and is made to express himself in these terms:

All those premonitions that I have ever had about men and their destiny, premonitions that have accompanied me from my youth on even unbeknownst to myself, are fulfilled and developed in Shakespeare's plays. It seems as if he dissolves all puzzles for us, yet without it being possible for us to say that here or there we have the key. His people seem natural men, yet they are not. These highly mysterious and artificial creatures act before us in his dramas as if they were clocks whose dials and casings are made of some special glass; they tell the hours as they should, yet at the same time we see the play of their springs and wheels.[6]

In this adaptation of the philosophically familiar image of the clock, Meister is suggesting that in profound art we are shown true general principles governing people's behaviour. Particular characters and their actions are perspicuously presented in a light that enables the spectator to discern their underlying explanatory principles. And something like this is just what is going to be needed if we are to make anything much in art of the Hazlittian elucidation of the theoretically profound. However, there is something about the way in which Goethe develops his simile that is misleading, since it invites the scrupulous and literally-minded reader to think that Shakespeare's success lies in presenting two separate items in his plays, first the particular actions of the plot (the hands and dial of the clock) and then the principles that govern them (the wheels and springs). And it will be thought objectionable that while the wheels and springs are logically detachable from the dial, such a detachment cannot be carried through for a man's actions and their apparent explanations. In the dramatic arts the actions are all that we are shown.

Yet if we attend to the idea that Goethe offers us of the clock-face being made of a special transparent glass through which we see the workings of the clock as we read off the hours, this disturbing sense of the image's inadequacy can be relieved. For what better picture could we have for the idea that in

Shakespeare's very presentation of his characters we see the driving forces that move them? What Meister is getting at is that Shakespeare shows us his people in the light of true general operating descriptions, and what he suggests is that his art is deep in part just because that light is one that incorporates Hazlittian depth about actions of the kind it illuminates.

It speaks in favour of this view of artistic depth that it should satisfactorily explain why we find it natural to say—as I did in this chapter's first paragraph—that depth is *embodied* in the work. In so far as literature and the other representative arts present something in a light that makes it plain why the represented people and events are as they are, they place before our eyes embodiments of general truths. No other way of talking expresses this idea so well. Furthermore, and returning to Goethe, we can now see why Meister should have been so puzzled to think that all mysteries are dissolved in Shakespeare's plays without a key to their dissolution being offered. To desire a key is to desire something that is detachable from the lock. Yet *embodied* depth is not detachable from its embodiment. It is rather more like a description of the lock itself which is so clear and precise that the need for a key to turn it is bypassed. To ask for a key, as Meister is inclined to do, is to ask for the wrong thing. What the arts provide is a perspicuous description of the lock, and that is what Goethe's more extended and better chosen image of the clock has to teach us.

Encouraging though these reflections are in the way that they show there to be no conflict between interest in generality and a concern for the particular, the proposal that they combine to deliver cannot really be correct. For if it were we should expect to have no trouble in understanding at least one way in which we can regularly identify art as profound. That is, there would be a simple transition that we could rely on which would allow us to pass from a claim that a work displayed depth of understanding of its subject-matter by the Hazlitt–Goethe model to the claim that it is on that account a deep work of art. Yet this transition does not seem available without exception. For instance we might well think that Isaak Walton's *Compleat Angler* or Boileau's *L'Art poétique* each handles its topic in a way closely akin to that outlined, but I doubt whether our admiration for either work is rooted in its depth. And should these two examples be found contentious I hardly think that the reader will find it difficult to think of others for which exactly the same difficulty will arise.

So far as I can see there is only one way in which the supporter of the Hazlitt–Goethe model might hope to meet this difficulty. He might try to say that the transition from a deep treatment of some subject-matter to the depth of the work itself can only be made over a certain range of topics, and that the inconvenient examples of Walton and Boileau are merely flawed by taking their themes from a range of subjects that do not generate deep art. However, as we shall see this suggestion cannot work, and what we shall be forced to conclude is that Hazlitt's account of depth is not the one to pursue.

Evidently it could be no easy matter to specify accurately any uncontroversial subject range that might be thought to be depth-permitting in art, but to attack the proposal which is offered that will not be necessary. For taking a hint from Meister's observations about Shakespeare, and remembering Pope's famous couplet apropos, we can be sure that if there genuinely is a restricted range of topics available to the artist, at the very least the topic of man himself must lie well within it. So we should expect that where a poem or other work of representative art displays Hazlittian depth of understanding about men we shall unequivocally recognize the work in question to be one of depth. But it does not seem that we always do.

Taking the suggestion first in the most literal-minded way, it is easy to think of counter-examples to the claim it generates. By Hazlitt's criteria there is no reason why Leonardo's anatomical drawings or some suitably composed verse study of human pathologies should not qualify. Yet it is hard to believe they do. Again, let us suppose that Zola's conception of heredity and social determinism had been more nearly accurate than we now know it to be, still it would be implausible to think of *Les Rougon-Macquart* as enjoying a profundity which as things are we find that cycle of novels to lack. The very fact that Zola's characters would remain, in M. H. Abrams' phrase, 'victims of their glandular secretions within and of sociological pressures without' would be enough to justify our withholding that claim from those books, however much we may admire them on other grounds.

It would be a natural enough thing to say at this point that what these examples show is that 'the study of man' should not be taken quite so simplistically. What that phrase really alludes to is how men see the world, themselves of course included; and what appears now to have gone wrong has done so because of the way in which Hazlittian obsession with systematic understanding has forced us to neglect this. Once we turn back to the non-absolute (though still objective) and the anthropocentric view of the world as Chapter 5 encouraged us to do we shall not be faced by embarrassing examples of the kind just given. The idea of deep theoretical understanding is far less restrictive than that suggests.

Now this criticism is certainly correct. The trouble is that it cannot simply be accepted while we leave everything else unchanged. For even when greater stress is laid on our experience of the world from the inside, so to speak, we cannot hope to get what we want within the framework of the Hazlitt–Goethe model. Not only shall we still be confronted by counter-examples to the resulting thesis about depth in art— by Pope's *Essay on Man* itself, perhaps, or by Ovid's *Ars amatoria*—but more seriously we shall also have to question whether the picture of depth itself on which I have been concentrating is the right one at all. For as long as we stick by it we shall be insisting both that depth in art depends on the existence of underlying principles in terms of which men's subjective experience of the world is to be explained, and that the interest we have in art of depth is carried by our interest in seeing how these principles actually operate. Either assumption can be fairly doubted.

In the first place we may well think that the ways in which our experience of various aspects of life is formed do not answer to stable underlying principles at all. Certainly when we come to explain why people think and act as they do, and restrict our explanations to the realm of the psychological, we do not seem to look for general principles at work. Rather we present the man about whom we are asking in the light of his own particular processes of thought. And then even if principle does play a larger role in accounting for the ways in which men do experience the world from the inside than seems likely, it is implausible to think that the arts notably interested in the display of such principles in action. For if they exist at all they are of such

a highly general and unspecific sort that we find them neither
mysterious nor in the abstract particularly engrossing. In art of
depth the focus of our interest is therefore not well seen as they
display of the particular case in the light of underlying
explanatory laws. It lies elsewhere, and for this reason I take it
that we need to supplement Hazlitt's rather scientistic account
of depth with one that better lends itself to application in the
arts.

III

Outside the arts, even in areas of theoretical study where it
makes good sense to seek Hazlittian depth of understanding,
we can also find ourselves speaking of those who have no
knowledge of general principles as men of depth. This is particularly noticeable when our interest in what they have to tell
us depends less on their ability to give us explanations than on
their capacity to predict. We may want to know what will
happen if this piece of metal is put to use in building a machine
or what we might expect this organism to do when exposed to
these others, and provided that a man can reliably answer this
sort of question over a wide range of his subject's behavioural
repertoire we incline to allow him a deep understanding of it.
To take another instance, the huntsman who knows exactly
what his quarry will do in given conditions of climate, of
terrain, and of physical exhaustion may be such a man, and so
too an old country herbalist who can reliably match his
patients' symptoms to the remedies at his disposal over the
range of disease and illness to which they are prone. In neither
case do we need to know whether huntsman or physician relies
on any general principles that might explain why his subjects
behave as they do. It is enough that he can regularly get things
right, and his performance may very well be no better with the
help of principles than it is without them.
    Nor ought it to be mysterious why we find the metaphor of
depth apt to describe such people. In order that the predictions
that they make or which underlie what they say be regularly
accurate the huntsman, doctor, or whatever has to make the
best possible use of the evidence available to him. He must be
able to get more out of it than do those of more restricted

understanding, and he must be sure not to misinterpret what evidence there is. In the first way his view reaches further than that of the rest of us, and in the second he sees the reality there is in the appearance. Hazlitt's phrase mentioning a cause 'lurking unsuspected beneath the circumstances with which it is implicated' is not so far amiss here, though in the present context it would be more accurate to leave causality out of it and to speak of reality being visible *in* the appearance rather than lurking *beneath* it. Anyway, in both respects we think of understanding of a situation approaching a limit, and our judgement of its depth again reflects our belief that the limit does not lie far off. It is perfectly true that our concern now is not with a terminus of explanation, but this provides no reason to think that the metaphor of depth is out of place. The terminus with which we are concerned—namely with the fullness of information that can accurately be gained from the data available in a given situation—is one around which our interests very naturally revolve; not the interest in *why* things are as they are but in *how* they are and in what they will in consequence of that come to be like in the future. There are other parallels with the kind of systematic theoretical depth discussed before, too. We still cannot elucidate it without reference to truth; it is obviously difficult to acquire, and it is a natural focus of much practically oriented observation of the world. So why should it not also find a favoured place in art?

In one way at least, one which I have already suggested is crucial, it is even better placed than its rejected rival to do so. For here there is no question but that the idea applies easily and naturally to art's prime subject-matter, to man himself and to his ways of seeing his world. Just as someone may display a deep understanding of animals by knowing what the individual will do in a wide range of particular circumstances, and how it will respond to a wide range of stimuli, so too he may have a deep feeling for men. Only there is a notable difference between what goes on in the two cases, and one on which everything that follows will depend. It is that whereas in the case of the animal world no essential reference to the mental is called for, when it comes to understanding men it is impossible for us to abstract from the way in which those we understand see the world, what they believe about it, affectively feel for it, and see as desirable to achieve within it. For what men do, unlike what other creatures do, they do in the light of their thoughts and feelings, and anyone who concerns himself to observe and predict men's behaviour cannot expect any regular success if he neglects these mental springs of action. But real though this difference between the various cases is, it does not make deep understanding of men something of a different order from that of the huntsman or the country herbalist. It remains of the same order, only it is understanding of something with a far more subtle and complex functional organization.

When we turn to the arts, matters are further complicated by the fact that our interest in understanding men always extends beyond the single represented individual. Of course it is quite possible for a man to have a deep understanding of one person alone and feel at sea with the rest. But in the arts we demand more than this. For what we expect to find there extends not just to the display of some particular imagined set of beliefs, preferences, and feelings, but needs to take in or rest on an appreciation of interesting possible ways in which salient aspects of life may really be thought of and internalized, and play themselves out. In practice here things are made more manageable by our readiness to concentrate on something less than the whole range of men's behaviour. Very often what is explored is the way in which a man's conception of himself and his world may be dominated by some form of a common affect like ambition or pride, or by the choice of a certain mode of life, and how these things may determine the sort of existence a man can have who lives under their sign. But still we should notice that even here we are very much engaged with the understanding of man, for each of these particular examples can be seen as marking out a restricted range of that subject, as picking out men who are affected by one or other of these sorts of experience. And apart from detailed appreciation of the ways in which men are affected by and come to see themselves as affected by these and comparable things, there just is no way of understanding them from within.

Putting these various reflections together we arrive now at a very different description of what profundity in art might be than was previously offered. It is that where we find a subject treated which is identifiable as man himself—even when

restricted in the ways just mentioned—we shall have a profound work of art if it is one that displays a deep understanding
of its subject. And that will be one in which the writer or painter
so treats his topic that from the view of it he presents he can be
recognized as exemplifying those conditions which make for
descriptive and predictive success in the relevant area. In
achieving this, he will present the world in such a way as makes
it apparent to his audience how a man of a certain sort may see
it, and bring to our notice the kind of complexity in a man's
subjective view of his situation that is liable to work as a
significant determinant of his thought and his action.

The chances for this proposal's success depend very largely
on its ability to face three objections. And of these the first and
most obvious is perhaps the least challenging. It is that our
interest in depth in art has absolutely nothing to do with
making predictions. What holds our attention is the illustration
of possible ways in which the world may be viewed, and not
with what figures in the work are likely to do in the light of the
way that they are shown to view the world, nor what course
people suitably like them outside the work are liable to find
their lives taking. Prediction, it will be said, is quite the wrong
notion on which to concentrate. But this objection is largely
beside the point; for the way in which the idea of prediction has
figured has simply been as a way of introducing the extensiveness of understanding in terms of which depth is explained. It is
not that in order to have a deep understanding of some topic we
must have an interest in making predictions about it. What we
do have to have is a grasp of the kind of information which
would make prediction possible. Even when, as in the arts, we
abandon all concern for making predictions, we may still have
to specify a kind of understanding that the arts display in terms
of what, if it were manifest outside them, would facilitate an
activity that has no direct place there.

A second criticism reaches further but still is not conclusive.
It is that the very particularity of the artist's concern does not
readily allow us to say that the understanding that is displayed
in art of depth matches up to the standard I have set. For in
presenting that standard I have emphasized the extensiveness
of the predictive ability that depth of understanding makes
possible. And that may seem to have no room here, for either we

cannot say of the individual work that it does display such extensiveness—it is too individual—or else we shall think that its possession can only be *inferred* from the artist's treatment of the single case. But then our interest in the work's depth will be of the wrong sort, based in some understanding that the work *indicates* and not in something that it *evinces*, where it is the second of these that we really care about.

Certainly we must not be forced onto the second horn of this dilemma. But that will only happen if there is no way in which we could meet the first, and there is at least one popular way of doing so that is suggestive. It sees the individual case as in some way universal. The protagonist of the work is no mere isolated individual, he is Everyman. Thus the understanding of his plight is the understanding of all men's plight, and for that reason the understanding on display in the work, which appears in highly particularized form, is of unrestricted scope. Hence it is requisitely extensive.

Once shorn of its unnecessary element of exaggeration there is something acceptable about this idea. What is exaggerated is only its claim to universality. Not only is that usually lacking, but it is also more than is needed. It would be quite sufficient if the understanding evinced in the work were of a suitably important typical sort, so that what we see happening in the particular case is recognizable as repeatable or else exemplifiable in circumstances that could be met with elsewhere. It may be true that it *takes* extensive knowledge to be able to display concretely and with conviction a typical complex of ideas and feelings or a typical mode of experiencing the world, but that is not what we are interested in when we come across art of depth. What we see is how the relevant mode of experience can typically work out in certain determinate circumstances, and this typicality can provide us with the extensity of understanding that is wanted. It makes available to us something that we can extend to a sufficiently large range of other cases.

Before I move on to the last objection I should put in two caveats. First, it might be supposed that by saying what I have I am forced to denigrate our interest in the particular and assimilate what it offers to the wider general interest just mentioned. This is not so. The particular case that is displayed fully warrants our interest and our attention; but what constitutes it

a study of depth is that it shows us something that can be
extended beyond itself. We do not have to explain our interest
in depth by direct reference to other cases, for the simple reason
that we acquire the vision of the typical case on the basis of this
one, but unless there were this extensibility depth would be
absent. So the claims of the particular case are not diminished,
it is just that we cannot say what they are without pointing
beyond it.

Second, it is important that the notion of typicality be not
misunderstood. In my use it has nothing at all to do with being
representative or common or average. Typical ways in which
our modes of experience are realized need not even be widespread. What matters is that they, like typical forms of an
illness, are salient among the varieties of form that experience
can take and consitute types around which particular instances
will cluster. To know what the typical forms of something are is
to be able to see in the instances we do come across features that
otherwise we might easily neglect. So the deep truths about
something that the artist shows us are well describable in terms
that Coleridge once used of genius. 'Like the moisture or the
polish on a pebble, they neither distort nor false-colour their
objects, but on the contrary bring out many a vein and many a
tint which escapes the eye of common observation, thus raising
to the rank of gems what has oft been kicked away by the
hurrying foot of the traveller on the dusty road of custom.'[7]

The last objection to be forestalled is this. It may be felt that
the course I have adopted leaves out the very thing that guides
our interest in profundity as we find it in art. It appears to omit
altogether our judging a work as one of depth by virtue of its
capacity to show us what to make of its topic when presented in
the way it is. Everything I have said has concentrated on the
way in which our understanding of something is accurate or
adequate, but this we might think is quite a different matter
from knowing what to make of what we are shown, and unless this
has its place the account must be defective.

However, I think that when we remember the emphasis I
have placed here and in earlier chapters on the anthropocentric
nature of the understanding that the arts provide, and on the
way in which they show us things through the ways in which we
and others are typically affected by them, it is far from clear

that this accusation hits the mark. Despite what is assumed to the contrary, there is here no clear way in which we can distinguish between sustainably understanding how a complex of thought and feeling is typically liable to operate, and knowing what to think about it. For the full understanding of these experiences cannot cut itself off from the judgements we make about them. Everything of importance about the resulting thought is given by way of descriptions which we see fitting what we understand, so when that understanding is suitably replete, it will contain what is necessary for us to know what to make of its object.

These three objections then can be met. Nor do I see any other reason for thinking that the proposal I have advanced is fundamentally unworkable, though it may of course well need further refinement. In the absence of that, confidence in the suggestion might be strengthened if it could only be seen at work, and while this is not the place for extended forays into criticism there is some point in testing it briefly against a couple of real cases. One I shall take from literature, the other from painting.

A minor figure in Joyce's *Ulysses* is Gerty MacDowell, a girl whose mind is essentially made up of genteel cliché. To show how impoverished is the sort of life open to one of her cast, Joyce needs to show how she thinks of herself, and in a thumb-nail sketch of her, seated opposite Bloom on the beach, he exhibits her as permeated and confined by fantasy of the most common currency:

She would care for him with creature comforts too for Gerty was womanly wise and knew that a mere man liked that feeling of hominess. Her griddlecakes done to a goldenbrown hue had won golden opinions from all because she had a lucky hand for lighting a fire, dredge in the fine selfraising flour and always stir in the same direction then cream the milk and sugar and whisk well the whites of eggs though she didn't like the eating part when there were any people that made her shy and often she wondered why you couldn't eat something poetical like violets or roses and they would have a beautifully appointed drawing-room with pictures and engravings—and the photograph of grandpa Giltrap's lovely dog Garryowen that almost talked, it was so human, and chintz covers for the chairs and that silver toastrack in Clery's summer jumble sales like they have in rich houses.[8]

To my mind it is incontestable that Joyce here offers us a deep view of one particular form of sentiment. He shows precisely how that mode of thought may dominate a life and how the world appears when under its control. In arguing for the importance to us of 'the sleazy shop-worn fabric of Gerty's little soul' one writer has noticed how we are here shown that 'when the very means for registering value are as coarsened and corrupted as are Gerty's we cannot avoid asking how honesty, decency, charity or any of the other virtues are possible on which any healthy civilisation is founded.'[9] Cleanth Brooks is surely right. And we might notice that what he says is not put just in terms of what we are taught to see about Gerty herself, but as a more general truth that we learn on the basis of this individual example. Through the accurate observation and presentation of the individual Joyce brings out how such sentimentalities can work themselves out, and once we recognize what he shows us for what it is, and so know what to make of it, we have taken one important move towards being armed against them.

Moving away from the literary, consider for contrast Masaccio's *Expulsion from Paradise* in the Brancacci Chapel. That we think of as a profound work because of the understanding it provides of the meaning for men of abandonment by God. What mediates this understanding is not just the despair of Adam and Eve stamped on their every limb and evident in their distraught gestures; more than that we are brought to realize how, in their despair, the world beyond the gates of Eden is bleak and unwelcoming to them. The painter has managed to intimate that the bleakness is not simply a feature the world has independently of them. In the absence of God's grace there is no other way in which they could see it. In their state, a state which we may also share, beauty and goodness have departed the world and departed it for reasons internal to those whose world it is.

What is here demonstrated in as compelling a way as paint allows is how men's well-being can depend on embracing an ideal that transcends our immediate interests—an ideal that is expressible in the language of religion as openness to the light of God. Nor is this thought available only to one already of a religious disposition. In the knowledge of the story of the Fall

and in awareness of the devotion of Adam and Eve to their own
desires we see in the picture how self-oriented gratification, and
rejection of any such ideal, can taint and make worthless the
world that men construct for themselves in self-absorbed states.
True, the demonstration is only compelling for those who are
prepared to see it, but to anyone who fully appreciates Masaccio's work the thought cannot remain entirely alien.

IV

We are now in a position to say why we expect depth in art to
resist those pressures that the passage of time exerts against its
retention of our attention: pressures that the last chapter
identified under the heads of displacement and disturbance. In
essence it is because depth answers better than the superficial
to interests that occupy the arts and which themselves are
constant over time. What has to be made out is that this brings
with it not just a persisting preference for the profound over the
shallow (other things being equal), but also a constant tendency
for the individual work of depth to establish and hold its place.

About the more general of these points there should be no
trouble. In Chapter 5 I argued that it is one central aim of the
arts to provide us with imaginative models for thinking about
aspects of the world, which are worked out and tested against
the detail of individual cases. A deep exploration of such matters is clearly better fitted for its task than is the less deep, for as
we have seen it is the deep rather than the shallow that provides
a fully sustainable view of the topics it treats. To suppose that
we might think as well or better of the superficial than of the
profound would be to embrace an incoherent set of priorities, to
prefer in full consciousness the less sustainable against the
more so.

But by itself this line of reasoning does nothing at all to assure
any constant interest in *particular* cases. Why should it not be
possible to allow that we have a *general* preference for the deep
over the shallow yet still to doubt whether the individual work
of depth has any marked tendency to hold its place? Might not
our interest at different times be so fluid that what engages it at
one time may well not do so at another? That this is not the case
seems to me to be no accident.

In the last section I endorsed a version of Aristotle's earlier-cited contention that the statements of poetry are of the nature of universals by way of saying that they show us individual examples of what is typical for men. An important consequence of this is that we shall have to resist the temptation to think that the individual instances of profound art must always enable us to recognize something of significance about ourselves, that is, about the individuals we are. For even though it may often be so, our situations may well not be of the types explored and so very often it will not. Hence we cannot say that because there is a universality of nature what the profound work of the past shows us must apply today and apply directly to ourselves.

Fortunately we do not need to rest on any such explanation being available. It will be equally satisfactory to set out from the observation that the understanding at which the arts aim must be understanding of ourselves only in the sense that it is understanding of the species to which we belong. And evidently such understanding extends to those whose ways of seeing the world are quite different from our own and often of a kind that we could not ourselves possibly embrace. Once we acknowledge these two things, that understanding is one prime concern of the arts, and that it stretches wider than the self, we shall have done all that is necessary to recognize that even if changes in our cultural climate over time make those who are different from ourselves even stranger to us than once they were, our desire for understanding can still extend to them. And that desire will be satisfied by sustainable representations of the ways in which such people confronted or might have confronted the world they met. To the extent that we turn our backs on individual cases of deep art for the reason that what they show us is no longer a picture of ourselves as we are or as we might be, we turn our backs on one of the major satisfactions that the arts have it in their power to offer us.

Someone might protest here that it is no a priori truth that people seek this understanding of themselves in the guise of understanding of the species. So perhaps we might abandon it. To this person my reply should be clear. The argument I have advanced does not pretend to be an a priori one; it does no more than to explain why it is rational to expect the deepest art of the past to survive for people who have the conception of art that we do. And since we do have an interest in an understanding of the kind described, it is reasonable to expect the art that delivers it to hold attention over time in the face of accompanying artistic and cultural change.

It might be asked whether this argument takes us any further than saying that there is just *some* ground for expecting deep art to survive, which is scarcely a very strong claim. Should I not go further than this and provide a reason that is active enough to ensure that it should regularly do so? But perhaps this is not needed, for appeal to what we might expect to happen has not been cast in terms of any single individual's reasoning but rather on what we might expect to happen within the institution of art. For it is difficult not to think that where the subject-matter in question is one that we acknowledge in advance to treat of significant possibilities that men may come to realize in their lives, the institutional interest is a very positive one. Again very little of an a priori kind need or should be said to constrain the subject-matter of art, but where understanding is what art aims at it is hard to imagine that it might come about that those artists with a capacity to see further and more accurately than others should abandon a concern with what they take to be the most revealing topics that touch on men's nature and experience of life. It is also hard to imagine seriously that these topics might change significantly over time. If these are constants we reasonably expect will hold, then our positive grounds for assuming art of depth to bid fair to survive are very strong.

Of course the question can also be asked why we should expect these insights to survive in the guise of art: for that could be thought of as an inherently unsure method of their preservation. But this doubt is unlikely to persist when we remind ourselves of three especial virtues that the arts enjoy and which make them a particularly well-favoured repository of valued understanding.

(a) Because of their very familiarity it is easy for us to give less than due weight to factors that are important in shaping our lives and determining our thought about their content. Coleridge observes that 'truths of all others the most awful and mysterious yet being at the same time of universal interest are too often considered so true that they lose all life and efficacity of truth and lie bed-ridden in the dormitory of the soul side by side with the most despised and exploded errors',[10] and he goes on to emphasize the arts' powers to resist this lightening of truth. 'In poems, equally as in philosophic disquisitions, genius produces the strongest impression of novelty while it rescues the most adulterated from the impotence caused by the very circumstances of their universal admission.'[11] In the ability of the artistic display of depth to preserve the well-known and important against the loss that familiarity brings we locate one sure root of its constant appeal.

(b) Secondly, obsessive preoccupation with generality and principle, sheer laziness, and stupidity can all work 'as blind(s) to keep out (nature's) strong light and shifting scenery from weak eyes and indolent dispositions'.[12] We are liable not to see the full complexity of situations in which we find ourselves, and liable not to appreciate pressing features of our circumstances and those of others. The particularity of the arts' presentation of generality allows them the power to alert us to these short-comings.

(c) Against the forces that make for corruption of our thought the deep work may stand fast because it holds before us in sharp focus ideas to which we may later recur in their most perspicu-ous definition. It thereby preserves them from the most com-mon forms of attrition. When Pope writes

> True wit is Nature to advantage drest,
> What oft was thought, but ne'er so well exprest.
> Something whose truth convinced at sight we find
> That gives us back the Image of our mind,[13]

the wit of which he speaks is not merely an adornment of thought, but a garment without which Nature could not reveal herself to us except dimly. 'What oft was thought' was scarcely thought with clarity till dressed by wit. It lies within the arts' power to make perspicuous what only the clearest-sighted can see unaided, and then to pass on to their admirers the percep-tions of the clear-sighted.

These truths should explain why depth is well protected against displacement as I introduced that notion in the last chapter. It is no harder to see why profound art is equally safe against the pressures that make for disturbance. We have seen that depth and truth cannot fall far apart, so that we shall recognize that the canonical interpretation of the deep work offers us something which non-canonical revisions will tend to move away from. This will be so whether the revisions involve overlaying original understanding with additional strata or stripping off elements that make it up. In either case truth will tend to be lost or obscured, and the precision of the original perception be dimmed.

In previous pages I have suggested that the truths presented in the form of art of depth enjoy a relative constancy, so it will not be open to one who favours the variability of interpretation over time, discussed in Chapter 3, to suppose that we adjust the interpretation of our art to match the changing nature of truth itself. For truth and correctness do not change. The most he can say is that over time we adjust interpretation to match our changing *view* of truth. This, however, is quite a different matter and of insufficient force to upset the present argument. If it is merely our view of what are the deepest perceptions concerning sustainable conceptions of possible experience that changes, then this view will itself be open to criticism and correction from the side of the reality to which it seeks to conform. Misapprehension of facts, omission of important concerns that bear on the issues discussed, and defects in arguments that are attributed to the author come to light as time passes and as the immediate appeal of the eroded or accreted reading is confronted with that which is properly canonical. The force of the usurper's appeal may temporarily blind us to the virtues of the legitimate reading but over time the power that it has in virtue of its depth will tend to reassert itself. Given that we have an interest in discerning what the deep work has to offer, and given that the depth it enjoys is something that is constant, attrition and encrustation upon the canonical reading are themselves liable to dissolution. Speaking of just such encrustations in his essay on Gérard de Nerval, Proust remarks that 'même de cet oubli qui l'abîme davantage, qui le défigure sous les couleurs qu'il n'a pas, un chef d'œuvre a tôt fait sortir quand une interprétation vraie lui rend sa beauté'.[14] Substituting 'depth' for 'beauty' the same holds true.

In either case then, be it that of displacement or of disturbance, the profound work of art is well placed to resist the pressures of time. This does not mean that no deep work can suffer in these ways. Of course it can, and I have not attempted to suggest otherwise. My claim has been that these works are *well placed* to survive, and we shall see later on that this conclusion is strong enough to support the inferences we hope to build upon it.

Chapter 8

Beauty

As with depth, so with beauty. It too is expected to survive time's passage, though why it does so is rather harder to describe, very largely for the reason that seven hundred years of philosophical turbulence about the idea have left us with very little understanding of it. After a string of failed attempts involving everything from simple realism through all sorts of subjectivism to even a shot or two at evaporative reduction we need to start again, for only when we have a defensible picture of what really does belong within the concept is there a chance of saying anything of interest about our attachment to things that fall under it. To begin with, then, some of the rubble has to be moved out, so I shall start with a little history, the dialectical utility of which should not be greatly reduced by its element of caricature.

I

Echoing a remark of Aristotle's on the relation between goodness and desire,[1] Aquinas implies that beauty is a property of objects distinct from our response to them: 'It is not that a thing is beautiful because we love it, but we love it because it is beautiful and good.'[2] On such a view attributions of beauty are true or false accordingly as the designated object does or does not have the property ascribed to it. Our response of pleasure or love is rooted in the object, but that response is not constitutive of the object's beauty; rather its beauty explains the response. It is natural also to think here that judgements of beauty are open to confirmation or disconfirmation by sensory evidence, and that the claims we make are sensitive enough to argument and discussion to merit the label 'objective'. What is more, we may be encouraged in our efforts to acquire discernment, for on Aquinas's view it makes good sense to think that by application and practice we may come to a knowledge of things' beauty, which otherwise we might very well not detect. All these are attractions of the realist position that need to be remembered and, if possible, preserved.

What made this stance unacceptable to later thinkers were the difficulties it encountered in meeting two challenges. It had to explain how there can always be an informative answer to the question: 'What makes this object beautiful?', and it had also to account for the apparently non-contingent nature of the connection between the beautiful and our loving attachment to the objects that display it. Its impotence on both counts fuelled the move towards the subject.

It is easy to think that there are only two possible answers to the question: 'What makes this beautiful?', and that neither of them is open to realism as cast in this style. Either we might cite a feature of the thing that *causes* it to be beautiful, or we might pick out a feature of it that is *constitutive* of its beauty. The first of these obviously will not do. If a man is interested in knowing what makes something beautiful he will be concerned to discern its beauty with the help of this knowledge. But if the relation in question is causal, as say between the lack of protein in a cat's diet and the dullness of its coat, there is no ground to think that knowledge of the cause will bring about perception of the effect.

On the other hand, making the explanatory feature constitutive of the object's beauty immediately suggests that there is some true identity sentence to be had of the form 'Beauty = . . .', and while there is certainly nothing amiss with the quest for such statements of identity,[3] it soon becomes apparent that no single simple choice fits all cases. In *De re aedificatoria*, Alberti offers us what is perhaps the most celebrated of all such identifications: 'Beauty is the harmony and concord of all the parts, achieved in such a manner that nothing could be added or taken away or altered but for the worse'[4] and undoubtedly as an expression of the High Renaissance ideal his choice is apt. But had it been present in buildings of the succeeding age, *concinnitas* could only have rendered them insipid, lacking in *sprezzatura*: depriving them of beauty, not promoting it. And we are forced to say this, for unless we do we shall be unable to understand as eulogistic, which they are, assertions such as are contained in Lorenzo Giacomini's funeral oration for Tasso:

He avoided that superfluous facility of being at once understood, and departing from common usage and from the base and lowly chose the novel, the unfamiliar, the unexpected, the admirable both in ideas and in words, which while artificially interwoven more than is normal and adorned with various figures suitable for tempering that excessive clarity, such as caesuras, convolutions, hyperbole, irony, displacement . . . resembles not so much a twisted muddy alley-way but an uphill stony path where the weak are exhausted and stumble.

Even though the aesthetic concerns of Alberti and Tasso were so very different we must surely say that both were authors of beautiful art, and this should teach us that the search for simple identities is a lost cause. If the best available candidates such as *concinnitas* and *sprezzatura* can live at odds, we should conclude that while either may justify the ascription of beauty, neither can be identical with it.

Then too it has always been felt to be a conceptual truth about beauty that we should love it or be otherwise attached to it. Any simple property of objects that might be selected as constitutive of the beautiful promises to make it a puzzle how this could be anything but a happy accident. Such identification also seems to make it impossible to explain just what call the beautiful object makes on us to come to love it if we do not already do so. If there is no theoretically well-established link between the object and our response to it there seems to be no hope of explaining why an object, however constituted, might be thought to demand a certain response from us, a demand that has been rightly felt to be a salient mark of distinction between the truly beautiful and the merely pleasing.[5] For reasons such as these then, the attractions of some form of subjectivism seemed overwhelming.

With notable exceptions, eighteenth- and nineteenth-century empiricists tended to accept a rigid dichotomy between the object and the subject, and to assume that because we need to do honour to the subject's response we must do so by concentrating on the subject alone. Taking his cue, like so many after him, from a misunderstanding of Locke's account of the secondary qualities, Francis Hutcheson was one of the first to make this move: 'Let it be observed,' he writes, 'that in the following papers the word *beauty* is taken for the idea raised in us',[6] and traces of the same view are to be found in the more influential writing of Hume, who in the *Essay on the Standard of Taste* (ed. cit., 139) observes that '[t]hough it be certain that beauty and deformity ... are not qualities in objects, but belong entirely to the sentiment ... it must be allowed that there are certain qualities in objects that are fitted by nature to produce those particular feelings.'

Much more fatefully for the subject, Kant too opens the *Critique of Judgement* in the same vein: 'If we wish to discern whether anything is beautiful or not we do not refer the representation of it to the object ... but to the subject and its feeling of pleasure or pain.' (§1.)

In the wake of such opinions as these it cannot really surprise us that lesser minds should be ready to speak of beauty as 'pleasure projected upon an object' (Santayana) or accept that 'When men speak of beauty they mean precisely not a quality, as is supposed, but an effect: they refer in short just to [an] intense and pure elevation of the soul ...' (Edgar Allan Poe, *Works* (New York, 1902), XIV-XV, 197.)

Like its rival, the unadorned appeal to sentiment has its attractions. If beauty really is 'an idea raised in us', we may well not be disturbed by the thought that different qualities in objects may give rise to it. As Moore saw, we have to recognize that '[i]t will never be true to say: this object owes its beauty *solely* to the presence of this characteristic, nor yet that: wherever this characteristic is present the objects are beautiful because they have certain characteristics, in the sense that they would not be beautiful unless they had them',[7] and the appeal to sentiment may have seemed the obvious way of doing so. Moreover, the original objection to the place that causality might play is now less urgent. For it appears that we only discern the beauty of an object if we put ourselves within the causal power of the qualities that elicit the response. Here, to find out what qualities these are *is* to bring about awareness of the object's beauty, recast of course in the language of sentiment. And given assumptions that we have seen came readily to eighteenth-century thinkers about the uniformity of human nature, it did not seem that these gains had to be paid for by relinquishing any claims to objectivity. If we all tend to respond to the world alike then we shall truly call those objects beautiful

that evoke the right response in most of us. Such was the
optimism of the day.

It is an optimism that a later and more sophisticated age
finds specious. To us it is apparent that unless the chosen
response is to remain insufficiently specific, we shall have to
characterize the sentiment that is supposed to turn the wheels
of theory in terms of its objects. Yet once this is done all those
difficulties that the move to the subject was meant to avoid will
reappear. Then too, the subjective account encourages us to
accept the unwelcome thought that if our common psychological response to a given object were radically to change, we
should have to say that it had then ceased to be beautiful even
though we recognize no change in the object itself. More serious
still is the difficulty that faces the critic of the arts, for it is his
business to persuade us to appreciate works of art for the right
reasons, yet he will be hard put to explain why his readers
should care very much whether their sentiments are properly
engaged as long as they are at least engaged. Nothing but cold
comfort lies there.

To those intent on preserving the importance of response in
the account of beauty, no way out of these difficulties offered
itself that pointed back to the original form of realism. The way
forward had to lie elsewhere, and it may surprise the modern
reader that as early as 1805 we meet the view that 'beauty' is no
more than 'a general term of approbation, of the most vague
and general meaning.'[8] Here an assertion that something is
beautiful is effectively deprived of all its cognitive content and is
explained instead as having only expressive force. The
significance of the predicate 'ζ is beautiful' thus reduces to the
point of evaporation. Evaluation does not simply supplement
description; it supplants it. Whether offered wholeheartedly or
not, such a position is still very much with us, and it is worth
noticing that in one recent book[9] it is claimed of such terms as
'beautiful', 'ugly', 'lovely', 'elegant', 'hideous', etc. that they
'are for the most part evaluative, used to express preference for
and against objects of aesthetic interest. . . . Distinctive aesthetic attitudes are expressed by the judgements that employ
them.'

All that needs to be said about these last assertions is that
they can only be true if at the same time we also find a cognitive

significance for the term 'beauty' to bear. The explanation of why we should approve of some objects of aesthetic interest rather than others must make reference to their very beauty, since unless it did so either we should find some other term lying better in the mouth than 'beautiful' or else we should not be able to rationalize our approbation at all. To accept this point is at once to recognize that somewhere between the rival extremes on which I have so far concentrated there has to be a stable resting place, and it is with the historical articulation of this midway stance that the next two sections will be concerned.

II

Hume's pondered account of beauty is found in the *Treatise of Human Nature*, at II. i. viii: 'Beauty is such an order and constitution of parts as either by the primary constitution of our nature, by custom, or by caprice is fitted to give a pleasure and satisfaction to the soul.' The great merit of his proposal is that instead of indentifying the beautiful with some 'modification of matter' (see Addison, *Spectator* No. 412, 23 June 1712) or some 'idea in the mind' (see Hutcheson above), it pinpoints the property in question as being complex. Beauty is a property of the object, namely the complex property it has of producing in the viewer a response to certain of its other properties.[10] The beautiful object is one that pleases men in virtue of its constitution. Why this is such a help we shall see in a moment, but first let us be clear exactly what it is that Hume is proposing for the sentence I have quoted is ambiguous in at least three ways.

One way of hearing Hume's sentence would be as saying that there is some particular order and constitution of parts, the same in all cases, which pleases us, and that it is this order that we call beautiful. Accordingly we might take Hume's words as saying:

(1) $(\exists o)$ (x) (Beautiful x iff. [In virtue of having o, x is such that (y) $\{\psi y \rightarrow x$ pleases $y\}$.])[11]

But this is both false and most unlikely to be what Hume meant, since he was perfectly well aware that different objects are beautiful for different reasons, or in virtue of their parts

being differently constituted in different cases. To capture this
thought we might rather write:

(2) (x) (Beautiful x iff. $(\exists o)$ [In virtue of having o, x is such
           that (y) $\{\psi y \rightarrow x$ pleases $y\}$])

It is important to notice here that the quantifiers are ordered
$\forall\exists\forall$. Each beautiful object, it is claimed, has some ordering
of parts or other that pleases everyone. Although Hume does
not say so this interpretation of his definition is obviously
preferable to a third alternative:

(3) (x) (Beautiful x iff. (y) $(\exists o)$ [In virtue of having o, x is
           such that $\{\psi y \rightarrow x$ pleases $y\}$])

For what (3) claims is that an object will be beautiful as long as
everyone is pleased by some order of its parts or other, and this
may happen when each person is pleased by a different order.
In that case it would cast no doubt on an object's beauty that no
two people could agree about what made it beautiful. It would
be enough that each man should have a reason of his own for
liking it, and this is neither true nor acceptable to Hume.

Of these three possible readings (2) is clearly the one to take
as a basis for refinement. However, before proceeding, notice
how well a formula of this kind is adapted to meet the objections
that lamed the extreme positions between which it is a mean. In
the first place it allows us to avoid choosing between a straightforwardly causal explanation of the applicability of the predicate 'beautiful' and an explanation constitutive of beauty by
reason of identity. It is not that the possession of the right order
of parts causes it to be true that the object is beautiful, for we
see now that the beauty and the order of parts are not independently identifiable as they would have to be if they were causally related. Here lies the true source of the earlier rejection of
causality. Nor is the object's beauty identical with this order of
parts. Rather Hume allows us to see that the thing's beauty is
supervenient upon its constitution, in that by having the right
constitution the object satisfies the whole complex predicate
that lies on the right hand side of the biconditional. That is
what it is to be beautiful, and that complex property is what
beauty must be identical with, and nothing less.

Secondly, room is made in Hume's account for the response.
It remains a necessary and not a contingent truth that the
beautiful object pleases us. And this is acknowledged without

at the same time denying that beauty is a property of the object rather than the subject. When properly appreciated, it is because the object is beautiful that it pleases; the logical form of 'x is beautiful' remains much as we expect, a predication upon x.

Thirdly, we now have a way of recognizing that different objects are going to be beautiful for different reasons without embracing the aesthetics of sentiment. We can recognize and accommodate the truth of Moore's dictum.

Lastly, Hume gives us a sure way of responding to Aquinas's Aristotelian slogan. It remains true that we love an object because it is beautiful, for only those loving responses are indicative of beauty in the object which are elicited from a constitution of parts that pleases everyone. Any other pleasure it gives us is immaterial to its beauty, and a man who gets his pleasure for the wrong reason does not appreciate the beauty of the thing he observes. But it will not follow from this that the object is not also beautiful because it pleases us. For what Hume tells us is that its pleasing us in the right way is just what its beauty does consist in. Aquinas was mistaken in thinking that the two clauses he opposes are incompatible, and it is Hume's merit to have given us a way of accepting both of them.[12]

Clearly Hume's account deserves to be taken seriously, but before subjecting it to criticism we shall do well to present it in the most favourable light possible that is compatible with Hume's own intentions. One feature not yet given any recognition is embodied in Hume's phrase 'fitted to'. Hume is careful not to say that just anyone in the right mental set would feel pleasure on viewing the beautiful object, for he is as aware as the next man that universal agreement of response is pretty rare and not to be expected. To mark this insight, let us accept fully the dispositional nature of the object to produce the response in us, and replace (2) with:

(4) (x) (Beautiful x iff. $(\exists o)$ [In virtue of having o, x tends to be such that $(y) \{\psi y \rightarrow x$ pleases $y\}])^{13}$

Thus there can now be occasions on which not everyone responds pleasurably to an object's constitution, without the judgement that it is beautiful immediately being false. In consequence it will make sense to try to get someone who does not respond to the object to come to see its beauty, an enterprise which would not be justifiable if his initial failure to do so were itself enough to rebut the original appraisal.

None the less, as things stand the disposition is not properly formulated as a material conditional, since so understood an attribution of beauty will be true if *no one* is in the mental set labelled $\ulcorner\psi\urcorner$. Imagine that some lunatic drops a neutron bomb powerful enough to kill all life but sophisticated enough to leave all buildings and machinery intact. Then while it remains true that St. Paul's is a beautiful cathedral, the Heathrow Hotel, which is surely ugly if anything is, will also enjoy that title. After the bomb has fallen, no one is in the right mental set and the analysans then is satisfied both by cathedral and hotel.

To remedy this defect we need to render the conditional not as a material conditional but in the subjunctive mode, and instead of (4) write:

(5) (x) (Beautiful x iff. $(\exists o)$ [In virtue of having o, x tends to be such that (y) $\{\psi y \;\Box\!\!\rightarrow x$ pleases $y\}$])

Then even if everyone were killed off the Heathrow Hotel would remain the monstrosity it is because it would be false that anyone who were in the appropriate mental set would find himself pleased by it. This Hume would certainly want to accept.

A third thing not yet made explicit is that we take pleasure in the beautiful object as a result of perceiving it. As things stand in (5), no more is said than that the embedded subjunctive holds in virtue of the beautiful object being ordered by o, and nothing yet said precludes it from being the case that some objects should have a constitution which for some strange reason tends to bring it about that people in the right frame of mind are pleased by the mere thought of them. So let us add that the pleasure in question is consequent upon perception, and for the sake of clarity make plain that this dependence is causal. We are pleased as an effect of perceiving the beautiful thing.

Taking causation to be a relation between events, and drawing on well-known proposals of Donald Davidson's about the logical form of event sentences,[14] we can comfortably express these two alterations in:

(6) (x) (Beautiful x iff. $(\exists o)$ [In virtue of having o, x tends

to be such that (y) (f) $\{\psi y$ & Perceives (y, x, f) $\Box\!\!\rightarrow$ $(\exists e)$ (Pleases (x, y, e) & f causes $e)\}$])

Complicated though this may look it does now say just what Hume must have had in mind. In prose less ambiguous and elegant than his, we say that on Hume's view an object is beautiful if and only if, in virtue of having a certain order of parts, it tends to be true that anyone with a certain mental set who were to perceive the object would be pleased by doing so, where this pleasure causally derives from that perceptual activity.

However close we may think Hume comes to getting right the form of analysis, a number of objections should persuade us that in filling out that form with content he is less than totally successful. (a) The response of pleasure that he offers us is far too anodyne, and it merely labels a problem without solving it to elaborate on the introduction of pleasure in terms of some other 'satisfaction of the soul'. (b) Even when the universality of the response is softened by introducing the dispositional clause, it is unwelcomely widespread. We often think that the beauty of many objects is accessible only to very few of us, and Hume with his insistence on a common psychology among men is unable to acknowledge that this is so. There is a certain tendency in his theory to make the appreciation of beauty far too easy a matter. (c) There is no reason to think that beauty is necessarily connected with the constitution of parts of an object. Many things are beautiful that have nothing at all to do with matters of organization or composition. (d) The verb 'perceives' is implausibly extensional. Obviously perceiving something is not regularly connected with any interesting aesthetic response, and it cannot be right, as Hume's view implies, that learning to appreciate the beautiful is a matter simply of strengthening a causal connection between perception as extensionally conceived and the elicited response of pleasure. For these reasons, whatever the merits of Hume's definition on the formal side, the precise understanding he offers us of the beautiful must be improved on.

III

A judgement of taste consists in calling a thing beautiful just because

of that characteristic in respect of which it accommodates itself to our
mode of apprehension. (*Critique of Judgement* §32.)
Pleasure in aesthetical judgement . . . is merely contemplative, and
does not bring about an interest in the objects . . . The consciousness
of the mere formal purposiveness in the play of the subject's cognitive
powers [i.e. imagination and understanding] in a representation
through which an object is given, is the pleasure itself. (§12.)

A proper understanding of Kant's account of beauty is interesting not only because it provides the starting-point for all serious
aesthetic theory after 1790, but also because it makes an
attempt on each of the various defects that leave us dissatisfied
with Hume, while preserving the virtues for which we want to
admire him.

On Kant's view, an object is beautiful when it is disposed to
produce in the subject who views it in a specific way a response
of a particular sort in the awareness of which we find pleasure.
Without commenting on the similarities with Hume let us note
the differences. First, the activity of the spectator is not, as it is
with Hume, simply that of receptively perceiving the object. He
has to perceive it in an active manner, one that Kant says
proceeds through 'the play of the cognitive powers'. Obscure
though the language is, it is not difficult to see what is meant.
According to Kant, the cognitive powers are those faculties of
mind which we apply to the manifold of sensation in the search
for objective experience. The imagination binds together the
data of consciousness in such a way as enables the understanding to bring them under a concept. In acquiring knowledge the
imagination is subservient to the understanding, but in contrast the two faculties are in equal relation in aesthetic contemplation. Here the understanding selects features of the perceived object for its attention and allows the imagination
actively to range over them *ad libitum*, seeking not knowledge
but simply a certain harmony. Thus if I contemplate a rose
aesthetically, I see the rose and view it in a way that allows me
to concentrate on some features of it rather than others, and to
take them up in an order that I myself choose. If the rose is
beautiful it will accommodate itself to this activity of mine by
evoking a certain response in me. If it is not beautiful this
response will not be forthcoming. By contrast with Hume,
intellectual activity is to the fore.

Secondly, Kant's analysis, unlike Hume's, does not equate the crucial response with pleasure, even though he says in the already quoted sentence from §1 that reference must be made to pleasure. The response is rather the feeling of harmony between subject and object,[15] and the pleasure that we associate with the appreciation of beauty is nothing more or less than the *consciousness* we have of this harmony, a mode of attention to the object that we wish to maintain (§§10 and 12). It remains true that Kant defines beauty in terms of pleasure, but pleasure in the response of harmony, not pleasure *simpliciter*, and this consciousness of the harmony between subject and object is far less vapid that Hume's simple 'satisfaction of the soul'.

Thirdly, Kant does not insist that beauty is always a matter of the constitution of parts of an object. His belief is that any feature of an object that is, strictly speaking, publicly knowable will do, and it is an unfortunate consequence of his understanding of Locke's theory of the secondary qualities that he thinks these features are exclusively formal ones. However, once we abstract from his weak epistemology, we can see that Kant's theory is at this point much freer than Hume's, even though in its actual application Kant fixes on much the same 'compositional' sources of beauty as does Hume.

Fourthly, Kant's view differs from Hume's in that it is easy for him to explain why we have to learn to appreciate the beautiful and why in some cases only few of us are able to do so. Once we realize that we are concerned with the response to a certain intellectual activity, we may easily appreciate that this activity is one we have to learn to exercise, and sometimes it may be difficult to engage in properly. Hence sometimes there will be beauties accessible only to few. Thus the four main weaknesses of Hume's analysis are overcome, but because the repairs are effected within a form that sticks to Hume's model we are assured that the virtues that come with that form are preserved.

As I have retold Kant's story it can be represented thus:

(7) (x) (Beautiful x iff. $(\exists \phi)$ [In virtue of possession of ϕ, x tends to be such that (y) (f) $\{\psi y$ & Views through imagination and understanding (y, x, f) $\Box\rightarrow$ $(\exists e)$ (Feels in harmony with (y, x, e) & f causes e & Pleasurable e)$\}$])

Before commenting on its adequacy let me briefly relate this interpretation of Kant's thesis to the salient 'moments' of his own analysis. These, it will be remembered, are that the judgement of taste is disinterested (§6), does not involve bringing the object under a concept (§9), enjoys an exemplary necessity (§22), and imports a purposeless purposiveness into our judgement of the object (§17).

These demands are all simply accommodated. The judgement of taste is disinterested in that '*x* is beautiful' has as its truth condition a claim about how people would respond if they viewed it in a certain way, a way in which the desire for cognition and the practical interests that cognition subserves are in abeyance. Since practical interests presuppose mental activity in which imagination is dominated by understanding, the judgement of taste precludes such practical concern. Hence it is properly called disinterested. Nor does it involve bringing the object under a concept, since what is essential to the judgement is the response of harmony evoked when the object is viewed in the right way. The response, however, is not one that provides us with any information about its object, and thus does not bring it under a concept. That this should be so is not incompatible with the claim that to say something is beautiful is true of false. To say that does tell us something about the object, but no more than that in certain circumstances it elicits this particular response.

Then the judgement of taste enjoys an exemplary necessity, being true only if the object disposes *anyone* who views it aright to respond with the response of harmony.[16] If I do not find the object beautiful that is no indication of its not being so. Maybe I am looking at it in the wrong way. The man who asserts its beauty commits himself only to a dispositionally weakened universal subjunctive claim. It is then up to me, his hearer, to satisfy its antecedent. Of course it has to be asked why I should bother to do so, and this is something that Kant discusses elsewhere (§42). We should not expect to find the answer to that question in the very analysis of the judgement of beauty. Finally, the obscure thesis about purpose is explained by saying that my feeling a harmony between the object and myself involves the thought that the object is designed (is purposive), but since it reveals itself in this way only when I contemplate it aesthetically I cannot say that it is designed for any particular

purpose. Its purposiveness is purposeless; it looks designed, but
not for anything in particular.

Maybe these last observations are of interest only to the
Kantian exegete. What is of more general concern is the correctness of Kant's analysis, in particular in so far as it advances
upon the views of Hume already discussed. On this score it
must regrettably be admitted that Kant's enterprise runs foul
of two substantial objections. The first is that, while Kant is
undoubtedly right in insisting that we cannot understand an
object as beautiful except we say something about the way in
which it is viewed, his particular choice for this task is far too
restrictive. It is false to say that beauty is only accessible to us
through *contemplation* of the beautiful object. As Paul Ziff has
pointed out,[17] we look at different things in different ways to
appreciate them, and contemplation is only one of these ways.
Thus sometimes it will be a matter of scrutinizing the object,
sometimes of peering at it, sometimes of examining it and
sometimes of observing it; and it would be misleading to think
that each of these involves the kind of interplay between imagination and understanding that Kant took to be paramount. If
we follow Ziff in calling all these various activities species of the
generic activity of *aspecting* something, we can say that Kant
made the mistake of defining the beautiful in terms of a particular species of aspection, namely contemplation, where what he
should have done was to have concentrated on the generic idea
itself.

It should not be thought that this is a change of only minor
importance in Kant's theory. Once we abandon the notion of
contemplation as essential to our understanding of the beautiful, Kant would say that the response of felt harmony can no
longer be introduced except contingently, since that response is
defined by him in terms of the contemplative activity. And if its
essential place in the analysis is given up he will say that the
peculiar pleasure that the beautiful object provides cannot be
retained. In consequence he would say that all claims of aesthetic judgement to objectivity will collapse. We must therefore
take care that any amendment to Kant's theory avoids these
dangers.

Secondly, the critic will urge that Kant's obsession with
harmony as the crucial response is unduly limiting. It is simply

untrue that appreciation of a beautiful thing must manifest itself in my feeling a harmony between it and me, and though it is perfectly proper for Kant to want to refine on Hume's response of unadorned pleasure, it will not be allowed that he has done so in the right way.

The justice of these two criticisms can be tested against an example of a kind that both Hume and Kant were inclined to overlook, but which a proper choice of aspection and response must be able to embrace. Consider our judgement that a detail of a painting is beautiful. On Kant's view it would seem that we have to select certain features of the detail and allow our eye to range over them in an order that we choose, hoping to find that when we do so we experience a harmony between that detail of the work and our mental powers. But this is quite ludicrous. For just because it is a *detail* we are most unlikely to treat it in this way. What is important is its relation to the rest of the work from which it is taken, not its self-standing relation to us. Kant notwithstanding, we feel that just because we do want to say that judgements of beauty about detail may be true or false as much as any other aesthetic claims, the connection that he makes between the feeling of harmony and objectivity of judgement must be secured in some other way than he proposes.

The upshot of my review of Kant, then, is that he shows us which path to explore. The importance of his work as an advance of Hume is to make plain that only through concentration on the intentional aspect of our perception of the beautiful object will we make progress. And just as he comes to identify the crucial response by first having selected as important a particular intentional act, so too may we hope to find it by first being clear about the sort of aspection that aesthetic interest in an object necessarily involves.

IV

One matter taken for granted by all these authors is that 'beautiful' is a predicative adjective. This is false. The same portrait may be a beautiful object to hang in this corner of the room—beautiful as an element of the room's furnishing—yet not be a beautiful portrait. The same predatory sea-bird may be beautiful as a predator, but not as a sea-bird. The attributive nature of the adjective may be expected to show up on both sides of our analysis.

What we have to analyse then is not the predicate 'ζ is beautiful' but 'ζ is a beautiful F', and I suggest that in the light of the Kantian demand that we concentrate on the intentional aspects of perception our task will be made easier if we start off by restricting attention to a particular choice for F, namely 'work of art'. By doing this we force ourselves to give full rein to the intellectual aspects of appreciation right at the outset, and we may hope to preserve the benefits this brings when, later on, we come to generalize the account offered beyond the arts. For the moment, then, let us ask about the truth conditions of the judgement that x is a beautiful work of art, and as an aid to doing this take a further leaf from Kant's book.

In writing about the arts Kant made two important observations, neither of which found any explicit place in his general account of free beauty. 'Art,' he says, 'has always a definite design of producing something' (§45), and then in an aside pertinently directed against a fashionable liberalism of his day, 'in all free arts there is requisite something compulsory . . . [some] constraint, without which . . . [we would] change [them] from work into mere play' (§43).[18] When we remember that he also thought 'Nature is beautiful only because it looks like art' (§45) it may appear all the more surprising that his general account of beauty bore no trace of these thoughts. We shall see that in putting them together our theoretical problems may be solved. But first let me concentrate upon the arts.

Works of art are artefacts produced by their creator under the guidance of an over-all intention. The artist's work answers, successfully or not as the case may be, to a determinate problem of design that he poses himself or entertains. It is the function of this over-all, publicly identifiable intention, together with more specific considerations, to control the marks that are laid down upon the canvas, the notes that are written, or the words that are chosen, etc. Quite how the guiding master-problem of a work of art should be specified is an important question of theoretical aesthetics, but one over which we need not pause here, since however it is done will make no difference to our understanding of the beautiful. All that we have to appreciate is that all works are of necessity

answers to some problem or other, that they are constructed to
fit some description that cites their over-all conception. So let
us write:

(8) (w) [Work of art $w \Rightarrow (\exists \text{ Problem}) (w$ answers to $P)$]

Kant's second remark is an expression of the thought that the
problem to which the artist addresses himself must be resolved
within a set of aesthetic constraints which I shall here call a
style. Only by reference to a set of stylistic constraints can we
sensibly judge that the answer the artist proposes to his over-all
intention is successful or not. Since artistry is to be thought of as
skill in matters aesthetic, Kant must be quite right in thinking
that a mark could count only as a doodle, as 'free play, not
work', outside any aesthetic bounds. So let us also accept:

(9) (w) [Work of art $w \Rightarrow (\exists \text{ Style}) (w$ is in $S)$]

For the sake of greater simplicity in what follows I shall from
(8) and (9) construct a complex predicate, 'being an answer to
P and in S', and assert (8) and (9) jointly as:

(10) $(w)(\exists P)(\exists S) (w$ answers to P and is in $S)$

With one more preliminary issue out of the way we shall be able
to state a partial account of beautiful art. This is that, in
consequence of the arguments of Chapters 3 and 4, only those
responses to works of art that derive from a proper understanding of them are fit to enter into the characterization of their
beauty. Unless I see the work as answering to the problem and
style to which it really does answer I shall misunderstand it;
and my response, however intense or rewarding for me, will not
bear on the truth of the claim that the work is a beautiful one.

Putting these various things together and for the moment
saying nothing at all about the nature of the response that is
involved, we can now offer a partial definition of artistic beauty.
The idea is that a work of art is beautiful if and only if, when
seen as answering to its problem in its style, it evokes the
appropriate response. This we can record, in the light of the
previous discussion, as:

(11) (w) (Beautiful work of art w iff. $(\exists \phi)(\exists P)(\exists S)$ [w
            answers to P and is in S & in virtue of possession of ϕ
            tends to be such that $(y)(f)$ {Aspects as answering to P
            and as in S (y, w, f) $\Box \rightarrow (\exists e)$ (Responds (y, w, e) & f
            causes e)}])

As far as possible, (11) follows the Humean pattern that we

found so helpful. But three changes have been made. The first consists in the insertion of a self-standing existential clause deriving from (10). This, it may be noted, is no part of the sense of 'beautiful' but has its provenance entirely in the appearance of the phrase 'work of art' on the left hand side of the main connective. Secondly, we have dropped the mental-set clause $\ulcorner\psi y\urcorner$ in the antecedent of the counterfactual. This has become redundant, since those who fully understand the aesthetic constraints within which the work is constructed and also understand the artistic problem which guides its construction will be members of a common culture. Sufficient community of mental set is thereby preserved. Thirdly, we may note that the intentional activity of perception from which Kant sets out is here refined without, however, setting limits to the kind of aspection that will be appropriate in different cases. The refinement comes in claiming that the relevant aspection must be one that views its object under the complex description that cites the work's problem and its style.

Having made these alterations, we are now better placed than before to improve on the suggestions of Hume and Kant as to the nature of the relevant response. Indeed, with things set up as they now are an obvious suggestion presents itself, quite different from anything that either of them was able to envisage. The response I have in mind is that which we experience when we recognize that the solution a work or art proposes to its problem within its own aesthetic constraints is just right, that, as Wittgenstein put it,[19] it 'clicks'. We see the work as satisfying its over-all aim. This surely was what Alberti was getting at when he said that the beautiful work is one in which 'nothing could be added or taken away or altered except for the worse'. Everything, we feel, is in place, and it is this feeling that is primitive to our aesthetic experience. We tend to teach people to recognize it by confronting them with beautiful objects whose problems and styles we explain to them, and we quite properly make use of it in our account of beautiful art.

It may well feel as if this sketchy indication of the response I am concerned with is somewhat question-begging, sounding no less obscure than the term 'beauty' itself. But this is an illusion. Outside aesthetics there are all sorts of situations in which we are confronted by problems to which we recognize a good solution. The feeling of satisfaction we have in this recognition is perfectly well described in these terms, and it is I think no accident that the word 'beautiful' comes so naturally to the tongue on such occasions. Nor should it be thought that the feeling of 'just rightness' introduced in this quite neutral way suggests that we are describing the beautiful in a manner that purges it too drastically of all aesthetic content. This is not so, since the response I have picked out must in the case of works of art be a response to an object as seen within certain stylistic (hence *aesthetic*) constraints. As far as beautiful art is concerned the full measure of the experience's aesthetic nature is thereby preserved.

A different hesitation that may strike the reader turns on our willingness to make comparative judgements of artistic beauty. One Raphael may be more beautiful than another; any Mozart sonata than any by Clementi. But if I am right in my identification of the response, in particular is I am right in connecting it with Alberti's idea that nothing could be altered except for the worse, it may appear that questions about degree cannot be asked, for that response is surely all or none. And this would be a mistake.

Even if we decline to speak of degrees of justice which we recognize in an artistic resolution of a problem, there are still ways in which we can accept the possibility of making comparative judgements of beauty without at the same time enriching the analysis of the positive beyond what is offered by (11). Of these the most attractive is to say that any response that falls under the head of a relevant recognitional event will be made relatively surely, immediately, intensely, easily, and so on, and it is some such feature or combination of such features of our responses, not explicitly alluded to in the analysis of 'beautiful work of art', that we rely on to permit comparison. As long as this is true, place enough is left for comparisons when they are made, but there is no need in the elucidation of the positive to declare what this feature is. That refinement impinges after all not a whit on the elucidation of 'is beautiful'.

This reaction has the one disadvantage that we can no longer explain in the manner of Hume or Kant why beautiful art should of necessity be attaching. Both thinkers, we have seen, defined pleasure into the response, Hume directly and Kant in terms of consciousness of harmony. Once we have rejected such a move, the only available way of getting pleasure into the analysis is to enrich (11) by insisting that pleasure (or some other form of attachment) must appear in the positive[20] as a base for securing comparisons when they are made. But this has not been done, and given the variety of other refinements of our recognitions apart from their pleasurability that might serve this purpose, such insistence could not but seem *ad hoc*. To make this admission leaves the question of the connection between beauty and attachment open and pressing. I shall turn to it again in section VIII.

A last comment on my proposal comes in the shape of a warning. It would be a mistake to think that it places too much emphasis on clarity of understanding and vision. That is, it must not be objected that it is unrealistic to insist that a beautiful work is one that can only be appreciated by someone who is articulately aware of its over-all intention and the aesthetic constraints that have guided its composition. That would be a mistake, for all that the analysis says is that a work of art is beautiful if and only if such a person would have the right response when viewing it as an answer to its problem and in its style. It says nothing at all about the less well informed. It is therefore quite compatible with the recognition that much of the time we have a dim understanding of many works of art that we find quite exquisite.[21] None the less, *full* appreciation of a work of art's beauty cannot be divorced from clarity of vision and accuracy of understanding. Since this is what we aim at, it must always be a rational desire to get ourselves into the ideal position. A man who says he recognizes the beauty of the work but does not understand it is one whose appreciation is in some way deficient. The deficiency must be made good by the exercise of intellect.

V

Let us now assemble the advantages enjoyed by the proposed analysis. Some have already been noted *en passant* and are simply mentioned for the sake of completeness; others we have not yet met.

1. Judgements of beauty in works of art are true or false. If

true they are made true in virtue of a property of the object. Confirmation or disconfirmation of the judgement is possible in the light of evidence we collect from our own experience, and also knowledge of well-informed responses. If we appreciate the work we love it because it is beautiful.

2. Due honour is paid to the importance of experiential response, since beautiful art is that art which in virtue of its sensible properties elicits a response from those who understand it. Because this response is one that can be intellectually justified and criticized, the original objections to the aesthetics of sentiment do not arise. In appreciation, experiencing the response is not enough; it must be experienced in the right circumstances, that is, when the work is properly understood. Hence the critic of art is not on this account made redundant. Nor shall we fear that if our tastes should radically change, objects that were once beautiful should cease to be so. For no change of taste will affect the truth of the embedded subjunctive conditional. Not to respond to the beautiful work is not fully to understand it. It is beautiful because we, the properly informed at least, love it for the right reasons.

3. The correctness of Moore's dictum is affirmed. Just because each work has its own problem and its own style, we should expect a just resolution of the task it sets itself to depend in different cases on different physical features. And we can see now very clearly why even if two works should have an almost identical physical conformation it does not follow that they are equally beautiful. For if they are correctly seen as addressing themselves to different over-all intentions, or are executed within different stylistic constraints (or both), the physical characteristics that make for success in one case may perfectly well determine failure in the other.

This connects with two other matters that have exercised practitioners of aesthetics. Kant remarks in *Critique of Judgement* §33, that 'the judgement of taste is not determinable by grounds of proof', and in §44 that 'there is no science of the beautiful'. There can be no criterion of beauty, if by that is meant some test independent of our responses, by which the beautiful can be identified. Nor can instruction be given for the creation of beautiful art. What satisfies the design he proposes for himself the artist must find out by trial and error. He knows that he has

to find a just resolution to his task within the chosen constraints, but what will do this cannot be stated for the individual work in advance of experience.

Secondly, works of art are often thought to be importantly
unique. One way in which this can be taken is that because
each work is the output of its over-all conception and its aesthetic constraints, only experience of it bears upon its assessment.
It is not a conceptual truth that each work is the uniquely
determined output of its problem and its style, since different
works can attempt the same designs within the same constraints, but given the premium we set upon originality in the
arts this reduplicative possibility is of little interest. It is not
something to which we might appeal in developing an aesthetic
science if, *per impossibile*, it were possible to develop one at all.

4. We can now easily explain why training and application
are needed in the appreciation of beauty. We cannot think of
the response that defines the idea of beauty except through
reference to the intellectual concerns that give rise to it. For the
most part appreciation of the arts consists in learning to see just
what these concerns are in the particular work before us, and it
would be ridiculous to think that in doing this we might reliably
rest by untutored intuition. But notice that this is quite consistent with recognizing that the response itself is not something
that can be taught. What we teach is how to see something as an
answer to a design. Having done this, the occurrence of the
response must be left to nature. It is the confusion of these two
things and the resulting concentration on the latter that leads
so many people to think that feeling is at odds with thought in
the arts. Nothing could be further from the truth. But this does
not mean that feeling should be abandoned.

5. In reviewing Theodor Vischer's *Kritische Gänge*, the novel-
ist and critic N. G. Tchernischevski observed: 'The sphere of
art embraces everything that interests man, what is of universal
interest in life, that is the content of art. The beautiful, the
tragic, the comic are only three more evident of the thousands
of elements that make life interesting: to enumerate them would
be to enumerate all the feelings, all the aspirations that engage
the hearts of men.'[22] This is correct. But it is also correct to say
that the term 'beauty' is the most general term of aesthetic
praise, one that can always be applied or withheld from any work

of art with propriety and relevance. Can we accept both of these claims? On the suggested analysis we can, for it tells us that the beauty of a work of art is just one property it has and a quite specific property at that. But because every work of art is of necessity conceived as answering to an over-all intention, the question will arise in every case whether the work has this specific property or not. In our assessment of art the question whether the particular work is beautiful cannot fail to be of importance. To this claim it is no objection that its centrality is belied by the notable absence of the term in critical discourse. For the critic is little interested in making the judgement *that* the work is beautiful, much more in showing *why* it is. He will concentrate on other features that it possesses. But this concentration is in the tacit service of the question why the work he studies is as beautiful (or as little beautiful) as it is. That issue can easily be discussed without employment of the term 'beauty' at all.

If it be objected that my elucidation overlooks the fact that not every successful work of art can be called 'beautiful', and that the word is in fact restricted to definite kinds of success, it may be replied that this linguistic matter reflects no more than a quirk of aesthetic history. One of the defects of taking the historical accident seriously is that it would deprive us of a concept which in aesthetics we urgently need, and for which role I have claimed the idea of beauty is well cast. Another defect is that since the word would be properly used only of successes in a particular range of styles, we should be hard put to use the term in translating the aesthetic vocabulary of other cultures. To make their sharing certain common styles with us the price of their possession of the concept of artistic beauty is to lay ourselves open to the charge of cultural imperialism: a charge we should be anxious not to invite.

6. In criticizing the views of Hume and Kant I claimed that neither of them was well placed to account for the beauty of artistic detail. This presents no difficulty to the proposal I have set out. For a detail of a work of art is beautiful to the extent that it is recognized as a successful resolution to the problem that it confronts within the constraints by which it is beset. The problem in the case of a detail is not of course to provide a resolution to the master-design of the whole work. Rather it

answers a sub-problem which arises in the resolution of the
master-problem. And the constraints which bound the adequacy of its solution of this problem are those that are presented
by the stylistic concerns of the whole, and also by the choices
that are made elsewhere in the work in its progress to the
realization of its over-all aim.

Sometimes, of course, we may pick out a detail of a work of
art that we do not think of as answering a sub-problem of the
work. It is just an arbitrarily chosen piece of the work. This we
may judge beautiful, but not I think *as* a detail of the work. That
it is a part of the work is then of no importance. Rather we treat
it as if it were a self-standing work in its own right. This piece of
fiction will in section VII provide us with a nice transition to
the understanding of beauty in the natural world.

7. It has occasionally seemed paradoxical that ugly things
may be beautiful, a reflection gracefully articulated by Celio
Calcagnini in a couplet on the *Discobolos*:

> Sunt quaedam formosa adeo, deformia si sint
> Et tunc cum multum displicuere placent

and although we may be more inclined than he to regard the
Roman copy of Myron's bronze as a work of unsullied grace,
the same sentiment appears apt when applied to the grotesques
of Bomarzo or to Guilio Romano's frescoes in the Palazzo del
Tè. Paradox however there is none, for we can now appreciate
that 'beautiful' and 'ugly' are incompatible only when the work
is judged according to one same problem and one same style.
Where we are willing to find the ugly object beautiful, that is
because as a satisfactory solution in one style to its over-all
design, allusion is made to a different style in which the object
jars. This effect is one that may be consciously striven for, and is
most likely to be achieved when the natural way of taking an
object is not the one that is indicated by the stylistic constraints
in play. Looking forward for a moment, we may say that the
incompatibility between beauty and ugliness must be represented as an incompatibility between the predicates 'beautiful as an answer to P in S' and 'ugly as an answer to P in S'.
Where P or S differ, beauty and ugliness may coexist in the
same object.

8. Finally, if my account of beautiful art is correct it will

conveniently explain the unease we sometimes feel when people attempt to say that some painterly or architectural styles are more beautiful than others. For what it suggests is that the issue cannot be raised in the way I have just put it. Beauty is not a feature of a style at all, but of works that are executed within the style. To talk of a style as beautiful can at best be a way of talking about its capacity for generating beautiful works executed in it, and this judgement of possibilities, particularly in cases where they are not actualized, is extremely tenuous.

VI

The last few sections have explicitly restricted themselves to the beautiful as it is found in art. Unless the analysis I have offered can be extended to cover natural cases of beauty as well, and extended in such a way as not to import ambiguity into the concept, my proposal will have to be judged a failure. Yet since the notions of style and problem have no place in nature it may seem inevitable that this judgement should be returned.

To avoid this objection let us first notice that it is a mistake to think that artificial notions such as those I have used can have no place in our thought about nature. That is just where they do have their place, not in nature itself but in our thought about it. The natural object is not one that comes into existence in God's studio as the construction of something answering to a problem posed within aesthetic constraints, but none the less it is perfectly possible for us to view it in that light. Only because this is possible can Ernst Gombrich ask whether a Chinese would not 'call that orchid "perfect" which corresponds most clearly to the rules he and absorbed? Do we not tend to judge human bodies by their resemblance to those Greek statues that have become traditionally identified with the canon of beauty?'[23] Only because it is possible could Oscar Wilde assert that:

Life imitates Art far more than Art imitates Life. This results from the fact that the self-conscious aim of Life is to find expression and that Art offers it certain beautiful forms through which it may realise that energy.

It follows . . . that external Nature also imitates Art. The only effects that she can show us are effects that we have already seen through poetry and in paintings. This is the secret of Nature's charm, as well as the explanation of her weakness.[24]

Having noted above that the *extensional* occurrence of '*P*' ('problem') and '*S*' ('style') derives solely from the presence of the phrase 'work of art' on the left hand side of the elucidating equivalence, by deleting this we can now extend the analysis to that of the expression 'beautiful *F*'. At the same time we can take the hint from Gombrich and Wilde (and indeed Kant[25]) and leave the *intentional* occurrence as it is. Doing this, we get the *generalized* form of the proposal:

(12) (x) (Beautiful F, x iff. $(\exists\phi)$ $(\exists S)$ $(\exists P)$ [Fx & In virtue of possession of ϕ, x tends to be such that (y) (f) {Aspects as answering to P and as in S (y, x, f) $\Box\rightarrow$ $(\exists e)$ (Recognizes as just to P & in S (y, x, e) & f causes e)}])[26]

Putting it like this, however, immediately gives rise to a problem which we cannot ignore. We have, it seems, secured univocity in the analysis of beauty at the cost of making every object beautiful under one description or another. For surely we can always find *some* style or other and *some* description or other to which *x* may be seen to answer quite satisfactorily, and once we do this we shall have to draw the conclusion that *x* is beautiful. Take for instance a poplar tree. It does not take much imagination to see that tree in a style that emphasized the vertical as fitting the description[27] 'tree'. Then (12) would encourage us to say that the poplar was a beautiful tree. And this is too cheap a victory.

The objection is serious and it does not find its solution by tinkering about with what we have on the right hand side. What it does teach us, I believe, is that we have to see the analysandum as more complicated than '*x* is a beautiful *F*'. It is more complicated than this in that room must be made in it not only for the kind of thing that *x* is, but also for the description and the style under which it is judged. Only then do we avoid the difficulty that any natural object will turn out to be beautiful. The assertion of beauty is to be understood as relative to a description and style and true if and only if, when viewed in that way, the object tends to elicit the right response. In amending (12) to accommodate this change, alterations have now to be made to both sides of the equivalence. Thus:

(13) (x) $(x$ is a beautiful F as fitting description D within
        aesthetic constraints C iff. $(\exists\phi)$ $[Fx$ & In virtue of
        possession of ϕ, x tends to be such that (y) (f) {Aspects
        as answering to D and as in C $(y, x, f)|\Box\mapsto (\exists e)$
        (Recognizes as just to D in C (y, x, e) & f causes $e)$}])

Allowing the form of 'x is beautiful' to be constrained in this
way by the demands of the analysis gets us over the difficulty,
but it may be thought that the cost is too high. For it will be said
that our judgements of beauty are surely *not* of objects as fitting
specific descriptions and as in specific aesthetic constraints,
and on a second count it will be urged that the new scheme
lends itself with difficulty to works of art. Since we have only
reached this point in search of univocity, this latter difficulty is
upsetting even if the first is not. Let us scrutinize these two
objections in turn.

It may indeed be true that we do not often explicitly specify
the relevant D and C of our aesthetic judgements. But then may
this not be precisely what leads to the difficulties we have in
resolving many of our disagreements about natural and personal beauty? Too often we find that we cannot agree over
aesthetic appraisals of a place or a person, and out of sheer
frustration are likely to catch ourselves acknowledging that
there must be some truth in the old adage that 'beauty is in the
eye of the beholder' or that 'de gustibus non est disputandum'.
In this we are not wrong, but we do incline to be right for the
wrong reason.

When we are concerned with cases of natural beauty it is the
beholder who selects the parameters of judgement. It is he who
decides what the relevant D and C are to be. In the case of the
work of art they are laid down in the shape of problem and style
chosen by the artist, and here the beholder has to follow, not
give the lead. So in this sense natural beauty *is* in the eye of the
beholder and we have nothing to say about the choice he
makes.[28] But it would be wrong to think that it follows from this
that judgements of natural beauty are not true or false. This
they remain, but relative to the choices that are made. Relative
to these choices the judgement is true if the subjunctive conditional holds, and false otherwise.

Having made this concession about indeterminacy, and
checked one misleading inference that might be drawn from it,

it is right now to insist that judgements of natural beauty are
not always indeterminate. In particular they are not often
indeterminate when all that is asserted is: 'That is a beautiful
F.' For we may surely take it to be a matter of conversational
implicature that where no specification is given the most
natural choice for *D* and *C* is to be understood. In the case of *D*
we shall generally understand to be implied the predicate *F*
under which the object is given to us, and for *C* it will be most
reasonable to select those constraints that are assumed by
speaker and hearer to be of common interest. If these fillings for
D and *C* are not in question, or are otherwise unclear, *then* we
may expect the speaker to say explicitly under what description
and within what constraints the object is being assessed. In
either case indeterminacy is restricted, so the first objection
may be dismissed.

The second objection disputes the applicability of our general scheme to works of art. So let us apply it and see how we get
on. For *F* we may expect to find a generic term like 'painting' or
'sonata' or 'portrait', and for *D* some artistic problem, and for *C*
some set of stylistic constraints in which the work is taken to be
executed. Thus on the left-hand side of the analysis we find:

(14)   *w* is a beautiful work of art as answering to problem *D*
          in style *C*, and on the right hand side:

(15) $(\exists \phi)\ (\exists S)\ (\exists P)$ (*w* is in *S* and answers to *P* and in
          virtue of possession of ϕ, *x* tends to be such that $(y)(f)$
          [Aspects as answering problem *D* in style *C* (y, w, f)
          $\Box\!\!\rightarrow (\exists e)$ (Recognizes as just (y, w, e) & f causes e)])

And it is at this point that it may seem that the scheme fails to fit
the arts. For nothing in what I might write down in the form
$\ulcorner$(14) iff (15)$\urcorner$ as an elucidation of '*w* is a beautiful work of art'
ensures that the *D* and *C* under which the work is judged
beautiful are descriptions and constraints that really apply to
it. To take a fanciful example, so far as the proposed analysis
goes a Venetian painting of the High Renaissance representing
St. George slaying the dragon might be correctly judged a
beautiful painting if anyone who were to see it as a surrealistic
representation of Salvador Dali waving a walking-stick at his
dog would find it just right. That is not what is meant by saying
of the Venetian picture that it is beautiful. What we have to do
is to connect the *D* and the *C* of the complex intentional

predicate of aspection with the quantified P and S that derive from the analysis of F (here 'painting') on the left-hand side. And this I think is easy enough to do without upsetting the univocity of the analysis of beauty that is proposed. For nothing prevents us from finally writing down as the analysis of 'w is a beautiful work of art':

(16) (w) (w is a beautiful work of art as fitting problem D in style C iff. $(\exists\phi)$ $(\exists S)$ $(\exists P)$ [w is in S and answers to P & In virtue of possession of ϕ, w tends to be such that (y) (f) {Aspects as answering problem $D=P$ in style $C=S$ (y,w,f) $\square\!\!\rightarrow$ $(\exists e)$ (Recognizes as just to $D=P$ and in $C=S$ (y, w, e) & f causes e)}])

This at once avoids the problem raised by seeing St. George in the wrong light and also allows us to answer the charge of ambiguity. The Venetian painting is not a beautiful painting when seen in the wrong way because then it is not judged according to the problem that really is its own. And as for the threat of ambiguity, this is surely staved off by seeing that the differences between (16) and (13) all derive from the differences that come from filling out $\ulcorner F\urcorner$ by 'work or art' rather than some other artefact or natural-thing term. Once we delete what flows from our understanding of the phrase 'work of art' in (16), what remains is the same in all cases. This is just what we want.

One last objection is this. In saying that it is a matter of conversational implicature that the filling for D and C should be assumed to be the most natural in the circumstances, I may be thought to have made way for a difference between the assertion that x is a beautiful work of art and that x is a beautiful natural object. For very often the most *natural* filling in the case of the work of art is of a problem and style that we merely *believe* the work to exemplify, rather than the one which it *does* exemplify. So on my account if only the surrealistic interpretation of the Venetian painting were the most commonly accepted it would appear to be true that the painting is beautiful when seen as a surrealistic work and false if seen as a Renaissance one. Just where, it may be asked, do the identities of (16) come from?

The reply to this is that our judgement of what is natural will depend on the kind of thing in question. Once it is plain that we are judging a work of art to be beautiful it will be natural to assume that speaker and hearer are both interested in the work from the point of view of its correct interpretation, and that, we have to acknowledge, involves the attribution to the work of an aesthetic structure that is independent of the spectator's choice and belief. It is natural therefore for the unspecified D and C to be assumed identical with this structure. Hence the identities in (16). Hence too the unconvincing nature of the putative counter-example. If the Venetian painting is claimed to be beautiful it must be understood that it is so relative not to its observer but to its structure, and whether we know what this structure is or not, it is mention of it within the embedded subjunctive conditional of the analysis that determines the truth or falsity of the asserted appraisal.

VII

The last section has suggested how univocity in the analysis is possible when the transition is made from the beauty of art to the beauty of nature. But to show how that may be achieved is not the same as to demonstrate that it must be done this way. My critic will rightly say that an argument is still owed to show that when we judge of a person's or a flower's beauty we are judging them within certain artificial canons, canons that we develop from our acquaintance with the arts. Initially it is not a very plausible suggestion anyway, and plausibility aside, what could the point be of behaving in this bizarre fashion?

In discussing the beauty of artistic detail I suggested we might be discussing either of two things. We might be judging something in a work of art as a beautiful detail of the work of which it is a part, or we might judge it *as if* it were a work in its own right. In the former case we are constrained by the structure that it carries from the work from which it is taken, but in the other case we are free. We can make of it what we like. Here surely is a kind of case that provides us with a smooth transition from art to nature.

The transition merely takes the form of noticing that the free application of canons of beauty learned from elsewhere is something that we engage in anyway. It is not something that is merely possible. It is something that we actually do. We try in the case of the free detail to see it as satisfactory, and our attempt to do this takes the form of applying to something that is given a set of standards that fit it well. To make it plausible that this is what happens in the natural case too we have only to find an explanation of the point of doing so. We have, that is, to explain why we should care that *nature* exhibits beauty.

My answer to this question is very tentative, and also very traditional. It was Kant's contention that 'to take an immediate interest in the beauty of nature (not merely to have good taste in judging it) is always a mark of a good soul; and that when this interest is habitual, it at least indicates a frame of mind favourable to the moral feeling if it is voluntarily bound up with the contemplation of nature' (§42), and sense may be made of this in the following way. A man who finds a way of viewing Nature in which he is bound to love it will through doing so find one way of overcoming that baneful divide between the subject and the world in which the subject lives. He will find in loving Nature an encouragement to his own integration in the world. If this is right we do not need a penetrating philosophical argument to show that morality is thereby furthered, as Kant supposed. We can simply say that it is a truth about human beings, of a psychological kind, that such attachments to the world as are furthered through the appreciation of its beauties encourage reverence for it and a respect for the claims that it makes against ourselves. Anyone who is conscious of the powerful forces in himself that make for selfishness cannot but find some solace in his possession of a power that can make it easier for him to love something disinterestedly that is distinct from him. To develop and exercise this power is to arm ourselves in one of the main ways at our disposal against the tyranny of self.

VIII

For the sake of my over-all argument I still need to ask why beauty in *works of art* promotes their endurance? Why is a thing of beauty a joy for ever— or if not for ever, at least of a notably non-ephemeral kind? To answer these questions I argue now that, conceived of as it has been here, artistic beauty is not just contingently attaching; and then that, because the roots of this attachment are what they are, the art that nourishes them well situated to withstand time's passage.

We saw above how eighteenth-century thinkers supposed the attaching nature of beautiful art was to be established. They inclined to fasten on the constitutive response that they took to analyse the idea.[29] Pleasure is integral to beauty, they would say, and it is analytic that we are not indifferent to what provokes it. This way with the question is no longer open. Having abandoned the traditional choice of elucidating response, we cannot suppose analytic truths about pleasure to be other than irrelevant. Perhaps this is as well, since not making pleasure central to the analysis we face no special difficulty in acknowledging the occasional (real, none the less) existence of beauties that do not attach but leave us indifferent, or even repel. The response of good fit I have put in place of pleasure leaves it nicely open whether we shall find all works displaying it to be attaching. That is what we want.

But is this thought consistent with my assertion that beauty is necessarily attaching? Yes, because while not all beauty in art compels devotion, those cases which constitute the norm must necessarily do so. Once that is established, it will be by reference to these normal cases that the power of beauty to survive will best be discussed. Non-normal beauty can be set aside as of little theoretical interest or importance.[30]

The normal case of beauty in art—that around which sound theory is constructed—must be found attaching because both the generation and the survival of the institution which is art is otherwise made incomprehensible. On any other supposition we try to imagine that the social edifice of art exists, while denying any regular motivation for its erection to those readers, listeners, and viewers on whose co-operation it depends. Unless what the would-be artist offers his viewers as beautiful is engaging enough not to leave them indifferent, they would have no cause to play their part in making his productions adequately public. Yet without this publicity these works could scarcely count as art at all, and the institution could not arise.

Again, we need to think of the normal case of beauty as rich enough in content to sustain the institution once under way. Now outside the operation of sets of stylistic concerns, conventions, and constraints it is extremely doubtful whether this could be achieved. But any actual set of stylistic concerns will themselves be the outcome of patterns of acknowledged histori-

cal development that only grow up where there exist expectations of a substantial sort about what may be achieved and
aimed at in the public arena. So the institutional persistence of
art, too, depends on expectations about what are thought of as
its central cases. And while expectations about what makes
art's public and continued existence something to desire may
well be variable, there could be no hope in supposing it always
to have a content from which we think ourselves repelled or
fundamentally detached. At the centre attachment is indispensable.

   This is to say nothing about why or how that peculiar recognition of good fit, in terms of which beauty has been explained
here, should generate attachment. It is just to point out that
however the idea is analysed its normal cases must do so. Now
it may well be thought that until fit and attachment are more
convincingly connected than they have yet been, the elucidating proposal I have made will remain deeply unsatisfying.
Why, one wants to ask, should we ever find (mere?) good fit of
work to problem and style a matter of much concern? Can this
really be the beauty that is so central to our concept and to our
practice of art? It is obvious that much that needs saying on this
matter has its proper place in critical discussion of individual
paintings, buildings, and poems rather than in the philosophical development of aesthetic theory. Still, something by way of
theory is called for, because in its absence we shall find it hard
to distinguish at all surely between those works that are simply
good examples of their kind and those that are beautiful as well.
The object that is experienced as being just right for its problem
and style might well be either, and that would not be good
enough. So the critic might say; and to see that his criticism
misses the mark will be to understand more about fit than has
yet been revealed. In any case, because his challenge is one that
is expressible in quite general terms it is only natural to expect a
response to it that enjoys a measure of generality too. So let me
distinguish between art that is representational and art that is
abstract, and attend quite generally to the beauty of each in
turn.

   In the above pages—and especially in section IV—I have
said nothing to preclude assessment of fit in the representational field from involving a judgement about the broadly

human or anthropocentric character of the represented world—of its emotional, intellectual, and even its moral nature. Indeed I have said next to nothing by way of description of this beauty-constituting fit at all. But it is plain that under the values of the chosen style the subject of the beautiful representative work will be shown in a certain light; and it should come as no surprise that our thought about how it is shown enters integrally into our finding the work just right for its problem and style when we do so. This being so, there can be no difficulty in distinguishing within the present theory between the good example of art of a certain kind and the truly beautiful instance, for this judgement of character is quite unnecessary on the first count, and scarcely dispensable on the second. If recognition of fit is indeed operative in both cases, the fit in question is different in each.

Now perhaps we can take the crucial step to supply the desired attachment. On the supposition that the anthropocentric character of the represented world has its part to play in our assessment of representational art as beautiful or not, it is inviting to surmise that to find beauty there involves our experiencing the represented world as—and quite deliberately I choose a rather bland term—coherent. This, I take it, is an element of our experience that is stable whether or not we find the work in question attaching, whether its beauty is normal or not. It is, on this view, something to which any judgement of representational beauty is sensitive. However when as here we are concerned with *normal* beauty, this coherence will be experienced as benign and non-alienating. Here, I think, is where we find the primary source of our attachment to it.[31] For the effect of distinguishing between the experience of benign coherence and the experience of coherence *tout court* is to force us to recognize that experience of the former kind is no more something to which we might be indifferent than is the pleasure that so occupied the thought of the eighteenth century. However, as I have presented the issue, this claim is not derived as an analytic truth depending on the meaning of the term 'benign coherence', but results instead from the actual character of our response of good fit to those representational works that we take to be normally beautiful. Without this benign aspect we should find them either too jarring to be beautiful at all, or else lacking in that warmth they need to have to make them theoretically central.

Before saying anything about abstract art I record two observations. The first is that stressing this internal aspect of fit is in no way meant to underplay the importance of other things that also enter into our judgement of representational beauty. Thus very often how the artist has handled his subject in the medium in which he is working is crucial too. But success here gives us a less clear line to a general source of attachment than it would if offered by the suggestion on which I have preferred to pick.

Secondly, it may be objected that these claims are to be had only at a cost—that is, only by abandoning any thought that aesthetic values are autonomous. Have I not spoken as if our interest in the beautiful lay in something quite different—effectively in the emotional and the moral? And would that not be a mistake? However, such a doubt misconceives my suggestion. On the contrary, these human interests are very much part of, not distinct from, our interest in representational beauty and as such they enter into our judgements of just fit. It will follow that as interest in their presence in art need not be an interest of a non-aesthetic kind. It is not that the aesthetic has lost its autonomy; it has retained it—only under a broader conception of its connection with the rest of our lives than some would like it to have. This is what earlier chapters have led us to expect.

About the beauty of the abstract arts we cannot take quite the same line. Lacking representational content they do not show us a world that is beautiful through being benignly ordered. That however does not prevent us from advancing by an analogous appreciation of the great width of scope that just fit of work to project has in these cases. It has long been recognized that abstract art exercises its power over us in large part by its potential for expression, and it would be consonant with what has gone before to discern a link between this kind of beauty and benign expressiveness. What is to count as this is a difficult matter, particularly since citation of individual states of mind would be too specific. Perhaps it comes near the truth to say that we experience the abstract as benignly expressive when the artist has managed to get us to see how his treatment of his material achieves a constellation of mental states that are expressed while inflicting no omnipotent violence on the material itself. He has humanized it in a way that renders it intact yet at the same time leaves no part of it untouched by the mind. The inner, the mental, touches the material at every point, and we feel that the whole contains no gaps. The result is that mind and matter match benignly, with no omissions and no violence. The benignity involved is not that of some particular state expressed, but a kind of accommodation between inner and outer that we experience as being just right. When this happens it is natural to feel that we have everything that could be asked for in general terms from this sort of art, though as before everything that is of detailed interest will have to be said at the level of the individual case. Thus these abstract beauties are well fitted to be regarded as normal once it is admitted that the desire to humanize the external world is something that is widely desired and something to be achieved through art. Responsibility for any failure of attachment at this point can be attributed to the spectator in the hope that he may come to make it good. It is not something to lay at the doorstep of the artist.

These paragraphs then have sketched out a claim that beauty in art of either kind, representational or abstract, is of necessity attaching in the normal cases. From here it is no great way to seeing why normal beauties generate attachment over time. The reason is extremely simple. We have a constant interest in taking into ourselves those forms of benign order which are displayed in these arts at their best. What is more difficult is to see why this answer is satisfying, and it will help to dispose of three obstacles to our doing so.

First, it might appear that this claim does no more than reiterate what has just been said, and that in consequence it cannot take the argument forward. Have I not already relied precisely on our always having an interest in taking these sorts of order within ourselves? Yet despite a superficial similarity, that assertion must be distinguished from the present one, that is, from the claim that we have a constant interest in what displays such order. The first of them makes no assumption that normal art will always generate a reason for us to give it our attention. The latter does. True, this last cannot be supported by what has gone before, but I have made no claim that it can.

Allow then that these claims are different. Does it not now cry out that the stronger of them is false? What could possibly encourage us to think that as cultural climates change the normal beauties of earlier times do generate such motivation? Do they not all too often elude our understanding? However, this question is one that we have dealt with before. The lesson learnt above has been that what is important is not whether these works demand our interest once we understand them, but whether they do so *prior* to our understanding them. If so, we should expect to direct our energies towards a full appreciation of them; if not, there would be little point in struggling for comprehension even if it could be had. In either case understanding is not what poses the problem.

Here we see what really does exercise the critic, and it is here that the most serious difficulty arises. He will say that as I have expounded the analysis—at least in the representational cases—it must very often happen that the work of the past cannot generate a reason for us to devote ourselves to it. For the possibilities it puts on display and whose nature admittedly accounts for *contemporary* attachment are no longer possibilities for us who view these works at a later date. What gave them their strength for the contemporary viewer—the benignity of what was a possibility for him—is something that in the present they can no longer call on to attach us. So even when we see the fit of work to project as involving a display of benignity, it will not be one that we should too readily rely on to ensure the work's survival. Once this defect in my argument is noticed I shall not be able to claim that normal beauties have a constant claim on our attention. Hence on the theory I have adopted I cannot explain their survival over time.

Certainly this criticism is to the point as the two previous ones were not. Yet it is mistaken. It relies on the erroneous and entirely egoistic assumption, criticized in the last chapter and in Chapter 5, that we are only rationally attached to what we take to be a benign sort of order that we ourselves might enjoy. That this is mistaken can be seen both by reflecting on our experience of the arts and on the assumption's rather dismal theoretical consequences. As for the first, if it really were true that only those beauties in representational art that show us how the world might be for us could reasonably engage and hold our attention, we should be at a loss to explain why we do in fact rightly prize so many of the finest beauties of the past. Very often the world they show us is not one which, as life is led, represents a possibility for us except in the uninteresting sense of 'logical possibility'. More theoretically, if it really were to be insisted upon that the real possibilities that generate a motive for interest were only ones that were possibilities for ourselves, see what the consequences would be. In the first place we should break down the publicity that is needed to keep the institution of art alive, because even though we are contemporaries what is a real possibility for me may well not be one for you. And then it is arguable that even for myself I could take no sure delight in a possibility for myself that was not a possibility for myself *in the present*. (What difference is there, after all, between a representation of a future possibility for me and a representation of a possibility for someone distinct from me? None, I should say. So if interest in others is to be kept at bay restriction to the present seems very probably needed.) All that this leaves free is the possibility that is now actual. Thus it could be said that the only rationally attaching kind of beauty in this solipsistic art would be one that merely replicated the individual's present world. And that could be of little interest, as absurd as Hegel's worm crawling after its elephant.[32]

The moral of these rather condensed reflections is this. If, as I claim, our appreciation of beauty does involve a judgement about the character of the represented world; and if in normal cases that world must be found to be in some way benign; then, because our motivation for attachment is not simply to the benign that we might find to be a good for ourselves, but also to that which anyone we can sympathize with might find so, mere distance from us of the possibilities that are displayed in the beautiful art of the past is incapable of blocking an inference to a constant interest in these works. So given that we have a motive for lending them our attention, it is likely that we shall want to see the desire it rationalizes fulfilled. Hence such art has a power to resist displacement and disturbance and is well calculated to endure.

This is to keep silent about the abstract arts. And my claim must cover them as well. This is not difficult. What has been said about the representational cases has largely taken the form

of setting aside obstacles to seeing why we should expect that
art to survive. In one way or another those obstacles turned on
thought about the content of that art. By contrast, abstract art
has no content—or at least not a content of this sort. It offers no
possibilities to the spectator which he might find engaging.
What I have said is that it offers him a certain match between
inner and outer, and that is a match that does not become
distant from him as time goes by. This match is one we always
seek; all we need is to make sure we understand how it is
effected. And we know already that difficulties about understanding are neither here nor there as far as the present issue
goes. So the call on us of abstract art is if anything easier to
understand than that exercised by its representational fellow.
It might strike us that when we look at particular cases we tend
not to find the beauties of older abstract art anything like so
elusive as the representational ones. They seem to speak with a
directness that is not enjoyed by their cousins. What that
suggests to me is that once we have given an explanation of why
in their case normal beauties are attaching, nothing else needs
saying about why they are expected to survive. For, issues of
understanding apart, there is nothing to stop them doing so.
Naturally one could say that sufficiently large changes in our
interests and concerns could bring this about—that we ceased
to find them appealing—but then do we seriously suppose that
if we stopped caring about finding articulated, expressive
match between inner and outer we should still have a live concern for the enjoyment of abstract art itself?

Chapter 9

Excellence and Stature

'. . . a notion which, like a good many others in art, has been heaped with ridicule. Namely the notion of Great Art. I believe it might profitably be revived.'

Paul Valéry, 'Reflections on Art'

I

In the Introduction I cited a stricture of Nelson Goodman's on paying excessive attention to excellence in aesthetics. That could suggest that matters of evaluation are of only the most marginal interest in our thought about art, and certainly some such reflection recurs influentially from time to time in the theory of criticism. If suspicion of its truth is not now allayed, energy expended on validating the critical inferences may well seem wasted.

One representative proponent of the anti-evaluative view is Northrop Frye, a critic who has repeatedly challenged the propriety of pursuing judgements of value about the objects of our literary attention.[1] To support his position he asserts first that such judgements do not express knowledge, but are 'mainly intuitive reactions to knowledge'; second, that they are conventional, reflecting the conventions of the critic's age and society rather than those of the poet he studies, and third, that they are 'indirect rather than direct', stemming not from experience of the work, but being derivatively superimposed upon that experience. On each count his arguments are insubstantial, but since they are fully representative of their kind, and are no worse than many others, they have a claim to our notice.

The first of these three charges depends on there being a dichotomy between expressions of knowledge and of felt reactions to knowledge. Historically viewed, the belief in such a dichotomy is the creature of a philosophical climate whose accounts of appraisive discourse are dominated by emotivist or ascriptivist doctrine (doubtless for Frye dominated by the writings of C. L. Stevenson). From a later perspective its appeal is weak. For why, it has insistently been asked, should we not admit that the vocabulary best suited to draw attention to and to praise works of art is best chosen from that segment of the language that serves to express knowledge about them? Quite generally speaking, are not the various functions of evaluative discourse best fulfilled by language that can assert something truly or falsely about the valued thing? Indeed, once our concerns and interests are fixed, it is hard to see how the language appropriate to conveying knowledge bearing upon them could fail to operate in this way. In saying that a poem or a painting is good or great I may admittedly provide no information about it that is independent of the knowledge I rely on to understand it, but this fact is not sufficient to reduce the standing of evaluation to mere 'intuitive reaction to knowledge'. Once we see that utterances well-suited to express knowledge may themselves have appraisive uses, we have no reason to infer that the evaluative portion of the critic's vocabulary cannot be used in a properly informative way. The divide that Frye assumes there to be between these functions is non-existent; hence the argument that presupposes it must fail.

If this point is well taken it effectively lames the second objection too. Recognizing that claims to knowledge *can* be expressed in language that is evaluative, we see that the charge that evaluation is 'conventional' (whatever that means precisely) loses its force. When the critic sets aside prejudice and bias, and forms his judgement not on misperception but on a proper (canonical) understanding of the work—as it is his task to do—we have no cause to think that his judgement is radically and objectionably subjective. Where Frye says that 'when a critic interprets, he is talking about his poet; when he evaluates, he is talking about himself, or at most about himself as a representative of his age' he either speaks falsely or else says something true about an unimportant set of evaluations, to wit those that are made on less than the best grounds, and which are for that very reason rebuttable. To make out his case Frye must restrict his attention to those evaluations which are not so deficient, and when that is done there is no room left over for what he calls 'conventional' evaluations. Maybe *they* are not 'subjects of knowledge', but that is not a feature they share with the more respectable members of their class about which he needs to be talking.

Of the three grounds of attack the last is the most serious. It rests, I suspect, on the thought that we can only come to sound appraisals on the basis of a full, first-order understanding of the work we are concerned with—which is true—and assumes that when that understanding is achieved nothing of interest could be added by evaluation. So, in effect, even when it is reliable, evaluation is superfluous, hence does not constitute a proper goal of criticism. What is questionable about this train of thought is the unexamined notion of *understanding* or *experience* on which it relies. What we are to believe is that the full experience of the poem is given before any evaluation is attempted. That is something that is superadded after understanding is complete. But just what is this understanding to include? To mention only a couple of notions that have occupied us in preceding chapters, if our experience is fully describable without reference to our perception of how a poem achieves its design within its chosen constraints, or without mention of the significance to us of its over-all aim, our understanding of the work will surely be less than full. Abstract from these matters and our experience of the work cannot be replete. On the other hand, once they are admitted we have let in (as the sequel will show) matters that are distinctly evaluative. So it is hard to say with all the conviction that Frye musters that we are here talking about something indirect, over and above the experience of the work itself.

A contention with which Frye's last argument should be opposed is that considerations upon which a full understanding or experience of art depends are not something on which judgements of value are simply superimposed; rather these judgements are partially constitutive of that understanding. So when Frye speaks of the full experience that a careful reading should aim at, judgements of value are not peripheral and not to be left out. This assertion is entirely consistent with the recognition that we give reasons for our evaluations of art in terms that are themselves non-evaluative and which are firmly among those that Frye reckons provide direct experience of the work. But to admit this is quite different from saying that our experience can be complete or adequate to the work if evaluative judgements are not made; or that the reason-giving relation that holds between this language and that of evaluation is one that allows the second class of statements full independence of the first.

The burden of my polemic against the anti-evaluative position is very simply this: we cannot hope to arrive at a complete understanding of any art in the absence of an assessment of its worth. As a matter of historical interest, and justice to Frye, it is noteworthy that elsewhere in his writings we see that this claim is not one from which he himself would always dissent. 'There is real truth', he writes, 'in the belief that the critic is deeply concerned with evaluation in separating the good from the bad in literature',[2] and he happily speaks of the best criticism producing 'the direct value-judgement of informed good taste, the proving of art on the pulses, the disciplined response of a highly organised nervous system to the impact of poetry.'[3] The difficulty is to reconcile these sober remarks with the dismissive line of thought just discussed. It cannot be done. If, as we should, we prefer the realism to the dogma, evaluation has to be accepted not merely as a proper part of the critic's concerns but as essential to the exercise of his activity. To secure the inferences concerning time's test that I am concerned with thus becomes a matter of theoretical urgency. Whatever we make of Goodman's original dictum as an observation about the course philosophical aesthetics has taken in recent years, it must not be used to justify systematic neglect of questions about artistic excellence and the stature of the artist's creations. To these topics I now turn.

II

From the premiss that a work of art has passed time's test the main inference we draw is one that I took care to state originally in anodyne terms. I said that the work is one legitimately thought of as being of high quality or merit. The anodyne must now give way to the specific, and we shall see how it is to do so only by finding a determinate form of this conclusion which the premiss will actually support. The output of the inference depends entirely on the weight that the initial input can be made to bear.

The most obvious candidate for output is the one suggested by the model that has guided the course of previous chapters. In the case of a car, a coat, or a clock there is nothing else to be plausibly concluded from their having worn well than that they are good objects of their kind. Their survival attests their proper functioning; and the goodness of these artefacts is just that. Apply this analogy to the arts as special kinds of artefacts and we are led to surmise that critical estimations of its works based on endurance must relate to goodness too. Hence we may think that even when the critic does not readily employ the words 'good' and 'bad' themselves in his judgements, the vocabulary of merit that he does use will permit of recasting in this style without significant residue. Evaluative language that can be so recast belongs to what I shall call 'the vocabulary of excellence', and it is a real question just how extensive this is. To take one instance, Yvor Winters at least believes that the term 'great' belongs to this vocabulary, for such literature he says is *good* literature, treating of subjects chosen from a range that lies close to our hearts.[4] The great is thus reduced to the good and would therefore fall within the language of excellence. And so perhaps with other evaluative terms too. Certainly, if nothing deters us from projecting the model of the goodness of artefacts onto the arts the call to reduce this and other evaluative terms will become pressing. However, leaving aside for the moment the plausibility of these individual reductions, there are at least two good reasons that prevent us from blindly following the analogy with standard artefacts.

The first is rooted in the fact that whereas cars, coats, and clocks have all a defining function, we know that the arts do not. True we saw in Chapter 5 that there are aims that they characteristically seek to fulfil and benefits that they typically provide, but when we ask ourselves whether some painting or poem is a good one or not, it is nothing answering to these aims or to the provision of these benefits that settles the question. To be told, say, that a lyric poem we prize is one of expressive sensitivity or is one that enlarges our understanding of some delicate feeling may well assure us that the poem is one that meets the aims of the art, but it is not to be told that it is a good one. As we shall see, this may very well not be true, and that is no criticism of the sensitivity it does display. So here it appears that the best thing that we might rely on to stand analogically to the defining function of standard artefacts is only dubiously related to goodness. In its simplest form the analogy breaks down.

The other reason for thinking that the conclusions of our inference should not be made determinate in the language of excellence is that that vocabulary is most happily used in relation to art of a specific type or category, whereas the test of time invites us to infer something about works of art as such, not *qua* works of a particular type. Thus choice of a specific conclusion cast in terms of goodness would misrepresent critical practice. Think how unnatural it is for a man of sensitivity to talk of a poem or a painting as being 'a good work of art'; naturalness only comes in speaking of it as a good portrait, or a good sonnet, or a good piece of genre. And it would be false to claim that what we learn from the long survival in our attention of such works is that they are good portraits, good genre pieces, or good sonnets. It may be of course that in the individual case we can sometimes arrive at these results, but when we do it is only as a result of having already derived some other conclusion. So excellence is too tenuously related to survival to serve our purpose. Again the analogy fails.

To confirm this last objection, reflect that one ground on which we allow a work of art to withstand time's pressures is that it displays depth of understanding. This is surely something that is true, when it is, quite independently of the profound work's belonging to the particular category of art to which it does belong. We do not say of an epic that survives largely on account of its depth that it is *ipso facto* a good epic poem. That evaluation points in quite a different direction, and once we see what that direction is, any temptation that we might still feel to cast the fully specified conclusion of our inference in the language of excellence will lose its appeal.

A judgement that something is good of its kind is very often made when the object is not flawed in any important way. As the lawyers put it, the judgement is a defeasible one. Thus an apple is thought to be a good one as long as it is not insect-ridden, shrivelled, pecked at by the thrushes, too tart, and so on. Similarly an artefact will be unflawed very often as long as it functions properly—whence the connection we made in these cases between goodness and function. Now when we reflect on the application of this idea to the arts, we can see that the idea of a flaw is much easier to introduce in relation to works of art *qua* works belonging to specific categories, than it is in relation to works of art as such. *As such* there are very few failings that a work of art might display which would unfit it for our interest, for the interests we have in the arts are so many and so diverse that it is quite unclear what property a work might have which would preclude it from satisfying any of them. Yet this is what we should be looking for if we wanted to treat goodness in the arts as a defeasible notion and at the same time divorce it from considerations of the specific type of work that is being judged.

On the other hand no such difficulty arises for assessments of excellence once they are made within a particular category of art. For works of particular types have type-bound demands to satisfy which, although they may resist precise articulation, are with patience and practice reliably enough internalized. Once they are so internalized we are able to judge of a sonnet, say, that it is flawed because its choice of theme is ill-matched to its formal constraints. Then, whatever its positive merits, we shall be unwilling to allow that the sonnet is a good one. Or, to take another example, we think it a failing in a novel that it should introduce a *deus ex machina*, or occurrences outside the order or nature (no failing in a fable, though) and when this happens, as, say, with the spontaneous combustion of Mr Krook in *Bleak House*, we perceive the work as a flawed novel,[5] and I suggest for that reason find ourselves less willing than we would otherwise be to speak of it as a good one.[6] Generalizing these examples, I propose that we recognize ourselves to be engaged with considerations of excellence primarily within the limits that are imposed by taking a work of art to be of a specific category. When we speak of a good work of art as such, this judgement will be one that is derivative from the more specific judgement, and defensible only if some such more specific judgement is available to us.

A full treatment of excellence in art is not to my purpose here, but as a prelude to the next section it will be helpful to point out how the suggestion I have made will explain one feature of our use of 'good' in critical contexts, which might otherwise cause some surprise. Very often we feel that little of substance is said of a portrait bust, or a love poem, or a line drawing, in declaring it to be a good one. We think we damn it with faint praise, and this thought can persist even when we extoll the work as excellent. What is happening here is that we are judging the work by standards which are not very exacting, judging it to meet more or less minimal standards. So that when it does come up to these standards we do not think of it as flawed —though we may still not think very highly of it. Now assessments of this sort are indeed of interest, but the interest is of a somewhat restricted kind: in place, for example, in the classroom where the apprentice is learning what he can about the construction of works of a given sort, or perhaps in the thought of the connoisseur to whom such information matters for the accuracy of his attributions. Not being teachers or connoisseurs ourselves, we demand in addition to these assessments estimates of works of art that range wider than do these limited critical comments. Hence, expecting that the strongest thing that can be said *is* said, when these are all we meet we infer that the more engaged appraisal cannot be sustained.

With this in mind it is easy to appreciate why it would be a mistake to cast the conclusions of time's test in the vocabulary of excellence. To do so would yield information that is pitiably weak. *Parturient montes, nascetur ridiculus mus.* For what we want these inferences to indicate is that the surviving work does have a serious claim upon our attention; and that information is not provided simply by the knowledge that it comes up to standards by which it is judged an unflawed member of its type. Thus on that choice of specification of the anodynely-stated conclusion, the main inference is rendered unserviceable.

So too are others of the arguments I listed in Chapter 1. To give only one example, I said we want to conclude that the more securely a work of art passes time's test the finer we take it to be. Now if 'finer' is understood to mean that the work more easily avoids the charge of being flawed, that it surpasses with greater ease the minimum standards for its kind than does the less securely surviving work, the focus of our interest in drawing the inference quite gets lost. For we are not for the most part interested in how easily or how nearly the work overcomes barriers to its success, but more directly with some more positive measure of its success. I conclude then that the inferences have to be cast in terms quite other than those of the vocabulary of excellence—and *ipso facto* to be cast in terms that are not reducible to that vocabulary. It follows then that if the inferences are to be made out at all there must be such a vocabulary available to us. It falls to the next section to show that this is indeed so.

III

Aesthetics has displayed a concern with the need for a different range of appraisive language, and one that is also freed from too intimate connection with the particular category of art, in classical and eighteenth-century discussion of the idea of *genius*. Many of the associations of this notion are admittedly somewhat alien to the modern mind, but in a suitably recast form they persuade one of the need for a different form of appraisive vocabulary.

In its origin the idea of genius is as far removed as possible from matters of craftsmanly competence that occupy the teacher and the connoisseur. A divinity invades the poet's soul (*Ion* 533, *Phaedrus* 245) and works in his stead. In this mythical form we even find an explicit connection with evaluative matters in Cicero's *De deorum natura* (2.66): 'Nemo vir magnus sine aliquo afflato divino numquam fuit.' But in these early appearances the idea of genius is not of great theoretical significance for the understanding of the arts. It is at most a contingent matter that the finest artistic work is produced under the influence of the gods, and certainly not a necessary truth. Nor can it be seriously maintained that the explanatory value of the myth in accounting for the production of great poetry is anything other than a sham. To be anything better, myth has to be replaced with something else, and such a step is first taken by Longinus in psychologizing the myth and ousting the gods. No longer does the poet hope to be inspired by supernatural forces; rather he gives expression to his own passions and bursts out with 'a wild gush of mad enthusiasm' (*On the Sublime*, VIII. 4). So psychologized, genius is appealed to in the explanation of the creation of the finest art late into the eighteenth century in, for example, John Dennis's *Advancement and Reformation of Poetry*, and Alexander Gerard's *Essay on Genius*.

Although a psychological account of genius is superior to a

mythical one, the explanations that it offers are none the less of the wrong sort. For the primary theoretical interest that we have in the subject is not the state of mind in which the finest art is engendered, but what it is that that art consists in. And an answer to this second and more pressing question cannot be given in terms of pyschological contingencies. It is only with Kant's *Critique of Judgement* that the discussion takes an altogether different turn, and that for the first time in the literature we find systematic arguments tending to show that genius and the finest art are indissolubly and non-empirically linked.

To establish the necessity of genius Kant argues that it alone enables us simultaneously to draw two distinctions which art theory cannot afford to abandon: those between art and nature on the one hand, and art and craft on the other. Without appeal to genius, Kant believes, we shall only succeed in keeping art and nature distinct at the expense of running together art and craft. Art is distinguished from nature by the fact that it is created in accordance with a plan: 'Art always has a definite design of producing something' (§45), and from this observation Kant goes on (uncontroversially enough) to claim that 'a product can never be called art without some precedent rule' (ibid.), by which he means no more than that in order to execute a plan we need to work in accordance with a conception (a rule) of how to proceed. And it is evident to Kant that out of these materials, plan or conception and rule of procedure, not enough is given to distinguish between art and craft. For craft, as much as art, aims at a definite design and therefore, like art, also presupposes rules in its construction.

To keep art and craft apart, then, he offers us a distinction between two types of rule for the production of artefacts: those that can be learnt and taught, and those that cannot. Genius he defines as a natural talent for the discovery of procedures of the second kind, and since it is they that are peculiar to art, whereas craft relies only on rules of the first kind, Kant concludes that genius and art are necessarily linked. Without the former the latter could not exist.[7]

Yet when we remember that for Kant genius invents rules that become *exemplary for others* (§46), that is, discovers the procedures which other artists follow in the execution of *their* works on becoming acquainted with them, we see how weak this argument is. If nothing will count as a work of fine art except genius participate in its creation, we are at a loss to explain how genius might be exemplary; for those disciples for whom it is exemplary are surely dispensed from its possession while none the less the works they fashion are undoubted works of art. If it is said in defence of Kant that all that is meant is that in its *origin* a rule or precept that becomes exemplary should not have been formulable and should require inventive power for its discovery, then the very same claim might well enough be made for the procedures that the craftsman follows in the production of his works too. Both in art and in craft, procedures for the execution of designs must once have been discovered, so appeal to genius understood in this more restricted way cannot be used to distinguish between them either.

Fortunately Kant has a second line of thought, this time more engaged with matters of conception than with those of execution, which looks more promising. In its barest terms his argument turns on our interest in the arts being of a different order than that which we have in the crafts. The interest we have in a craft object is ultimately grounded in the utility that the particular sort of object it is has for us; its beauty is subservient to its function, and is very largely decorative. In the case of art, though, our interest in the object is rooted in the thought that the work expresses, and Kant thinks that it is the task of genius to express in art such thoughts as sustain our interest in it—thoughts that in his writings go under the name of 'aesthetic ideas', and which stand ever in need of constant elaboration.

Like its predecessor this contention of Kant's also involves genius in making the distinction between art and craft and thus underwriting the claim that the arts are necessarily the creation of genius. But even if this is how Kant would wish to be understood—at this late stage of the *Critique* he has somewhat lost hold of the over-all structure of his argument and interpretation is not simple—it is neither adequate to the task, nor does it best deploy the consideration on which it turns. Obviously, even when the term 'genius' is generously construed we shall not want to say that *every* work of art is a work of genius, but at most that what Kant calls 'beautiful art' is so. And if we train our sights, as Kant did, on making the distinction between art and craft, the limited observation about the necessity of genius for the creation of *beautiful* art will not immediately avail us. Just as beautiful art is distinct from craft, so too is non-beautiful art; and if all that Kant maintains is that genius is necessary for the production of beautiful art we are still some way from showing that the production of art itself is impossible without it.

But this need not be the end of Kant's argument. For if we remember that for the purposes of drawing the distinction between craft and art he has available to him the heteronomous appeal of the one and the autonomous nature of the other, we can see that he might perfectly well claim that genius is necessary for art, not as a condition of drawing the distinction but for the purpose of ensuring that it is not an empty one. That is, he might claim that while artefacts are works of art only if we have a disinterested attachment to them, there can only be such things if at least some of them are works of genius. And while Kant does not in fact argue along these lines, it is not difficult to see how he might have done so. It is, after all, very plausible to claim that in the absence of genius it would be impossible for us to account for the actual existence of art: for the establishment, that is, of an autonomous institution of art whose members we can reliably identify as its works. Alternatively, and in addition, even when we waive considerations about the genesis of art, it is an attractive thought that without the effective presence of something that only genius supplies, the autonomous survival of the institution over a period of time would be incomprehensible. If in addition we suppose that the idea of genius introduces into our thought about the arts a range of evaluative vocabulary that is not a part of the language of excellence, then such a development of Kant's reflections on this subject would yield just what we are looking for, a way of showing that without such a discrete vocabulary the concept of art could not get off the ground. The question is, of course, whether such an argument can be made good.

It is common for historians of the subject to conjecture that our earliest art derived from representations that served magical or ritual purposes. What prevents us from thinking of these things as proper examples of art has nothing to do with their lifelikeness, or the primitive skill with which they were made, but is simply the fact that we cannot see them as part of a publicly established institution of art. For it is only if we can assimilate a particular artefact to such a publicly recognized undertaking that we shall be able to defend an identification of it as a work of art against challenge. To identify it as a work of art is to say of it that it has a self-standing, non-utilitarian interest, and unless we can rely on the knowledge that such interests are publicly recognized, such a suggestion about a particular object would have to be treated as false, or at best as unsubstantiated. To call it a piece of 'art' would then be to say little more about it than that we knew not what it was for.

So the very existence of art involves its having an institutional character, hence implies that some works of art must evoke an interest that is sufficiently engaging for such a public institution to arise and become established. And what such an interest centres on can only be (i) the skilful execution of some design or (ii) some conception that is sensuously realized in some medium. These two, execution and conception, seem to exhaust the possibilities. And of this pair it does not seem realistic to say that the first, taken by itself, is powerful enough for our purposes; for however aesthetically accomplished we might suppose the execution of some design to be, it is difficult to imagine that in abstraction from the *point* of the design sufficient public interest should focus on the work for the activity it exemplifies to become an institutionalized one. The highest degree of executory aesthetic skill can be put to the most trivial ends, and in a community where this supposition were thought to extend right across the board, we should be hard put to justify a claim that we had really understood what was going on in the name of 'art'. To avoid imputing collective irrationality to that community we would rather say that what they were doing served some end that we did not appreciate,[8] not that the end served was an artistic one.

On the other hand, once we see a representation as realizing not just some aesthetic skill of execution but a conception of the world that has a non-subjective claim on us, then it becomes possible to explain how it is that the work might autonomously engage our interest and be of a kind that it makes sense to identify as belonging to a social institution of its own. Then and only then does it become possible for us to say that art has severed its connection with ritual, or magic, or some other heteronomous interest. And this severance we see depends on the artist being able in his work to make available to us a certain demanding thought, which is just what genius consists in on Kant's second account of the matter. So we have an argument to the conclusion that unless some representations are works of genius the distinction between art and craft would be an empty one. Without it there could exist no geniune art at all: not merely no 'beautiful' or outstanding art, but not even any that we could judge to be mediocre or negligible.

A parallel reflection permits us to argue that even if in some unexplained way the institution of art were to become established on a slighter basis than this, it would be unrealistic to suppose that it might continue in existence unless sustained from this source. For how could it do so? The alternatives seem to dwindle either to the mere elaboration of themes in terms of which we suppose the institution to have got off the ground— which is here to relegate the problem to the domain of mystery— or else to the development of technical skills for their own sake, the rationale of which, when divorced from any thought of what might be achieved with their aid, is of insufficient power to prevent the hypothetically established, autonomous institution from collapsing into a heteronomous one, or from withering away altogether. So I conclude that the persistence of the institution of art as well as its genesis supposes that we see the arts as necessarily aiming to elaborate thought of a sort to which we attach common public importance. If genius is a capacity to achieve this end, then Kant is indeed right in thinking that genius and the concept of art are inextricably intertwined.

But what has all this to do with the need for an evaluative vocabulary that is distinct from that already discussed in the last section? Why should the introduction of genius help at all here? The answer is that the conceptions that individual works seek to realize must themselves fall within the scope of evaluation. If they were not to do so, then we should be unable to mark a distinction between those thoughts to which we do attach importance and those to which we do not. In the absence of that distinction art would again become impossible. Yet it is evident that these evaluations cannot simply be chosen from the vocabulary of excellence I have spoken of above. For if they were so chosen we should only be able to talk in terms that enabled us to assess whether or not a particular conception of the world as mediated through some work of art made the work a good one of its type. And we have already seen that such assessments as this do not commit us to an interest that goes far beyond the achievements of, so to speak, minimum standards, an interest that only begins to occupy us when we know that something more demanding can be achieved. What we should have excluded would be a capacity ever to comment on the extent of the human achievement of art, and under that regime, with all evaluation bound to a category, it would be impossible for us either to identify the product of genius, or if, *per impossibile*, that could be done, to explain it as being of any significance.

The moral then is this. The existence and survival of the institution of art seems to be possible only on the supposition that we have a way of talking about the arts in evaluative language that takes us beyond assessments of their works that are reducible to the vocabulary of excellence. The argument that I have used to show this has been conducted quite independently of any consideration concerning the test of time, and without making any attempt to say what that language might be. If it can now be identified and shown to be free of the limitation that we saw infected the language of excellence, we may finally have located determinate conclusions for our initial critical inferences that stand some chance of subsequent legitimization.

IV

Both in the arts and elsewhere we praise something not only as being excellent of its kind but also as being of stature. I shall argue that terms within this range—in particular 'great', but by implication also 'mediocre' and 'negligible'—are irreducible to evaluations of the former sort, and in consequence that to say of some work of art that it is good of its kind and that it is great is to say two logically unrelated things about it. Further, we shall see that the nouns that go together with adjectives of stature do not have to be those that assign a work to its category. We can as well say that something is a great work of art as we can that it is a great sonata or a great epic. Since it is also true that works of stature are well fitted to ground and sustain the institution of art, there is good reason to think that we have suitable specification in this vocabulary of the conclusions that we are looking for.

To say of something that it is of great stature is to apply to it either literally or, more usually, figuratively, an estimation of size. The Great Bed of Ware, Trinity's Great Court, and the Great Wall of China would all be ill-named if they were anything other than large. But to be large in size and to be great in stature are not the same, for nothing is great if, in addition to being large, it is not outstanding in respect of its size. That is why it imposes itself on our attention.

One reason for which we judge something to be outstanding in size is its being larger than the average member of its kind. This is Kant's explanation of that ordinary greatness with which he contrasts the 'absolute greatness' that he believes to constitute one sort of sublimity—i.e. 'mathematical sublimity' (§25). But this will not do. For a man, a house, and a tree (all Kant's examples) may well not be great in size even though they are larger than average. That would not ground their being outstanding. Something different is called for.

An alternative might be that the great is that which is outstanding by reason of being among the largest examples we know of a certain sort of thing. For our acquaintance often goes beyond the merely larger than average. Though this is often true, and though it would explain why we find it outstanding, the suggestion cannot be properly elucidatory of greatness of size, since our knowledge of objects of a certain sort is often found to change over time. Yet we do not want to say that an object that was at one time truly great might be falsely so called as our acquaintance with the class is relevantly enlarged. This proposal is no more comfortable than the other.

At least in the case of things belonging to natural kinds, there is a third alternative which I find more promising. The size of a thing can be estimated as outstanding not just in relation to the average, nor in relation to the range of our acquaintance, but in respect of the natural possibilities for its kind. Animals, plants, and trees can grow no larger than a certain maximum size, and

it is open to us to say that a large object is great when and in so
far as it approximates to this maximum. A great oak tree is one
whose size is not to be surpassed by oaks; similarly with men
and fishes. I submit that it is this idea of a possible maximum
which lies at the bottom of many of our attributions of greatness, both when we speak literally and when, figuratively, a
concern with physical size is not what guides our interest.

To extend the idea literally beyond natural kinds of thing is
not always very difficult. For things are limited in their size not
just by their internal laws of growth, but also by external
natural forces. Consider a building, say. Given the particular
sort of materials of which it is constructed and the techniques
with which it was built, there will come a point beyond which
its size cannot be increased without the edifice collapsing. This
is just what happened to the nave of Beauvais Cathedral in
1284 and to its steeple in 1573. So we could judge a building—not a natural kind of thing—to be great as it approaches
the maximum possible for its constructional type. (This relativization to type gets round the difficulty of finding the truth-
value of attributions of greatness changing as we learn how to
build bigger, using new materials and new techniques.) Yet
another way in which greatness of size is estimated—often
when we are dealing with artefacts—is relative to the largest
size a thing can be and still fulfil its function effectively. A great
beer glass for instance is not just a vat-sized glass. Made for the
individual drinker, its size would be limited by consideration of
what a thirsty and large-bellied man might possibly get
through in a draught or two when he set himself to it.

Discussion of greatness of size is of interest here only in so far
as it can be used as a basis upon which to rest the figurative use
of the term, and it may be objected that there are two good
reasons why this is not possible. The first is that once we leave
the literal domain we often find ourselves saying that an
achievement is a great one where there just is no maximum
available by reference to which its greatness can be estimated;
and secondly, it may be felt that once we leave the literal
domain where estimations of size are clearly non-evaluative, we
find ourselves speaking in a way that is nothing else. The
differences are just too marked, it might be thought. But are
they?

Consider the first point in relation to a claim that a man is a great general. Obviously we are not judging him by his size. So what is being considered? As a rule, when we speak figuratively of the greatness of an F, the property we fix on will be one which counts as a virtue in Fs. So, on my account, we are saying of the general that he is as gifted as a man could be in winning battles and in staving off pressing defeats.[9] But, the objection runs, what can ground the truth of such assertions? For there seems to be nothing very much about winning battles or avoiding defeats that is easily assimilable either to the natural internal limits of growth that govern the maximum size of plants, or to the external law-like constraints on the maximum size of buildings of a given type. And if there is no such thing here as a maximum then our general will not approach it whatever feats of generalship he performs. In that case my proposed extension of the literal notion of greatness would yield a falsehood (or at best not yield a truth) where a truth is what we need.

The force of this objection depends entirely on our willingness to concede that claims of maximality are assertible only if they reflect something such as a natural law that fixes them quite independently of our judgement. This is indeed just what was relied on in the case of the plant and the building. But the reader should here recall that *other* estimation of great size where the relevant maximum is set by reference to our purposes. A great artefact I said is often one that is as large as it could be and still serve its purpose, and it is some such move as this away from natural law that will help us now. For where independently-given natural standards of maximality are not available, judgements of greatness are assertible on the basis of commonly accepted conceptions of people's capacities that are founded in wide experience and in the failure of attempts convincingly to imagine capacities of the relevant kind being more highly developed. In the case in point there is nothing more to being as good as possible at winning battles except winning them in situations that we recognize to be challenging and which are as demanding of the military strategist as any that we might devise. In these circumstances our preparedness to judge a general as being as gifted as could be is what makes it assertible that he is so. *Nota bene*, this is not to say that our judgement that he is a great general is self-confirming. It is not.

For our judgement is open to argument and to being tested by
experience and the development of strategical thought. But the
arguments that test our judgement need not rely on the holding
of truths that are entirely independent of our readiness to make
it. So much, then, for the first difficulty about the figurative
application of my elucidation.

The second obstacle I mentioned demands an explanation of
why an estimation of greatness involves no evaluation when
taken literally, whereas figuratively it always does so. But so
put, the objection is overstated, for sometimes an attribution of
literal greatness does have a positive evaluative use, and sometimes a figurative attribution does not. Suppose that in an alien
culture the gods' wrath is believed to be placated by the erection of
idols, and that the larger the idols come the surer is their placatory
effect. To be told in such a context that a great idol had been carved
could be very naturally, to be told something carryng evaluative
force.[10] If size in such objects is desirable, and if we have an
exemplar before us that is as successful as any could be, then *ceteris
paribus* we have one by which we cannot be set high store if we want
those things. On the other hand, where the property in virtue of
which something in itself undesirable is made outstanding, the
usual positive evaluative use of the term 'great' is unavailable.
This is so as much in the figurative realm as it is in the literal: think
of great criminals, great perverts or great poseurs.

What this suggests is that the term 'great' enjoys a positive
evaluative use when and only when the property in virtue of
which the person or achievement assessed is one which makes it
outstanding of its type (is a virtue in Fs), where the kind of thing
assessed is one that we want or approve of. A runner will be a
great one if he excels in respect of something (speed or stamina,
say) that counts as a virtue in a runner, and in a culture which
values running it will be available to us to use the claim as a
positive evaluation. But if running were undesirable then a
great runner would not be one of whom we think well, any more
than we esteem highly a great seducer such as Don Juan, a
great simoniac such as Pope Nicholas III, or a great traitor
such as Judas.[11]

Let us now apply these suggestions to art. A work of art will
be a great one when in a way that approximates to the limits of
possibility—judged as we judge it—it displays a property

whose possession we account a virtue in art. From the earlier discussion it emerged that when the work is considered *qua* work of art rather than as a work of this or that particular category, these properties will be of a sort that we might draw on in theory to explain the generation and survival of art as an autonomous institution. Not surprisingly, if my argument has been correct, we shall be primarily inclined to find greatness in the arts where matters of conception are involved rather than merely matters of execution. (In the case of goodness, by contrast, it seems that it is often considerations of execution that are to the fore rather than those of conception.) And since we think that to become institutionalized the arts must be capable of providing important benefits through the virtues that great art displays, it is a natural consequence that art's outstanding examples should enjoy our close attention and our deep admiration.

In the light of these claims we can now see how to take Kant's dictum that the products of genius are exemplary for others. For what he is telling us, and telling us quite rightly, is that art of stature necessarily leaves its mark on what follows it. Great art is bound to be influential. For if a man achieves something that brings him close to the limits of what we believe possible in a field in which we have a deep interest, he will be as likely as anyone to extend our conception of what really can be done in that sphere. To create a work of stature may remind us that what we believed to be possible really is possible.[12] But this is not all it does. In addition, it will be influential because the realization of previously unrealized, but assumedly possible, goals comes to form an important element in the mental set of those who come later and work in the same field. It makes for a consequent readjustment and transformation of the goals they set themselves. To take an example outside the arts: once our belief that a four-minute mile could indeed be run was shown to be correct, the knowledge that the feat had been performed became an important factor in explaining why thereafter it seemed so unremarkable to repeat and so often unremarkable to improve on. Its achievement raised the question of where the limits of possibility really lay, and in consequence we set ourselves targets which before 1954 would have seemed quite unrealistic.

In a more marked way the same thing happens when we express ourselves hyperbolically by saying that a man's achievements surpass (what we take to be) the bounds of possibility. His work shows us something which we had not even thought to be a possibility. In the arts such achievements are influential often because they show us previously unavailable modes of expression and thought which are impossible to neglect in either of two ways. They may be so because we find ourselves internally compelled to make explicit use of the innovation the man of genius introduces; alternatively, if we refuse to avail ourselves of his discovery, its very absence is of note in our own work and thereby gives it an allusive significance which otherwise it could not have. Art of acknowledged stature can therefore scarcely fail to be of influence; genius cannot but be exemplary.

This defence of Kant may seem to give rise to a difficulty acute enough to jeopardize progress. For if genius is exemplary in these ways, will we not find that as our conception of the artistic possibilities broadens over time, our assessments of artistic stature are subject to change? One and the same work may once (judged as we judge it) be rightly seen as a great one from its original vantage point, but equally rightly a less great achievement when judged with hindsight at a later date. Alternatively, of two different works, originating at different times but similar in structure and appearance, the one may seem of stature and the other merely mediocre. As Reynolds put it: 'the truth is, that the *degree* of excellence which proclaims *Genius* is different, in different times and different places; and what shows it to be so is, that mankind have often changed their opinion upon this matter,'[13] and should this not puzzle us?

The answer is one that by now we should have learnt to expect. No threat arises on either score. The historicist account of art forces us to recognize that the greatness of an achievement can only be estimated by reference to the modes of thought against the background of which it arose.[14] If the bounds of possibility have indeed been extended, that will make no difference to the proper estimation of the earlier work. That will remain a great one. Only the later work that does no more than age its predecessor will not be great. For the modes of thought by which we judge it have changed, and in the circumstances of *its* production the very fact that it relies on the existence of a model invalidates its claim to greatness. Again Reynolds gets this just right:

When the Arts were in their infancy, the power of merely drawing the likeness of any object, was considered as one of its greatest efforts. The common people, ignorant of the principles of art, talk the same language even to this day. But when it was found that every man could be taught to do this, and a great deal more, merely by the observance of certain precepts; the name of Genius then shifted its application, and was given only to him who added the peculiar character of the object he represented; to him who had invention, expression, grace, or dignity; in short, those qualities, or excellencies, the power of producing which could not *then* be taught by any known and promulgated rules.[15]

We need only be careful not to draw from this passage the invalid conclusion that the reported belief of Reynolds's first sentence was a false one. It was not. On the other hand the common people of the second sentence do speak falsely.

V

To make the discussion of these last pages more vivid I now offer four illustrations of ways in which the thesis about art of stature may apply.

(1) Consider first Vasari's discussion of the infancy and growth of graphic art in classical times. As he describes it, both the Greek artist and his public had a clear enough conception of what was possible to one seeking to draw or paint natural likeness; only until the work of Apelles no proper knowledge was available of the means whereby these possibilities might be made actual. With its discovery the limits are touched, and the resulting work is evidently of great stature: 'In the . . . works of Zeuxes, Polygnotus, Timanthes and the rest, who only employed four colours, the lineaments, outlines and forms are unreservedly praised, though doubtless they left something to be desired. But in the productions of Erione, Nicomachus, Protogenes and Apelles everything is so perfect and beautiful that *one can conceive nothing better*; for they not only painted the form and gestures of the body with the highest excellence, but the emotions and passions also.'[16]

(2) While in this case is was possible for the contemporary Greek to articulate the limits to which the search for natural likeness might aspire, this is not always so. We are just as likely to find greatness in the works of those who explore to the limit the possibilities offered them in a given medium and a given style, but which limits we cannot so readily antecedently formulate. We recognize only *ex post facto* that their explorations have brought them up against the boundaries of the medium and the constraints of style which their art adopts. For that limit is determined by their own or others' inability, working within the same framework, to create further notable work. A good example of this is provided by Beethoven's last keyboard writings, of which Charles Rosen has written that 'their universe is the language they have shaped, whose nature and limits they explore, and in exploring, transform.'[17] In the great piano sonatas from op. 101 to op. 111, as in the *Diabelli Variations*, we recognize the attainment of limits of significant keyboard writing composed in the style formed by Haydn and Mozart, a recognition surely signalled by Beethoven himself in his resigned remark that 'the piano after all is an unsatisfactory instrument'. In retrospect it comes to us as no surprise that the next noteworthy step in music should be taken only with a dissolution of the forms elaborated in Vienna in the half-century that began in 1775, for in the middle of the 1820s the old language is so transformed that it no longer makes much sense to speak of identity of form with what has gone before. Even though we could not state these limits, we see with hindsight that no more could have been done.

(3) Contrast with this case one where the goal to be achieved is formulable *ex ante facto* easily enough, though its realization appears to be beyond us, because the natural limits set by the materials and techniques in which the work is projected just do not permit it. Success here involves what we judge to surpass the limits of possibility and not simply to touch them while remaining still within their bound. Just such a challenge was presented in 1420 by the prospect of erecting a cupola over the drum of S. Maria del Fiore, enlarged before that date by Francesco Talenti to a size greater than that which would still have been possible to bridge using standard forms of internal wooden scaffolding. Contemporary report tells us that 'the

difficulty of having to span such a great and high vault was
already evident to the minds of the builders. To them it seemed
that in respect of both height and width . . . not only was the
necessary expenditure of wood and money daunting, but by
reason of its very difficulty almost impossible, *to speak more
accurately, absolutely impossible*.'[18] Brunelleschi's achievement did
not, of course, consist in the construction of practicable scaffolding out of cheap wood. His technical discovery lay in the use
of a mural structure that dispensed with the need for scaffolding
altogether, and it did indeed make his building a great one. But
the reason why it is a great building does not rest with such a
technical discovery; what gives the vault its sublimity is in part
at least the *thought*, rooted in the technical facts, that such a
marvel transgresses the limits of the possible and the resulting
experience of that vault as unspannable. This experience may
be less evident to us that it was to Brunelleschi's contemporaries; none the less it remains an important element in a true
appreciation of the work's stature.

(4) Lastly, there are cases in which we are not able, as
audience, to anticipate the artist's goal before its achievement,
and of which we also want to say, even *ex post facto*, that the
achievement involved the artist surpassing (what we take to be)
the bounds of possibility. In his *Problems in Titian*, Panofsky
finds it convenient to adopt the customary division of a great
artist's activity into early, middle, and late periods, and
explains them there respectively as 'that in which [the artist]
defines his attitude towards tradition, that in which he origi-
nates a tradition of his own and that in which he outgrows the
tradition established by himself, and thus attains a sphere no
longer accessible to others'.[19] If we apply this to the use of
colour in Titian's very last works— to the Munich *Crowning with
Thorns*, say, or the *Nymph and Shepherd* in Vienna— we see why it
should have been impossible to say what Titian's art aspired to
before he discovered the path he was taking. Passing beyond a
use of colour as something adhering to the objects shown or as
determined by the colouristic pattern appearing on the panel
or canvas, in his work after 1560 he conceives of colour 'as if it
were something diffused in space and merely concentrated and
diversified in individual areas'. It is within the guidance of this
new and quite unforeseeable conception of colour that we meet

that 'indescribable glow or shimmer (first the glow, then the shimmer) which is the signature of Titian's *ultima maniera*' and which forcibly brings to mind the felicity of his proud motto: *Natura Potentior Ars*, 'Art is more powerful than Nature'.

VI

We noticed before that an adequate choice of vocabulary for the specification of our conclusions had to meet two requirements. It must be usable in abstraction from consideration of the category of the particular work of art to which time's test applies, and it must also not be reducible to the vocabulary of excellence. We can see now why it was right to say, as I did at the start of section IV, that both of these demands would be met by conclusions stated in the language of stature.

'Excellence' has been treated as having, in its application to the arts, a defeasible usage.[20] Our assessments are made relative to what we think of as a flaw in art of a certain kind. Stature, on the other hand, is estimated in relation to the achievement of a perceived limit, where what sets the limit and guides our concerns with such maxima is ultimately our imaginative capacity for enlargement of the boundaries of actual and possible experience. It will therefore very often be quite irrelevant to the correctness of our judgement of a work of art as fulfilling this last aspiration that it should be thought of as coming up to standards that are implicit in its being a work of the type that it is. Hence we are inclined to think of great art as such, independent, that is, of the particular category to which it belongs.

This is not to deny that we do sometimes say that this work or that is a great sonnet or great portrait; but generally that judgement is derived from three separate pieces of information: first, that it is a sonnet, or a portrait; second, that it is a great work of art; and third, that portraits and sonnets are works of art. This seems to me the standard way in which these judgement are made. Perhaps there are other cases where we make an assessment of a work in relation to precisely the sort of virtue that can be displayed by some particular category and no other. But if so they are rare.

From this difference between excellence and stature alone it follows that the one cannot be reduced to the other. A work of art may be of stature without being good of its kind, and vice versa. What allows us to call a work a great one is its achievement in a domain which attracts and sustains our interest in the arts. It may do this without being a good work, for its success in exploring the boundaries of what we regard as possible in the former way is quite compatible with the commission of faults that prevent the work being thought of as an unflawed example of its type. Very often works we think of as great are indeed flawed, but in their greatness transcend their deficiencies. So clearly greatness in art does not entail goodness, and stature does not imply excellence. Since it is also plain that goodness does not entail greatness either, it follows that the two vocabularies are requisitely independent of one another.

With these two conditions met we are now in a position to construct an argument taking us from the premiss of survival of art to a conclusion about its stature. That is matter for the next chapter. Before embarking on that, however, it will be useful to tie up a number of loose ends that have been left in the previous pages.

I mentioned above Yvor Winters's attempted reduction of the great to the good in the literary sphere. Great poetry was supposed to be good poetry about a topic of human importance; and good poetry he took to be that which effects an appropriate match between the rational statement that the poem makes and the emotional resonance of the language that makes it. Now we can see how mistaken this idea is. For great poetry need not be identified in terms of its subject-matter at all— though of course this can be of importance— and the match between statement and feeling might be appropriate but in no way criterial. As long as a poem offers a treatment of some matter, be it directly of human importance or not, that sustains our interest in that art, and takes us within sight of the acknowledged limits of what we feel to be possible within the medium, we are dealing with writing of stature. It is a simple application of what has been said above to see that such an achievement is logically independent of the goodness that is marked out by saying that the poem is excellent of its kind, or even that it enjoys that specific virtue in terms of which Winters casts poetic excellence.

My discussion of stature has largely concentrated on matters I have collected together under the heading of conception, while my treatment of excellence has focused on matters of execution. But this is not meant to exclude the possibility that works of art may achieve stature by means of outstanding execution. For all I have said, masterly execution may be a feature of a work that underwrites our interest in it and plays a part in accounting for our autonomous interest in the art that exhibits it. None the less, it should be plain that this is not the standard case and it could not really be so. For execution stands, in the end, in the service of conception, so that our interest in it will in large part be dependent on our having a prior attachment to what thought it seeks to reveal. It is a general truth, I believe, that the art we regard as being of stature should take us beyond mere matters of execution, even if sometimes that is what holds our gaze and admiration.

Although I have explained the idea of stature in terms of the interests that great art answers to, only by implication have I said anything about the appeal to us of great art *over time*. Once the idea of greatness is relativized to the circumstances of the time in which it is achieved, and once we remember that so much of the great art we know was created in times very different from our own, it may seem that there is no clear reason to expect that the art which is correctly identified as great in relation to a set of interests that are those of people distinct from us should be of pressing interest to us too. But this is appearance and not reality. For one thing, in many ways the interests we have today are to a large extent the same as are our predecessors', deriving as they do from a common nature and from social circumstances differing from theirs in only superficial ways.[21] But even if not too much weight is placed on our similarities with them, and the differences between their ways of thought and ours are by contrast emphasized, there remains a clear and straightforward interest for us in the great achievements of the past even when no mention is made of the real and quite legitimate curiosity about it that so often moves us. It is that in the arts of different periods we are shown many different ways in which the world can be viewed. We cannot, of course, adopt them all, for the adoption of one view of the world excludes the adoption of others. Yet awareness of the limits to which various possible ways of thought can be taken cannot fail to have a bearing on the view that we ourselves eventually come to adopt. Only if we have a full understanding of the alternatives that are open to us, and of those that are real alternatives to ours though maybe not open to *us*, can we make the best of our own ways of thought in the articulation of the world that is ours today. So in its own right, both directly and indirectly, the great art of the past has a *present* claim to our attention. And this remains true even while our explanation of its greatness will often involve a kind of relativization to the circumstances of its period and its production.

Lastly, I said at the beginning of this chapter that our having an interest in the evaluation of art was an integral part of its critical appreciation. This is as true of evaluations of stature as it is of evaluations of excellence. Appreciation of art is depleted unless we view its works against a background of estimates of what might have been achieved within the limits and conventions within which they operate. Were we to try to abstract from such comparative interest it would be hard to apply coherently many of those predicates upon which a proper aesthetic description of the individual work depends, as should appear from the detailed accounts given above of the ideas of depth and of beauty. Furthermore, since it is just such matters as these in which, in the individual case, greatness consists, to disclaim an interest in evaluations of stature could only be carried through at the cost of detachment of interest from that wherein greatness consists. As we have seen, that kind of detachment ultimately brings into question the arts' very existence and survival.

Chapter 10

The Test Legitimized

The time has come to offer an informal though abstract argument that will take us reliably from knowledge that a work of art has passed time's test to a conclusion that it is a work of stature. As we go along we shall see that it will not yet be possible to do this unrestrictedly and for all surviving art, but even to provide a legitimization of the critical inferences that are concerned with works of beauty and of depth will help us to move forward.[1] Greater generality will be secured in Chapter 11.

I

Were we dealing not with art but with simple artefacts—coats, cars, clocks, and the like—the following argument, [A], would be available:

[A.]   (1) Any well-wearing artefact of type T, having a defining function, efficiently satisfies that function

        (2) Any artefact or type T efficiently satisfying its defining function is a good one of its type

_____

Hence   (3) Any well-wearing artefact of type T is a good one of its type.

This argument is valid. (3) cannot be false if (1) and (2) are true. Furthermore it is sound, since (1) and (2) are true. In addition, the conclusion may well be necessarily true, since the premisses from which it follows are themselves arguably necessary; and a valid deductive argument with necessarily true premisses has a necessarily true conclusion.

Such a pattern of thought is what we might expect to guide us in the attempt to justify time's test by treating the arts as analogous to simple artefacts. But two established truths prevent us from applying [A] to the arts. First, art has no defining function; and second, our critical conclusions are not to be stated in the language of excellence. Nevertheless, we have said that if art has no defining function it does have sustaining aims; and if the language of excellence will not serve us, the language of stature looks apt to stand in its place. So an argument [B], closely parallel to [A], suggests itself:

[B.]   (4)   Any art passing time's test satisfies art's sustaining aims

             (5)   Any art satisfying the aims of art is art of stature

Hence   (6)   Any art passing time's test is art of stature,

where (6) expresses, in a requisitely specific form, the first and most important of the conclusions enumerated in anodyne terms in Chapter 1. Is this the reasoning that is to underwrite our critical practice?

The answer must be 'no'. For while [B], like [A], is valid enough, it is very dubiously sound; and soundness is essential if the inference is to do for us what we want. Ideally we look to the test of time to provide knowledge that a passing work is a great one. And any justification of this test that does not regularly permit us to do this will not be adequate to what we want of it. Now, on the basis of [B] we might hope to apply time's test to some particular work of art w with a view to establishing knowledge that it is a great work, and reason, by means of a further argument, [C], that that is what it is:

[C.]   (6)   Any work of art passing time's test is art of stature

             (7)   Work of art w passes time's test

Hence   (8)   Work of art w is a work of stature.

We have no qualms about the validity of this reasoning, and hence no qualm about the derivation of the information contained in (8) from argument [B] together with the further premiss (7). But unless we have good reason to believe (8) is true we shall not *know* it is. If the grounds on which we assert it are simply those in the premisses (4) to (7), and if these premisses are not themselves well-founded, their deductive relationship with (8) is cognitively unsatisfying.

Indeed, we have no grounds for thinking that the premisses

are well-founded; for, as I said, [B] is dubiously sound. The form of its premises (4) and (5) is that of universally quantified propositions, $(x)(Fx, Gx)$; and such propositions are false if there is a single case of an x which is F but is not G. Surely we have no reason to doubt that it is possible to find at least some cases either of works which pass time's test without satisfying the aims of art, or of works which while satisfying those aims are none the less not works of stature. Hence we will not be justified in believing the premises of [B] to be true as they stand, and therefore not justified in believing (8) even though the argument which gets us there is deductively unimpeachable. Having insufficient reason to believe (8), we cannot know it, so if time's test is to be underwritten by this deductive train of thought rooted only in the arguments [B] and [C], its conclusions will not regularly furnish knowledge.

A further inadequacy of the suggested procedure is to make time's test insufficiently surely projectible into the future. Even if we should not succeed in finding in the art of the present or the past counter-examples to (4) or (5), we have no a priori reason to think that the future will not provide them. So we have no reason to think that the universally quantified claims will hold true in the future even if they have not yet been falsified. But our justification here of time's test must be seen as a legitimization of its *continued* use by critics beyond the present; so unless we can establish projectibility of the test into the future as well as its proper past use, the over-all argument will turn out to be distressingly trivial, merely one of an ever-receding historical interest.

To meet the demands for knowledge and projectibility, and otherwise cause as little disturbance as possible, we might hope to replace the premises (4) and (5) by two others which will not be falsified by the occasional case of works which satisfy the aims of art without being of stature, or which pass time's test without satisfying those aims. Correspondingly we should expect to replace the conclusion, (6), by a matching, weaker conclusion. Such alterations are recorded in [D]:

[D.]   (9) It is reasonable to believe (4)
             (10) It is reasonable to believe (5)

Hence   (12) It is reasonable to believe (6).

Even if some argument is to be had for thinking that (9) and (10) are true—which I shall soon try to show—it is patently obvious that this weakening of [B] does not leave us with a deductively valid argument—at least not unless we can rely on something other than the logical powers of (9) and (10). If there is a deductive inference to (12), we must also be able to call on some true principle about the notion of *rational belief* by which (9) and (10) may be shown, with the help of (4) and (5), to imply (12). And it may appear that there is such a principle to hand, a principle which I shall dub the *Principle of Deductive Cogency (PDC)*. Loosely stated, this asserts that it is rational for a man to believe the deductive consequences of his rational beliefs. So that if someone rationally believes p and rationally believes q, and if furthermore p and q together entail r, then it is rational for him to believe r.[2] In one form or another this principle is certainly attractive, and for the moment I shall set aside discussion of it and concentrate on the use to which it might be put if it were acceptable.

Applied to the premisses of [D], *Deductive Cogency* will now allow us to infer (12), for it enables us, as desired, to rely on the information that (4) and (5) together entail (6). And that was something that [D] itself had to ignore. A further application of the same principle to knowledge we have of the particular work of art will finally give us the evaluative conclusion that we want about it. Thus we have now available an enthymematic composite argument [E]:

[E.] (9) It is reasonable to believe (4)
      (10) It is reasonable to believe (5)
      (11) (4) and (5) entail (6)
Hence (12) It is reasonable to believe (6) (by *PDC*)
      (13) It is reasonable to believe w (assumed on the
           passes time's test   basis of evidence
                                             about w, say)

Hence (14) It is reasonable to believe w is a (by *PDC* on (11)
           work of stature   and (7) which
                                                together entail
                                                that w is a work
                                                of stature).

Suppose now I act on a simple rule of acceptance: 'accept what it is reasonable to believe'; then by this argument, if I accept that some particular work w does pass time's test (something which on the relevant evidence we may suppose it reasonable for me to do—hence (13)), it will be reasonable for me to accept that w is of stature. So the inference that we make from my initial well-founded belief about the work having passed time's test to its being of stature is legitimized. Moreover, it may easily be appreciated that it is legitimized in a way that requisitely enables me both to acquire knowledge of the work's stature, and to do so in a manner that can be satisfactorily projected into the future.

Knowledge poses no problem. For if we have the information that it is reasonable for me to believe p, then (roughly) provided p is true and I have relied on no false information in coming to believe that p, my rational belief will be an instance of knowledge. Now although no justification has yet been given for thinking that (9) or (10) are true, the obstacle that held us up before plainly does not apply. For whereas (4) and (5) would be false if there were single cases of works which satisfied art's sustaining aims without being works of stature, or works which passed time's test without satisfying art's sustaining aims, this is no longer a relevant consideration. Unlike 'all Fs and G', 'it is rational to believe that all Fs are G' may well be true even though there be some Fs which are not G. And since it was the thought that even a single counter-example to the generalization might emerge in the future (if it has not done so already) that cast in doubt the projectibility of the test into the future, the weakening of the argument along the lines proposed permits projectibility as long as the support that is to be offered for (9) and (10) is of a suitably temporally-neutral kind. What is needed is to provide this support.

Certainly there are grounds for believing at least restricted versions of (9) and (10), namely (15) and (16), where consideration is given only to those works of art which have survived on account of their possession of one or other of those two aesthetically important properties already discussed, beauty and depth.

(15) It is reasonable to believe that if a beautiful or

deep work of art passes time's test, it satisfies the
aims of art

(16) It is reasonable to believe that if such a work does
satisfy the aims of art, it is of stature.

Given the truth of these two claims then a matching restricted
conclusion, (17), looks within our grasp, as both validly and
soundly derived from the premises:

(17) It is reasonable to believe that if a beautiful or
deep work of art passes time's test, it is of stature.

We could not ask for more.

Consider first (15). Previous chapters have yielded these
truths:
(a) while the arts have no defining functions they do have
sustaining aims; (b) works of beauty and depth offer us goods
that satisfy these aims; (c) works of beauty and depth are well
placed to survive the pressures of time. I submit that taken
together these three pieces of information offer solid enough
support for (15). When a work of beauty or depth survives over
time, we must be able to find an explanation of why it does so,
and failing any other account of the matter the only reasonable
thing to believe is that its survival is rooted in precisely those
features of it which make it well placed to survive, that is, in the
fact that such works, through their beauty and depth, offer us
goods which in our culture it falls largely to the arts to provide.
So, of individual works of beauty and depth, it is reasonable to
believe (unless, of course, we have special grounds for thinking
otherwise) that when they survive in our attention they satisfy
the sustaining aims of art in one way or another. That is what
(15) says.

As a step in the advance towards (16) we may allow that the
better embedded an individual work is in our culture—a notion
I insisted on in Chapter 1—the fuller we may take its offering of
the goods it brings us to be. For again, we need an explanation
of why the work has passed time's test *as well as it has*; and what
alternative is there of a general kind to that offered by the
significance of the appeal it makes to our interests? That, after
all, is what we have seen to explain our having the arts as a
social institution in the first place, and it is only natural that we

should believe the degree of success the work achieves over time as giving us some measure of the importance to us of its offering under this head. So as a corollary of (15) we have (15)′:

> (15)′ It is reasonable to believe that the better the beautiful or deep work of art survives time's test, the greater is its compliance with the arts' sustaining aims.

Now with confidence in the acceptability of (15) and (15)′, we are well on the way to accepting (16). For the more significant is the compliance of a particular work with the aims of the art, the readier we shall be to claim that it is a work of stature. What else could we say? Were we to surmise that the good offered us by the work did not measure up to that standard, we should then reasonably expect some detachment of interest mediated through the ordinary pressures that make for the displacement of the work from our attention. Yet here we are concerned with the case in which the work is *ex hypothesi* well embedded, so that these pressures have been ineffective. Why else should this be except that the work is of stature? Of course we may find extraordinary factors at work that give us a different explanation, but then they are *extraordinary* factors and hence no threat to the claim that (16) expresses. Hence (16) is as well supported as (15). So if the argument from (15) and (16) to (17) is valid, we have no reason to think it is anything other than sound. And since nothing in this reasoning turns on temporal considerations, the desired temporal neutrality of the supporting argument is assured. Hence its conclusion can be used—and used projectibly—in further sound arguments about individual beautiful or deep works of art that pass time's test, to the effect that they are works of stature.

But is the argument from (15) and (16) to (17) valid? Everything is all right as long as the *Principle of Deductive Cogency* is acceptable. And one may think that surely if there are any acceptable principles about rational belief that are a priori true, this will be one of them. Yet for all its attractiveness I do not see that it can be maintained. As I have stated it so far it plainly will not do. All I have said is that it is rational for a man to believe the deductive consequences of his rational beliefs. Yet I may have reason to believe p and reason to believe q, where p and q

together entail r; and quite independently have good reason to believe $\sim r$. In this situation, iterated application of *Deductive Cogency* will make it reasonable for me to believe a contradiction, $(r \& \sim r)$. Obviously this consequence cannot be allowed.

We might think to overcome this objection by simply insisting that the Principle be stated so as to allow the acceptance only of consistent sentences, only of the self-consistent deductive consequences of one's rational beliefs.[3] But this restriction will not prove strong enough to prevent one from accepting some beliefs which it is difficult to allow we should. To see this, it is helpful to consider a familiar example in the literature of this subject, that of a large and fair lottery.[4] Suppose a friend of mine, James, buys a ticket and loses his stake when the draw is made. Just because I know what a large lottery it is and that there has been no unfairness about it, I can truly say that I *knew* James would lose his stake. That is what we would say, and not just something weaker, e.g. that we knew it was highly likely that James would lose his stake. Since my knowledge is based only on the information I have cited, I must have had reason to believe James would lose, for otherwise my assertion that he would lose would not be an expression of knowledge. Now since the considerations which give me reason to think that James would lose are exactly the same as those which would give me reason to think that the other participants would lose, by the same argument I have reason to believe of each of them that he too will lose. And since I might know who each ticket holder is, and know too that together they comprise the totality of ticket holders, I could by application of the *Principle* as stated above conclude that it is reasonable for me to believe the non-self-contradictory claim that everyone who holds a ticket will lose. That is surely unwelcome.

It will not help here to object that even if the sentence 'Every participant in a large and fair lottery will lose' is not self-contradictory—not, that is, of the form '$p \& \sim p$'—it is at least inconsistent, it being impossible that the lottery should both be fair and that everyone should lose. For I doubt whether fairness would be affected if one ticket put into the draw should not have been sold. And in such a situation, when that is the very ticket that wins, I might indeed have known of each single participant that he would lose. Then, if the *Principle of Deductive Cogency were* correct, I should be able to conclude *without inconsistency* that everyone would lose, and in the case of a large enough lottery that would surely be irrational. (It will, of course, make no difference if such a lottery be adjudged unfair: the belief under consideration would still be irrational, even though a self-consistent deductive consequence of rational beliefs.)

Unfortunately, there is no reason to think that there is any simple and natural emendment to the *Principle* to be found that is both generally acceptable (not just a case of special pleading) and also able to conduct the transition from (15) and (16) to (17). So I reluctantly conclude that (17) is not a truth that could be substantiated in the deductive way I have been contemplating.

Nevertheless, since it has been emphasized on several occasions that we should not expect to find anything stronger than defeasible support for time's test,[5] this failure need not perhaps be found too disturbing. Even if there are no true principles of rational belief with the help of which (15) and (16) may be shown to entail (17), the arguments I have adduced in favour of the two premisses do surely make it hard to see how the antecedent of (17) might be true unless the consequent were so too. This thought may be seen as the core of a different and better solution of my puzzle than that which we have had to reject.

In support of (15), (15)′, and (16), I argued in effect that the truth of the various conditionals' consequences would generally provide the best explanation of their antecedents, and that where there are no special reasons for thinking some other explanation to apply we should adopt it. Since this is a generally acceptable strategy for inductively establishing the acceptability of a contingent conditional, we may argue for (17) in just this way: first by making out that the truth of its consequent would provide an *adequate* explanation for its antecedent's holding, and then by showing that this account of the matter is preferable to the available alternatives. If successful, these two moves show that the hypothesis of stature provides the best explanation for art's surviving time's pressures. Hence our readiness to accept (17). And where there is no special reason to think that some other explanation is at work in the particular case, we can, by reapplication of the same argument, come to know that the particular beautiful or deep work of art is a great one.

The case already made out for accepting (15), (15)', and (16) should persuade us that if it were true that a beautiful or profound work of art is of stature and as such outstandingly complies with important sustaining aims of art, that would be a perfectly good explanation of why it should both claim and retain our interest over time. Hence it would provide a good explanation of why the work has been able to survive the pressures of displacement and disturbance, and therefore to resist time's pressures. So nothing else need be said now to assure us that the hypothesis of stature is adequate to explain survival. But of course adequacy itself is not enough: for the mere fact that a hypothesis H would adequately explain data $D' \ldots D''$ does not give us any reason to think that it is what does in fact explain those data. We must often choose between competing adequate explanations, and the condition of our accepting one of them in preference to the others is that it should provide a better explanation than they of the various alternatives to hand. Any choice other than the best or the strongest is inductively non-inferable.[6]

That the hypothesis of stature does indeed provide the best account of survival can be judged by recalling earlier discussion of the weaknesses of the four alternative ways in which theorists of art have attempted to explain its survival through time, by recalling the way in which they have drawn on these alternatives in forming their attitudes to the critical inferences I am seeking to justify.

First, there were those theories that sought to explain survival while at the same time explaining away the critical inference based upon it. The persistence of art in our attention was put down to some psychological drive quite unconnected with the aesthetic merits of the work that absorbs us. In the particular example I discussed, the drive was taken to be a desire for self-validation, but other choices to be found in the literature would have served equally well to illustrate this theme. As we saw in Chapter 2 n.1, I. A. Richards in the *Principles of Literary Criticism* (Ch. xxix), and Julian Hirsch in *Der Genesis des Ruhmes* both appeal to what they take to be something like a natural psychological law of imitation and behavioural conformity for this purpose. But variation in the details of the arguments need not concern us. For apart from the contempt that these trains of thought display for the critical intellect, in their presentation of men as witless cultural lemmings, they all suffer from a defect that makes them acceptable only as arguments of the last resort. I refer to their rejection as irrational of the critical phenomena associated with the survival of the individual works or art, that is, to their rejection of the critical inferences themselves. This rejection of our common practice automatically makes these theories less powerful over all than one which is both adequate to the explanandum (survival) and also endorses it as well founded. Hence they are not inferable in preference to the theory of stature.

Second there came the suggestion that survival might be put down to the development of talent or taste on the part of artist and critic. The works that survive do so because they are more advanced. But this idea turned out to be objectionable for the reason that if progress is conceived of as being linear, our present judgements of stature based on survival would have little claim to future stability; whereas if progress is more realistically thought of in pluralistic terms, the stylistically transcendent nature of the inference is then obscured. So explanations that appeal to progress in either way are less satisfactory than what is offered us by a theory which does not suffer in either of these two ways. Although no attempt is made this time to explain the critical inferences away, some aspects of our practice emerge as unjustified. Again, this puts the mooted theory in a weaker position to claim our assent than one that does not make our behaviour indefensible.

A more popular explanation of survival accounted for it by reference to the multivalence of some (the best) art (See Chapter 3 section III). Yet that view turned out to presuppose a concept of art whose identity-criteria are avowedly ahistorical. Apart from the threat the proposal offers to the idea of our needing to *understand* the artist's work, and hence, I suggested, to the very idea of art itself, it has turned out to be fundamentally incompatible with a justification of the critical inferences we make. So again, if we test the strength of the explanation of survival against (*inter alia*) the preservation of these practices, multivalence does not seriously challenge the preferability of its major rival.

Last, I left hanging in the air an updated version of Johnson's and Hume's theory of obstacles, obstacles to be overcome by the exercise of a common sense. In essence, the suggestion was that correct understanding of art asserts itself against bias over time, and that works which survive do so because when properly understood they truly merit our interest. At the very least we know from our earlier discussion that this story required supplementation, but its ultimate explanatory adequacy could not be properly assessed before a stand was taken on the correct identity-criteria for art. In the light of the historicist view, which a fully articulated concept of art encouraged us to adopt, it can now be seen that the Johnsonian position is far weaker than it may originally have appeared to be. ·

The crucial difficulty is this: on the only tenable understanding of the premiss that a work of art has withstood time's test, we must assume that it has been tested *under its canonical understanding*. It is only when this understanding is given that survival can properly be spoken of at all. Yet once this view is taken there is no explanatory advantage to be gained from the supposition that correct understanding asserts itself over time, or that, as F. N. Sibley put it, true judgements about the work are those that converge over time. For correct understanding is exactly what canonical understanding is. What Johnson and Hume tell us has no explanatory power at the point where it needs it most. In this respect the modern version of the old theory of obstacles suffers from exactly the same defect as lamed its predecessor. It is brought upon the stage at just the wrong time, and its power is quite exhausted before it is called on. While the order of exposition has made it impossible to push this point fully home before, it is noteworthy that it was clearly foreshadowed in one of the queries raised earlier about the Johnsonian thesis. It was asked how that thesis might be applied to those cases of art which are well understood from the very start, and for which the idea of improved understanding over time is otiose, having no role to play in the explanation of the retention of our interest. To that question there was no Johnsonian answer. Now we can see that this question is not one that applies merely to a sub-class of the arts, but embraces the whole body of art. Hence the remoulded theory of obstacles never begins to explain what it is required to.

A further difficulty for the theory is accentuated by the

commitment to historicism. Whatever success it is to have, Johnson's view depends on our accepting that over time understanding converges on correct interpretation. Yet, as a general thesis, this plainly lives at odds with the perception that, as time passes, retention and even achievement of proper understanding are powerfully threatened by the forces of erosion and accretion. So when Johnson's defence of time's test is updated to account for survival in terms of the achievement of proper understanding, it has to be asked why the understanding that asserts itself over time is the proper one when in fact it is. To this question Johnson (and Sibley) have no worked out answer. That has to be supplied from elsewhere. And when I said earlier on that however great our sympathies with the Johnsonian position are it would require supplementation, what I was alluding to was the supplementation that would be demanded at just this point. It is the task of the theory of stature to make good this deficiency. And because it *is* a deficiency in the eighteenth-century justification of the critical practice, that attempt on our problem constitutes no more of a barrier to the claim that (17) is the best explanation of the facts than do the other three rejected alternatives.

This completes my review of the various alternatives offered in the literature as rivals to the account of art's survival proffered here. None of them, we see, casts in doubt the claims of a theory of stature to offer the best general explanation of survival when it occurs; so it looks as if there is no reason to withold assent from (17). Nevertheless, a sceptic might think that not enough has yet been done. For, he will say, merely to have shown that one alternative is better than a number of others is no ground in itself for thinking that it is the best that is available to us. And that is what is required. May it not be that there are other undiscussed alternatives to hand, at least as powerful as that which I have proposed (if not more so)? If this is indeed a possibility, does it not call in question the claim that (17) is the best option before us, and hence the claim that it is rationally acceptable?

The answer is 'no'. For the admission that there is such a possibility concedes nothing more than that it is consistent with what we otherwise take ourselves to know that another alternative better than that already canvassed should turn up. But in effect this is no concession. For it gives us no reason to think that there is in fact such an alternative to hand: only that it is not ruled out by anything yet said. Since it is no part of what I claim that (17) should express a necessary truth, it cannot rightly be demanded that this possibility be discounted before we accept it. The one thing that the sceptic might do to confound the argument here advanced is actually to produce a particular proposal which explains the survival of the arts more satisfactorily than does the theory of stature, or a reason for thinking there really is one that has been overlooked. Since his complaint does not take this form, and since search reveals no further alternative, the sceptic's worry can be dismissed. It is thus in order to accept that works of art which on account of their beauty or their depth pass time's test are works of stature. And having accepted this, when we come upon some *particular* such work of art that has withstood the test, satisfying the conditions set out in Chapter 1, we can, in the absence of any special explanation of another kind, reasonably conclude, and therefore come to the knowledge, that it is a work of stature. This was the first of the inferences I sought to underwrite. And this, I claim, is now achieved for those works of art of the restricted class so far discussed.

II

Confidence in the argument just developed will be increased if it can be extended to cover the other, secondary, inferences of Chapter 1. It will be enough to say something brief about each of them, remembering that their acceptability is likewise restricted by the same limitation to works of supposed beauty and depth. When we come to inferences based on failure to survive, it will be natural similarly to limit the claims here made to works defective in point of beauty or depth.

'Art's canonical survival over time tends to confirm the aesthetic judgements on the basis of which the work is appreciated. If it is originally praised on account of its beauty or depth and becomes suitably embedded in our culture, because every opportunity has been provided, though not taken, for us to withdraw these judgements, we have the best reasons that we could have for thinking them correct. Our own confidence in them is thereby reinforced. Because we expect error and mis-perception to be factored out over time, and expect that in those cases where we have a strong interest in its recognition judge-ment converges upon truth, the very fact that ascriptions of beauty and depth are maintained in the face of time's pressures provides good (though defeasible) evidence for the correctness of our judgements when they mirror those of the past. It should be noted, though, that this argument (like those that follow) is of necessity limited to cases where the interpretation that gives rise to the judgements under considerations is stable and canonical. If that is something quite unknown, we shall need to use agreement in judgement, first in the manner of Hume, Johnson, and Sibley as evidence of such stability, and only then as evidence of the judgements' truth. The confirmation then secured is necessarily somewhat weaker than in the former case.

In an entirely parallel way, survival of the work against the trend of early unfavourable criticism encourages us to reassess that criticism. We are likely to explain it away as based on misperceptions of the work and failure to understand what are the conventions within which it operates. Again the principle that carries the conclusion is that earlier unfavourable judge-ment is too difficult to combine consistently with the facts of survival and embeddedness that have since accrued. These facts demand explanation, and the way it is provided by the hypothesis of stature combines ill with retention of the early views. This is particularly marked when the passage of time not only gives us good ground for saying that the early view was in some respect wrong, but also enables us to see why it was so natural for the mistake to have been made at the time. This perception is frequently provided by the historical perspective that the later eye enjoys.

Though highly accomplished, a work that fails to sur-vive—fails, that is, for reasons other than loss or destruc-tion—may be said to be lacking in some important way. We know that there is no great puzzle about this. The accomplish-ment that is shown by the artist may well lead us to judge the work to be excellent of its type, but as we have seen this does not permit a straightforward inference to survival. On the other hand, it is a safe enough bet that *if* the work had merits outstanding enough to allow us to think of it as a work of stature we should expect it to demand our attention beyond the period of initial success (if it enjoyed even that). As it is, the work that passes unnoticed or fades into oblivion is one which we can reliably, though of course controvertibly, judge not to sustain a claim to be of stature. Such a lack is quite real, but it may not be articulable as a lack of any determinate kind.

Persistent failure, just like continuous passage, will confirm earlier judgements and will correct initial critical over-enthusiasm by the mechanisms outlined above. It may of course be true that continuous neglect makes it *difficult* for the unjustly forgotten work to re-engage our attention, but there is no general ground for thinking that the true merits of individual works are bound to be, or even in general likely to be, smothered beneath the weight of neglect. In a society which prizes the goods that the arts make available—that is, in a society that fosters the institution of art—we expect men of discernment slowly to raise to the surface unjustly submerged treasures. Given this expectation and an insight into its reason-ableness, we have no choice but to endorse the neglect of long neglected works. But to endorse neglect is not to turn our minds against revival. We merely resist revival in default of convincing experimental evidence: and it is proper for us to do so.

When we compare works of art on account of their varying success over time, it is easy to see why it is acceptable to think more highly of that which survives better; in consequence, proper to think highly of that which is better embedded in our culture. For if we acknowledge that survival itself responds to artistic virtue and vision, we shall rightly incline to say that the better and deeper is that survival, the greater the claim on us of the art whose virtues make its success possible. Hence we properly look for a stature in the embedded work that the less embedded art is not expected to possess. Hence the rational feeling we have that this surviving work has important merits of an order that the failing work does not; and that a failure to withstand the test is tantamount to a failure by that test.

These secondary inferences need occupy us no longer. Once the first of their number is secure, the others are straightfor-ward enough. However, I have repeatedly said that their leader is so far legitimized in only a highly specific way. Consequently, the subsidiary inferences too cannot yet enjoy more than conditional support. It must be the business of the next chapter to ask how the preceding arguments may be more widely extended.

Chapter 11

Sentimentality, Vulgarity, and Obscenity

To be of more than restricted interest the argument of the last chapter has to be generalized. As it stands, it only permits inferences to be drawn from survival that is rooted either in beauty or in depth. So nothing can be concluded yet about art whose longevity is otherwise grounded; nor can the inferences comfortably be used when we remain ignorant of survival's source. This was a limitation anticipated at the end of Chapter 4.

It is evident that the previous pages contain nothing deductively powerful enough to generate the desired extension; nor is there any prospect of finding anything that will. As I have stressed before, it is defeasible not fail-safe support that is wanted. Furthermore, it would be a mistake to try—in the manner of Chapters 7 and 8—to provide it by (very probably tedious) discussion of yet other candidates for survival, in the hope of exhausting the range of qualities that give rise to it and of showing each one to be satisfactorily inference-permitting. In the first place, there is no reason to think that such a list could ever be known to be complete; and, more seriously, without any idea of which cases remained undiscussed at any given point along the line, no piecemeal success could provide impressively better support for the desired generalization than we already have.

Instead, an oblique approach recommends itself. We know that the hypothesis of stature has already proved to have the *capacity* unrestrictedly to explain survival of canonically understood art against time's pressures; we know also that no more plausible explanation of the phenomenon than this forced itself on us when it was grounded in beauty or depth. In these circumstances, provided that no better explanation can be found for survival in general, and provided that we can find no easy way of generating counter-examples to the unrestricted claim we are interested in, I suggest that it would be irrational not to accept it. As for the first of these two conditions, we have seen just now how little attractive are alternative competing explanations of survival that do not appeal to merit (of which stature is a species). So here we need only worry about the second of them, that which canvasses the possibility to finding traits that appear engaging enough to warrant that art's survival but without giving rise to any claim that what embodies them is art of stature. And that, it might be felt, is a worry far less easily disposed of, for those qualities that supply the title of this chapter, sentimentality, vulgarity, and obscenity, immediately come to mind as enjoying just that character. Whether they attract us personally or not we would be rash to deny that they exercise widespread and pretty constant attraction for many. Nor can we deny that this appeal gives the works that carry them considerable purchase against the erosions of time. Even so, they do not support the critical acclaim that great art evokes. So here it seems there is a real obstacle to face.

I

An initial clue to the nature of sentimentality is that there is no distinct feeling or content of thought that passes under that name. What qualify are our standard feelings of grief, anger, pity, and so on, and the thoughts internally associated with them. This is not to say that every occurrence of such feelings and thoughts is sentimental. That would be absurd. They are sentimental when they are felt or entertained in a particular way. Sentimentality is properly seen as a *mode* of feeling or thought, not as a feeling of a particular *kind*. The task of elucidation is to characterize that mode by describing the way in which we sentimentally think and feel what we do.

Another thing we know is that sentimentality is always open to criticism. There is always something wrong with it. Whereas for any standard affect there will be situations in which it is quite appropriately felt or in which not to feel it requires explanation, in the case of sentimentality there are no situations the proper perception of which demands a sentimental response or in which its absence needs to be accounted for. The thought in which sentimental grief or pity about something is grounded will always be defective in some way, and I surmise that in its essential defectiveness we find a pointer to its nature.

One property that lays thought open to criticism is falsity. Another, quite compatible with thought's truth, is lack of evidential justification. Now while it is certainly true that when I sentimentalize an object something in my thought about it will be false or evidentially unjustified, these faults, either singly or together, do not capture its essence. If, seeing you knocked down by a car and mistaking you for your brother, I feel sympathy for him, I need not do so sentimentally. Again, if my love for you is rooted in the true but in fact unjustified thought that you cherish me, my love is not on that account a sentimental one.

These two defects of thought are naturally enough envisaged as arising in the course of truth-seeking enquiry. I have supposed myself to form the belief that your brother is hurt and that you cherish me under the guidance of a quite general desire to believe what is true. But we have only to remind ourselves that this is not the only desire that contributes to the formation of belief[1] to see that the deficiency of thought that is characteristic of sentimentality does not arise under the aegis of this particular overarching desire. For given that a belief of mine is so formed, when it is pointed out to me that it is false or that I am not justified in holding it, I shall abandon it or at least suspend belief. If nothing else sustains such errors than my desire rationally to believe what is true, they die a reasonably swift death. By contrast, a man whose grief, anger, or love is sentimental will tend to resist the correction of the thought on which his emotion rests, and this very recalcitrance suggests that what holds the thought in place is not a desire for truth and knowledge but something else— a desire that can be satisfied by seeing the object in a false light. Hence the crucial belief about it is not so much mistaken as arrived at as a result of active false-colouring. And we can perhaps descry the element of purposeful activity in the formation of feeling in the way we speak of ourselves actively *sentimentalizing* something rather than simply passively finding ourselves with a sentimental view of it.

What then is the desire under whose guidance sentimental thought is conducted? Doubtless there are several answers to this question. The most straightforward seems to be that what the sentimentalist seeks is the occurrence of certain enjoyable emotions. And since no emotion can be felt except as supported by a certain thought about its object, an appropriate thought has to be entertained for the sake of the pleasure. Where the object itself does not properly support that thought I shall have to contrive it by projection. Thus for instance I may sentimentalize a duckling before eating it by falsely representing it to myself as eagerly waiting for the pot, and in doing so make possible a gratifying feeling of benevolence towards the bird and the natural order to which the bird belongs.

A more interesting case—and surely as common in its occurrence—is that in which what is desired is not so much a gratifying feeling as a gratifying image of the self that is sustained by a fabricated emotion. As before, what makes the emotion possible is a thought about its object (which may or may not be the self). Take for instance those very common objects of sentimentalization, children and domestic pets. Projecting onto them an exaggerated vulnerability and innocence, I encourage myself to feel a tender compassion for them, one I may make use of to support a view of myself as a man of gentleness and fine feeling. And the temptation to sentimentality here is obvious, for it is far harder to be a man of fine feeling by proper response to the objects around me than it is to fabricate such a characterization of myself by some factitious projection. Indeed, provided that the feeling I generate is one that does underpin the character I want, sentimentality may offer me the added advantage that I may not need to go on and actually do anything about it. My aim is achieved in the feeling.

It must not be thought that only those emotions which we experience with pleasure make for sentimental thought, for once the structure of the phenomenon is clear it is evident that this will not be so. Even when we do not find them pleasing, anger or indignation for instance can easily be fitted into the pattern just illustrated. Thus a man who idealizes a distant political cause may be sentimentally angry or indignant when one of its exponents is extradited from the country, even though he does not experience these feelings with pleasure.[2] What may happen is that in demonstrating against the extradition he may sustain a view of himself as righteous and just. His anger is fed by his sentimental view of the cause, and while it may bring him distress, it also works to enable him to take a gratifying view of his own character. In the same vein it is no more difficult to imagine self-gratifying jealousy or hatred even though these emotions are far more painful to experience than anger or indignation. So my jealousy could support a pleasing view of myself as a man of grand passion, and my hatred for some luckless neighbour serve to endow me with a gratifying heroism that otherwise I would not take myself to possess.

What we see in these various cases is how the sentimentalist achieves a certain kind of gratification by false-colouring an object in his thought. A fuller description would undoubtedly attempt more precision. It would in particular tell us more about typical ways in which the sentimentalist acts, and would show how very often his activity has a protective function, so that what is achieved through the false-colouring of the world that he goes in for is reassurance in a world that is found unsettling. He tends to protect himself against the resistance of other things by softening them down, filing down their uncomfortable edges, or makes what is in truth rather alien and off-putting quite docile to his wishes and tastes. Thus when the advertizers of David Hamilton's *Le Jardin secret* hold out that book of popular photographs as containing 'images d'un monde où le spectateur peut contempler la fragile beauté des jeunes filles aux premiers instants de leur éveil à la féminité; monde heureux qui ne connait ni violence, ni viellesse, monde d'élégance et de beauté, refuge contre les rigeurs de la réalité,' they collude with the photographer in offering the reader a world in which he is comfortably and protectively cocooned. The appeal of these popular shots would scarcely be comprehensible if they did not encourage fantasy to deny the reality of a world in just the odious ways the publicity so glutinously describes.

However, it may seem that the description of sentimentality I have offered is too wide, for it suggests that almost any gratifying self-protective fantasy projected onto the world will be a sentimental one. And that is surely wrong. For example I may find myself unable to understand the work of some difficult philosopher, Kant, say, or Wittgenstein, and rather than admit that the fault lies with me, rather than abandon my pride, I may accuse the author himself of bad faith and of passing off as deep insight what is in fact little more than empty babble. Here I protect my pride by discovering in imagination the confidence trick that has taken everyone else in. In consequence I represent the frustration arising from my own limitations as justified anger, and protect my self-esteem by detection of the intellectual fraud. Such a situation may appear to mirror those just set out, but it would scarcely be one in which I have sentimentalized the work of Kant or of Wittgenstein.

It is evident that this kind of case cannot be dealt with by pointing to some unacceptable harshness in the emotion that is involved. We have already noticed that *any* emotion can on occasion be sentimentally entertained— though it may well be that in some cases the object of the sentimentalization and the object of the emotion differ (as in the case of hatred that I mentioned). However, it may be right to suggest that what distinguishes the sentimental fantasy from the other one is its tendency to idealize its objects, to present them as pure, noble, heroic, vulnerable, innocent, etc., and that feature is quite absent in my mistreatment of Kant or Wittgenstein. There I went in for no idealization at all and have instead projected onto the obscure philosopher a kind of malevolent intent that permits me to divert frustration away from myself.

With this emendation made, my tentative suggestion is that a sentimental mode of thought is typically one that idealizes its object under the guidance of a desire for gratification and reassurance. Derivatively, emotion is sentimental which is supported by such as thought. And we can see that such an attitude is one that may be directed not only towards other people and abstract causes, as my illustrative examples have shown, but also towards the self and, at the other extreme, towards the inanimate natural world.

For an example of the former, consider Ruskin's remarks in 1865 to the cadets of the Royal Military Academy at Woolwich:

You don't understand perhaps why I call you 'sentimental schoolboys' when you go into the Army? Because, on the whole, it is love of adventure, of excitement, of fine dress and of pride of fame, all of which are sentimental motives, which chiefly make a boy like going into the Guards better than into a counting-house . . . So far then, as for your own honour and the honour of your families, you choose brave death in a red coat before brave life in a black one, you are sentimental.[3]

To put it more fully than Ruskin did, the young man will be sentimental in his action if he goes into the Guards because by doing so he sustains a picture of himself as grand, glorious, honourable, and dashing in contrast with the mediocre and drab fellow he may dimly suspect himself to be. The idealization of Army life makes it possible for him to love and admire himself and incidentally at the same time does something to ward off the uncomfortable prospect of banality which is the lot of most. To accept that lot, to accept what Ruskin calls life in a black coat, is what would be truly brave, for as Ruskin sees it it is based on fact and does not enjoy the support of illusion that the sentimental young guardsman relies on.

Exactly the same structure can be discerned in the other case too, in that of the sentimentalization of the natural world. Typically we find this when we project onto an inert and separately existing world a warm concern for our human welfare and a tender amenability to our desires and needs. Instances of the strategy are to be found throughout the work of the Romantic poets, and one instructively complex example is supplied by Matthew Arnold's 'Dover Beach'. There the poet, put in mind of the ebb of Christian faith by the grating of the pebbles on the shore, apostrophizes his mistress in the lines:

> Ah, Love, let us be true
> To one another! for the world, which seems
> To lie before us like a land of dreams
> So various, so beautiful, so new,
> Hath really neither joy, nor love, nor light,
> Nor certitude, nor peace, nor help for pain;
> And we are here as on a darkling plain
> Swept with confused alarms of struggle and flight
> Where ignorant armies clash by night.

Now undoubtedly it is sentimentalization of the ego, and not of Nature, that we first detect here. Lover and mistress are presented as engagingly forlorn and bereft of all comfort but what they offer each other. What makes them forlorn is the departure from the world of faith, whose presence we are given to understand previously extended to Nature herself. With its departure the natural world cannot but be bleak, alien, and comfortless. *This* view of nature is not sentimental. What is sentimental though is the view on which it relies for contrast; the view that when the tide of faith was full Nature did minister to our needs and desires, and that we are now to be pitied because this is no longer so. Here we have a case of one piece of sentimentality facilitating another. For if it were clearly recognized that Nature is unchangingly inert, and therefore just as much capable of attaching the poet now as before his loss of faith, its distance could not be made a source of self-pity. The poet would not be able to think of it as having abandoned him. It is the suggested breakdown of the first idealization that makes way for the second. Both are gratifying, and both give the poet an easy picture of himself that is insulated from the more precise and better sustainable— the painful— view.

Before taking up the main thread of the argument, I add to this description of the standard cases four additional comments which are all provoked in one way or another by Michael Tanner's 'Sentimentality', the only treatment of the topic that the philosophical literature has recently provided.

(*a*) Commenting with favour on Oscar Wilde's *aperçu* that sentimentality is merely the bank-holiday of cynicism, Tanner suggests that there is no merely casual relation between the two, but a genuinely internal one. This I doubt. Of its essence cynicism refuses to see good where good is genuinely to be found. It consists in the representation of real good as an illusion. In contrast sentimentality fabricates the good where it is felt not to be, or felt to be in inadequate strength. Admittedly both attitudes involve a distortion of reality— but in opposite directions. The one may always exist without the other, and *contra* Wilde there is no a priori reason to expect the sentimentalist to be a cynic at heart. More easily we may expect the cynic to be sentimental— not believing in the existence of the real good he has to fabricate one if he is to find it at all.

Perhaps, though, we might think that the sentimentalist is cynical in a different way, using a fantasy as a support for feeling while being unprepared to rely on it or take it seriously as a basis for action. Only if there is any cynicism to be found here, that will have to involve the readiness to admit (or at least recognize) the pretence that is being practised (e.g. Prince

John's cynical disregard of his promise of pardon to his brother's opponents in *2 Henry IV*, IV, ii.). But this is something that the sentimentalist can scarcely do, for to admit that his feeling is baseless will come uncomfortably close to abandoning it.

(*b*) Tanner himself is happy to associate sentimentality and self-deception, and the description that I have offered makes it understandable why we should find it unsurprising to speak of the two in the same breath. As time passes the realities of the situation which confront the sentimentalist are likely to make it harder and harder for him to guard his fantasy against the incursion of truth. So he will need to protect his thought in cunning ways to sustain his feelings and the gratification they offer. But to do this successfully he needs to have a very shrewd idea of what the realities are which pose the greatest danger. So the deeper his sentimentality lies, the more likely it is that it will involve self-deception (and the less likely it will involve my second sort of cynicism).

(*c*) What appears of crucial importance to Tanner is the mind's passivity in relation to the feelings. 'The only activity that the sentimentalist manifests naturally is, one might say, the activity of rendering himself more passive.' (134.) At the very least this claim requires considerable redefinition, for we have seen how important it is to the sentimental that the light in which the world is seen should be that of the thinker's own making. Activity of the mind there certainly is, only it is not an activity that is adjusted to reality itself. That deficiency however does not render it passive, merely misplaced.

(*d*) Finally it may be objected that for all its applicability to some cases my characterization cannot but be somewhat parochial. Is not the reality of the concept too indocile to admit of such schematization without risk of damaging falsification?' (127.) In the arts especially, and in them particularly in music, we may feel a need to move in different ways altogether. And since it is with the arts that I am chiefly concerned, my account of extra-artistic sentimentality, however accurate, may appear to provide only the slightest help in rebutting this counter-example to the general thesis I am aiming to defend.

It can be conceded here that we have to treat sentimentality in the different arts in different ways. But this may not be all that worrying. In the representational arts at least we can make the transition from the extra-artistic cases as I have described them with no difficulty at all. For they either show us without sentimentality what is in itself thoroughly sentimental—as does Shakespeare in Othello's final speech: 'then must you speak / Of one who loved not wisely, but too well . . .'—or else they exhibit sentimentality by inviting the reader to collude with the author (or painter or sculptor) in adopting a sentimental view of his subject—as does Dickens at the end of *Oliver Twist*: 'I believe that the shade of Agnes sometimes hovers round that solemn nook, I believe it nonetheless because that nook is a Church and she was weak and erring.' In the musical cases, however, where there is no available object onto which an idealization can be projected or shown to be projected, a different line must be taken, and it is here that the danger of disintegration foreseen by Tanner seems to be at its greatest.

This fear can be disarmed. In speaking of music as sentimental we are speaking *metaphorically*. Music cannot be literally sentimental, for unlike novels or paintings or sculptures music does not typically convey a thought about anything. Now in metaphorical speech the point of assertion is not truth but aptness; we say something which is perhaps literally false (though certainly not always so) but which is none the less illuminating. By the often patent falsity of what is said our attention is drawn to something in the object which we would otherwise not see in quite that light. Thus in the case of music we speak falsely in saying it is sentimental, but in doing so draw attention to the way in which the gratifying emotion evoked is less than fully answerable to the music itself, rather as emotion does not properly answer the object in the kinds of literal case discussed above. The musical case therefore does not involve a different idea, just a different way in which the same idea can apply. And since we have to explain the impotence of sentimentality in the arts to upset the generalization of the larger argument, we can hope to do that by reference to the literal account of sentimentality, and need only consider the metaphorical cases in its light.

II

Confronted with the widespread presence of sentimentality in art, one may think the desire to generalize the argument of Chapter 10 is vain. Deplore it though we may, we cannot really deny that many people have and always have had a penchant for the second rate and for such easy gratifications as the arts have it within their power to provide. It then comes as no surprise to find perennially popular poetry, painting, and music that is grossly sentimental, art whose survival cannot be accounted for other than by reference to what is sentimental in it. So how can it be hoped to justify the fully general claim that what survives in art is of stature? Whatever else we may be unsure of, at least we know this: even enduring sentimentality resists that evaluation.[4]

To defuse this counter-example and its counterparts in the cases still to be discussed I shall rely on a principle for which I have not yet argued, and which I call the *Principle of Transparent Understanding*. What it maintains is that over time we may properly expect the source of art's appeal to us to be recognized for what it is. And in due course we shall discover that application of this principle to sentimental art makes its chances of survival far slimmer than the objection of the last paragraph supposes, or else ensures its survival to be of a peripheral kind unfit to serve as a suitable counter-example to the general argument. Before we descend to details, however, something must be said on behalf of the principle itself.

Raptly engaged by a book or a picture, a man may know what it is about the work that engages him. Or he may not. To his eyes it may be either transparent or opaque. If it is opaque, we shall think that even though he does not perhaps misunderstand the work, his understanding of it leaves something to be desired. He has not fully worked it through; he has not entirely appropriated it. In consequence, if he is of a dedicated and inquiring disposition we shall expect him to seek to replace the opacity in his view by something more transparent. This expectation is no mere reflection of individual psychology. It derives from (i) a general theoretical truth about the arts—on which I have relied in earlier chapters—that we cannot explain their significance except as consisting in something of importance that they have to show us, and (ii) the consequential conclusion that understanding and appreciation are inseparable from one another.[5] Success in appreciation therefore depends on our aiming at correct perception; and the pursuit of this aim cannot be detached from eventual recognition of what we see when correct perception is achieved. Once the path of understanding has been initially entered there is no point short of this goal at which it might be rationally abandoned. So, as a general rule, we have to think of ourselves as aiming at transparent understanding and as adopting it as the model of understanding on which appreciation is based. Furthermore, we must also suppose that this aim is one that is capable of satisfaction, because otherwise we should represent ourselves as self-deludedly committed to explaining the value of art by reference to an understanding that we had no reason to believe might be reliably secured. Put these observations together and *Principle of Transparent Understanding* is within our grasp. For while transparency will never be a priori guaranteed in the individual case, at least it must be a proper expectation that the sources of art's appeal will in fact transparently show up to persistent efforts to realize its significance.

My line of reasoning here may be thought objectionably ideal, and unsound as a basis for further argument. By way of dissent it will perhaps be said that true insight and limpidity of understanding are often difficult to achieve, and that the popular success of much art in fact rests on perception that is not all that laboriously won and which easily remains less than clear and distinct. So there may be no inconsistency in admitting the wider thesis about the value of the arts' connection with transparency and at the same time maintaining that art which is sentimental, vulgar, or obscene may well attract us over time without it being generally apparent what lies at the source of their appeal.

In this there is much that can be admitted. Only to do so is not to abandon anything of importance. For while no very great weight has yet been placed on it, it will be recalled that it was one important element of my account in Chapter 1 of what it is for art to pass time's test that not just any continuum of popularity will do. And since it is with such art alone that we are here concerned, it is that art which must escape the *Transparency Principle* if the present objection is to be effective. What we saw before was that survival can properly be adjudged secure only in so far as the enduring work is *well embedded* in the culture of which it is a part. And this condition, I contend, cannot be satisfied except by fluke if the character of the embedded object is other than transparent to us. If this is right we shall see that the rule of transparency, while it may not run everywhere, is effective where it needs to be, namely where the test of time is passed. In other cases we may have less faith in its rule, but there we cannot be so sure that the condition of embeddedness is well enough met to be sure that critical inferences are to be based on persistent success.

Why should we think that deeply embedded art is not open to the present objection? The answer lies in our understanding of the concept of embeddedness. Embedded art is that which plays an organizing role in a true account of our culture and of our conception of it. It exerts influence on the artistic production of succeeding key figures within the culture, whose own work can be fully understood only by reference to it. Equally it tends to mould the critical canons of those whose voice over time shapes effective public taste. Even if this idea is vague, what is abundantly clear is that to be embedded a particular work of art must exercise those who, in aesthetic matters, we see as having the sharpest eye and most steadfast gaze. Other things being equal, they are those who take the culture forward and give it the shape that it has and that we see it as having. Hence it is anything but absurd to think that since they are the best equipped to see the objects of their study for what they are, and the most concerned with accuracy of vision, to their eyes at least the true nature of the embedded work's appeal should normally be transparently revealed. If they do not standardly traverse fully the path of understanding, no one does. Once this is conceded nothing is lost by elsewhere allowing the effectiveness of transparency to be tempered with realism, as the objection insists that I have failed to do.

By itself the transparency of understanding, however effective, cannot take us very far. It allows us to assert only that we may expect embedded art to reveal the sources of its appeal, whatever they may be. And it may appear, to someone who sees sentimentality as a counter-example to my general claim, that this poses no threat. Why should sentimentality be any different from beauty or depth, both of which we hope to recognize transparently when we come across them?

The answer is largely provided by the description of sentimentality given in the last section. From it we know that in the non-abstract arts[6] sentimentality will usually involve a false-colouring of reality. And we know also that the benefits that we look to sentimentality to provide depend on our not explicitly recognizing that the false-colouring is ours. To recognize that it is ours is to admit that it has no basis in fact, and thus to deprive it of its effect. Now I suggest that it is highly likely that one thing that will prevent us from sustaining the self-deception that is needed for sentimentality to exercise its appeal is the recognition that what offers us the desired projection is actually sentimental. And that is just what the *Principle of Transparent Understanding* yields. Hence unlike the beautiful or the profound, if a sentimental work has aspirations to become embedded it will get picked up in the trawl of transparency and its claims to hold our attention will be undermined, since they cannot be sustained when once their source is recognized.

The argument is not foolproof. But at least the obvious hole in it can be made good. It will be said that while the *Principle of Transparency* insists that we shall eventually recognize sentimental art as sentimental, it does nothing to persuade us that those who enjoy transparent understanding will see what they understand in the way my description of sentimentality presents it, even on the supposition that my analysis is correct. For a person can perfectly well recognize that a view he holds is a sentimental view and *still* gain comfort from it. The mere recognition of the sentimental for what it is does not undermine its claims: what is needed for that is something different, a thorough developed grasp of the concept, and it will be said that is something I am in no position to trade on.

Formally speaking the objection is quite correct. But it can be avoided. For we really do not need to have a full and articulated account of sentimentality to disarm it—we just need a shrewd one. And while philosophical talents of a high order may be required to articulate *exactly* what goes into a full understanding of the concept, there is every reason to think that those who are in a position to determine the embeddedness of their art will have a shrewd enough grasp of sentimentality if anyone has it. Among them persistent failure to see that the sentimental is generally harmful and self-deluded must be the

exception rather than the rule, and we can therefore rely on
their ability to put together transparency of understanding
with a sufficiently firm grasp of this concept to insulate sentimentality in the arts from deep entrenchment. Thus I conclude
it constitutes far less plausible a counter-example to the general
claim I am defending than it sets out to be. Of course we can
admit that sentimentality is perennially popular, but now we
should be able to say with some conviction that its popularity is
unlikely to account for the survival of the same works over time
so much as the existence of a series of different works whose
attractions fade on being recognized for what they are. Where
on the other hand the same sentimental works do endure, we
should expect them to do so not as embedded in the culture but
as clinging to its edges. Then again it cannot be conveniently
used against my claims, for there the art that embodies it does
not withstand the test of time as it has here been understood.

III

We apply the term 'vulgar' to a man's manners, tastes, opinions, and character. In respect of each vulgarity can be displayed in numerous ways. If for no other reason than this the
scant literature of the subject does little to provide a cohesive
account of the idea. It seems obvious enough that we should
start with etymology. Vulgar behaviour is what is typical of the
mass of the people. However, this common observation, once
treated as definitional, has always appeared to be ham-strung
by the questions: which population is contemplated? Which cut
constitutes the mass? No one should think that to call someone
vulgar is simply to assimilate him to the Greek *banousoi*, or the
Roman *vulgus*, to Arnold's Populace, Marx's lumpen-
proletariat, or to Ortega's mass. Many men from each of these
groups have certainly been vulgar enough and no discovery
that the typical modes of thought and behaviour of the chosen
model had in fact been mistakenly identified could falsify that
truth. Yet that is what we should have to expect if such an
assimilation were what the word really intended. Since a parallel consideration tells against the rather more plausible idea of
making the relevant mass that of the vulgar man's own time,
whatever that might happen to be, it seems that our under-

standing of vulgarity cannot be fixed with the help of historical reference at all. Hence it might be thought that the etymological hint cannot take us very far.

But wrongly. For that hint will be preserved if it can be analytically detached from particular reference altogether. To do this we have to find an established, commonly shared conception of the mass which is temporally neutral, which fits the mentioned exemplars reasonably well, and which is rich enough to provide a basis for our understanding of vulgar thought and behaviour. And one such conception can, I think, be constructed on the basis of three relatively uncontroversial elements.

(i) Thinking of a man as belonging to the mass, we regard him less as a particular individual than as a member of an undifferentiated body. The mass, to our common way of thinking, is and always has been homogeneous.[7] This homogeneity is not so much socio-economic in nature as one found in patterns of thought and action. But in calling the mass homogeneous I do not simply mean that its members think and act alike. That they might quite fortuitously do without reference to one another, in ways that have no tendency to mark them out as members of the crowd. What is of greater importance is that these common patterns should arise in response to a desire of each man not to be distinguished from his fellows, or should at least in part be causally explained by the fact that others think and behave in similar ways too.[8] In homogeneous thought the independent call of fact and the cogency of a man's own reasoning are subordinate to his desire for identification with (or acceptance by) others and to his desire for the confidence and self-esteem that this can bring.[9] That this homogeneity is a settled element in our conception of the mass is evident in the literature, most recently perhaps in David Riesman's *The Lonely Crowd*, but visible also early in the last century in de Tocqueville's observation that under American democracy 'every citizen [is] assimilated to the rest, is lost in the crowd, and nothing stands conspicuous but the great and imposing image of the people at large.' (*Of Democracy in America* (1831).)

(ii) Not, of course, that socio-economic considerations are entirely irrelevant. It is common to the examples of the mass we started with that their members are drawn from the lower orders of society. Usually mass existence has been fostered by poverty, and the social inferiority and subjugation consequent upon it. But we need to remember how frequently it has been stressed that these features are conceptually detachable from the existence of the mass—in the 1830s by de Tocqueville, fifty years later by Arnold (*Culture and Anarchy* (1883)), and fifty years later again by Ortega (*La rebelión de las masas* (1929)) and Jaspers (*Die Geistige Situation der Zeit* (1931)). What cannot be detached though are the limitations of mind that poverty and social subjugation bring with them: ignorance, lack of intellectual sophistication, and the deficiencies of an inferior education. Together with the element of homogeneity these features of the mass mind ensure that its thought should crystallize around an intellectually undemanding centre. For the sake of homogeneity the crowd's intellectual endeavours must lie within the compass of all (or at least of the vast majority), and they are therefore rightly to be thought of as weighed down by the drag of a low common denominator. It might even be thought an a priori matter that the mass should have a low centre of intellectual gravity; for were that centre raised, the pressures making for homogeneity would be slighter and men would consequently be less inclined to depend on likeness to one another for self-confirmation. In those circumstances we might speak less of a mass than of a community.

(iii) We presume the mass to have an internal cohesion that does much to shape its attitudes to the world that lies beyond it. Men adhere to the mass in part through an inability to find a sense of their own worth without doing so. To those who do turn to mass ways of thought for this reason, the very existence of alternative and implicitly critical tastes, aspirations, and opinions seems to harbour a threat to the benefits that association with the mass brings. Hence we should not be surprised to find among the mass a deep hostility towards these alternatives, which functions to strengthen the group's internal ties. To view the alien with distrust and fear, and to be unable to meet its challenges, reinforces a man's reliance on the group he recognizes as clearly his own.

These three features then, homogeneity in patterns of thought, its crystallization around an undemanding centre, and self-protective cohesiveness, together yield a temporally neutral picture of the mass that fits our original exemplars well enough. On the basis of this framework we can proceed towards the vulgar itself by projecting out from it a cluster of characteristics that pick out a distinctive cast of mind. It will then, I suggest, be this cast of mind which, when revealed in a man's action and thought, enables us to identify him or them as vulgar. The desired connection with etymology is then preserved through the projected construct without falling to the original objection.

It is hard to believe that the three forces just identified will not tend to promote in those subject to them a natural preference for the sensory over the intellectual, and for the concrete and practical over the abstract and theoretical. They foster men who find themselves more at ease with the shallow and simple than with the profound and complex; men who sympathize more swiftly with the coarse and obvious than with the refined and subtle. They will naturally promote the conflation of the quantitative with the qualitative and make it attractive easily to sacrifice the goods to be gained from precision of thought for the immediate satisfactions accruing to the loose and unreflected. Further, because of the self-protective nature of the mass, it will be natural for the mind that the mass breeds to respond more readily to what is flattering than to what is challenging. Hence it will be an easy prey to complacency and self-satisfaction, prone, as Arnold put it, to 'insist on the prime right and satisfaction for each one to affirm himself, and his ordinary self to be doing and doing freely as he likes', prompted and guided by 'disbelief in right reason as a lawful authority'.

Much the same characterization is offered by Ortega in his contrast of the *vida noble* with the *vida vulgar*. Mass man, he writes (Ch. VII), is accustomed to appeal to no superior instance. He is satisfied with himself just as he is, ingenuously tending to pronounce good whatever he finds within himself—opinions, tastes, desires, and preferences—except where purely contingent circumstance constrains him to do otherwise. 'Left to himself he is hermetically enclosed within his own circle, incapable of attending to anyone or anything, believing that he is sufficient unto himself and, in sum, self-willed, intractible and unmanageable.' (112–13.)

Finally, because of the difficulties the mass mind encounters in making out grounds on which one choice of value should be preferable to another—any ground, that is, that reaches beyond the fact that it is already endorsed by others—we expect vulgar taste to be influenced by changing fashion and the immediate appeal of novelty rather than soundly grounded in stable tradition. Furthermore, because nothing in the content of choice finds firm root, the chances are that, lacking all else, sincerity of feeling should become the sovereign value, finding its natural expression in entertainment and diversion that depends on no lasting commitment to discernment, discrimination, or self-awareness. (See Richard Hoggart, *The Uses of Literacy* (1957)).

Now, to understand our speaking of the individual act or thought, or even the individual object, as vulgar, we need only make a connection between it and a cast of mind such as that just described. To this end, let us say then that those deeds or thoughts or objects are vulgar which reveal the agent or thinker to whom they appeal to possess a mind of such cast. The individual act etc. is thus revealed as vulgar not by its possession of some intrinsic set of features that it displays but because of what it tells us about the kind of person whose act or choice it is.

That is my suggestion. But so far little I have said goes beyond mere presentation. Support that is other than merely descriptive of something we intuitively recognize is thin. So to bolster up my proposal it is worth showing how it fits a number of common insights about vulgarity, the first three of which I take from the best discussion in the literature I know, from Hazlitt's essay in *Table Talk* (1823) entitled 'Of Vulgarity and Affectation'.

Considering a proposed identification of vulgarity with some simple trait such as coarseness, ignorance, or awkwardness, Hazlitt objected that none of them (and by implication no combination of them) need be vulgar in themselves. Caliban for instance is coarse enough, but surely he is not vulgar. Hazlitt's own expedient here is to back up such a feature by reference to a psychological root or motive. Thus he claims that vulgarity's

essence consists in taking manners, actions, words, opinions on trust from others without examining one's own feelings or weighing the merits of the case. It is coarseness or shallowness of taste arising out of want of individual refinement, together with the confidence and presumption inspired by example and numbers. It may be defined to be a prostitution of the mind or body to ape the more or less obvious defects of others, because by doing so we shall secure the suffrage of those we associate with.

What is surely striking about this passage, however, is that while each description is apt enough, together they lack any clear unity. The proposed psychological root is different in each of the three attempts that is made; and even what is supposed to spring from the various psychological motivational forces is presented as very open-ended. We are consequently given no hint as to how either roots or branches of the concept are properly to be closed off.

On the indirect approach I have adopted this difficulty does not arise. The rich variation in the concept's extension that Hazlitt emphasizes is given a rough cohesion by reference to the admittedly imprecise and certainly incomplete idea of a cast of mind, the nature of which is initially fixed by reference to a schematic understanding of the mass, as etymology suggests. The very variety that puzzles Hazlitt is even something that we should expect to encounter on the ground that a stable cast of mind is liable to manifest itself in different situations in different ways. None the less its manifestations retain a unity through the way in which the stable cast of mind they reveal is conceived of as generated.

'An opinion is vulgar that is stewed in the breath of the rabble—nor is it a bit purer or more refined from having passed through the well cleansed breath of a whole court.' A notable merit of Hazlitt's proposals is that they each succeed in detaching the vulgar man from too close an association with any particular class. And this virtue must be carried over into any more successful account. Happily this demand is met, for the cast of mind by reference to which vulgarity is characterized is one that a man can come to possess in ways that are causally unrelated to his origins in any particular class. Room is also allowed for a man to be one of the people without adopting a mass mentality. Social origin no more condemns a man to vulgarity than does his vulgarity fix his social origin. Moreover we also retain, as we must, the distinction that Hazlitt draws between the vulgar and the common in pointing out that "'tis common to breathe, to see, to feel, to live—nothing is vulgar that is natural, spontaneous, unavoidable'. So however common the vulgar mind might become it would not be that which constituted its vulgarity. Those universal things that Hazlitt here lists have no relation at all to the homogeneity, the low intellectual centre, or the protective cohesiveness, which in the end have to bear the weight of the description proposed.

'There cannot be a surer proof of a low origin or an innate meanness of disposition than to be always talking and thinking of being genteel.' It might be thought that the paradigm from which Hazlitt sets off is one that my own proposal cannot match, and one which therefore undermines it. Is not the ostentatious distancing of himself from the crowd that a man insists on by conspicuous display of wealth, or of social position, or of select information, designed precisely to escape from the toils of the homogeneous mind? And does not such egregiously vulgar distance *reject* the very cast of mind that my account essentially relies on? It is interesting that Hazlitt himself immediately makes an observation that might seem to offer us a way of handling this apparent difficulty: 'One must feel a strong tendency to that which one is trying always to avoid. Whenever we pretend on all occasions a mighty contempt for anything, it is a pretty clear sign that we feel ourselves on a level with it.' That is, despite their rejection of it, the ostentatious and snobbish are indeed of vulgar cast; and, disliking that, publicly insist on not being so. However, this explanation, pertinent though it may often be, cannot be quite generally correct. All questions of self-awareness aside, if it were right, we should have to say that vulgarity of character is invariably displayed in the attempt to distinguish oneself from the crowd—provided one is motivated by a fear of belonging to it. Yet there is no reason to think this is so. Spurred on by fearing to be vulgar a man may honourably and even insistently strive to better himself without actually displaying vulgarity in doing so. After all, one who feels himself to be vulgar need not inevitably be so; and his fear of vulgarity does not always commit him to it. Indeed, a man's openness to the fear may often show it to be groundless.

The truth of the matter is not far off. The man who thinks he can establish himself as other than vulgar by dissociation from one or other of those conditions that promote the growth of the vulgar mind—poverty, say, or social inferiority, or ignorance—is making a vulgar error, and in doing so reveals the very cast of mind he seeks to distance himself from. This error of taking what favours vulgarity for vulgarity itself, and the consequential attempt to escape vulgarity by display of what promotes its contrary is one that will be made by those whom we recognize as coarse and insensitive, by those who are equipped with only a shallow conception of and feeling for true gentleness and excellence. So Hazlitt's paradigm furnishes no counter-example to the account I have proposed. Rather it accurately describes one way in which I am committed to saying that the vulgar mind is revealed.

Leaving Hazlitt aside now, we may also gain some support from contrasting this unitary account of vulgarity with the more customary plural analyses that are offered. John Bayley, for instance, has claimed that 'of all possible terms in aesthetics ["vulgarity"] is perhaps the most ambiguous',[10] and what prompts him to this assertion is the perception that there exist—apparently unrelated—both vulgarity that we endorse and applaud and vulgarity that we deprecate. But if these phenomena really were unrelated it would be pretty extraordinary that they should so regularly be picked out by the same term. At this point the present scheme enjoys a flexibility that its rivals lack. For what it suggests is that vulgarity will be deplorable when behaviour manifests a vulgar cast of mind in circumstances and ways in which more exacting standards should run. On the other hand we shall rightly welcome the vulgar—in exactly the same sense of the word—when the standards to which it responds make no higher demands. As an example of the latter we might consider public seaside architecture. The entertainment that it houses is boisterous, hearty, and direct, robustly self-confident, and full of zest. What housing for it could be more suitable than the vulgar pleasure palaces and piers of the last years of the nineteenth century? Would constructions of a different character have avoided the dangers of facelessness or of sheer hypocrisy?[11] None the less the cast of mind that they embody and to which they most naturally appeal need not be discontinuous with that displayed by more deplorable vulgarity; for it is one projected from the same roots. Ambiguity is not called for.

While there exist both vulgar good and vulgar bad we feel that the first is recessive to the second. An adequate account of the concept should show us why this is so. On the present suggestion, vulgarity has been presented as stemming fundamentally from certain limitations of mind, and while it may be readily admitted that not everyone can avoid it and that it is not always damaging, we cannot think of it but as a limitation to transcend. A fully developed grasp of the idea of vulgarity will be impossible unless we understand its manifestations as falling towards one end of a scale, the polar term of which is recognized as enjoying a fineness that its counterpart lacks. And it is inherent to our understanding of fineness and of the refined that it has virtues that the coarse does not. Where we have no special reason for preferring the coarse— as sometimes of course we do— possession of the concept of refinement will only be surely attributed to us if it goes hand in hand with a willingness to make refined (though not over-refined) choices. So to see certain behaviour as vulgar is to set it— either directly or by association[12]— in a range of comparisons which those who self-consciously operate the concept cannot unreservedly embrace. It will at bottom be for some such reason as this that we feel Bayley to be on to something important when he says that 'I am vulgar' is not a possible pronouncement. I may perhaps say it truly of myself,[13] but if I do I almost certainly convict myself of having a less than perfect grasp of what I say. If I fully understood it I would hardly suffer from the limitation of mind that makes what I say true.

IV

Does vulgarity as it appears in the arts present a more worrying counter-example to the desired generalization than sentimentality? First, it is obviously true that despite the openness of the vulgar mind to the vagaries of fashion, the survival and enjoyment of vulgar art over time is a real possibility. Secondly, when it is truly what is vulgar about that art that accounts for its success, we should be reluctant to think of the works that embody it as works of stature. For it emerged from the discussion of Chapter 9 that stature-grounding features will be of a kind on the basis of which we might plausibly project the establishment and survival of art as an autonomous activity. This is scarcely possible in the case before us, for the ends that vulgarity most typically subserves are entertainment and distraction, ends, that is, which enable the mind to lose itself and be absorbed in what is commonly and unreflectively enjoyed. These are hardly ends that we might in all consciousness embrace. So to all appearance the vulgar is at least as great a threat to my argument as sentimentality. It will be more so if it cannot be disarmed.

As before the move to make is one that challenges the equation of mere survival with the unequivocal passage of time's test. For even though it endure vulgarity, like sentimentality, has little claim to be able to satisfy the condition of embeddedness that we know to be essential to the critical premiss. This is true both of what I have called the vulgar good and the vulgar bad. As for the vulgar good, we know from the earlier discussion that the *Principle of Transparent Understanding* will apply. If the vulgar is successful, we shall expect it to be recognized for what it is. Moreover, among people who are best placed to effect embedding we may properly expect to find a shrewd, if not fully articulate, grasp of the nature of the features that underlie artistic success. Now from what was said at the end of the last section, a proper grasp of vulgarity sees it in contrast with what is more refined and sees it as unable to aspire to finenesses to which we are committed and which we would not abandon for its sake. Hence where it really matters the vulgar is seen as at best of limited worth. And that fact sharply exposes the works whose appeal turns on their vulgarity to the pressures that time generates. We shall expect it to be displaced in our attention by art the value of which we find less limited. If the vulgar good is at best of restricted worth, the vulgar bad will correspondingly, under the rule of transparency, be recognized as badly deficient. Hence it will be ill placed to become embedded at all. In either case the reservation with which the vulgar attracts our attachment must be reckoned to move it towards the periphery. For that reason its occasional long lasting success does not pose any intolerable threat to the wider argument. Vulgarity and sentimentality here go hand in hand.

Nevertheless it might be felt that this line of reasoning is far too cavalier. Does it not neglect the all too obvious fact that our own age has witnessed an unprecedented ascent of the vulgar—even maybe the self-conscious vulgarization of our whole culture? Can it be seriously maintained today that the vulgar is resistant to embedding?

For all its appeal this challenge is somewhat imprecise in its intent and demands to be taken in at least two different ways. First, remembering that we have so far been speaking only of the possible embedding of the single vulgar work in what is pre-eminently and ideally a non-vulgar culture, we ought to say that the salient place of vulgarity in our own day cannot be offered as evidence of embeddedness of single instances. Of those it is perhaps too early to speak, and care must evidently be taken not to confuse the prevalence of vulgar art in general with the embeddedness in the culture of particular cases. By itself, the mere prevalence of vulgarity allows us to conclude very little. So taken in this way it is uncertain how effective the objection might in fact be. Certainly it is not conclusive.

Alternatively, we might hear these questions much more radically, as suggesting that we have already come close to throwing over large-scale commitment to the fineness against which the vulgar is offset, and close to abandoning (except at the periphery) what might withstand the drab, the strident, and the monotone. Even if this new regime is not at present quite to hand, is there any reason to think that it might not really one day arrive? Then my resistance to the partial embeddedness of vulgar art will seem a trifle thin, for it will have taken over the culture and have rooted itself deeply within it. Then, if not now, the generalized inferences will not reliably hold.

Here finally we approach the issue of how sound the previous reasoning will be in circumstances very different from those so far envisaged. Discussion of this matter must await the next and final chapter, and nothing need be said now to rebut the challenge it poses. All that I have here sought to do is to provide inductive grounds for our customary inferences under circumstances that we clearly recognize now to hold. I do not thereby commit myself to their continuing to hold no matter what changes take place in the ways we think about ourselves and arrange our lives. What we can say in advance of such changes coming to pass is that if, and when, they do we may indeed be forced to give up our inferences. But it should not then surprise us if we find that a large number of other things have changed as well.

V

The third member of my unsavoury trio is obscenity. Uncertain about the details of my understanding, I do little more than present a proposal about one rather special aspect of this topic and offer a number of comments to make the proposal look attractive. Someone who thinks that I am mistaken in supposing myself to have accurately located even one facet of the obscene may none the less feel that I am talking about a real phenomenon that merits attention. I myself find no apter name for it springing to mind.

My proposal is this. In general the obscene is what invites us to self-abandonment through the breaking of some taboo. And a species of obscenity that easily finds its place in art is the deliberate and seductive degradation of what are proper objects or reverence or love, a degradation that unfits them for our attachment. So what we feel should be loved or revered is obscenely treated when those responses are deliberately inhibited by some alluring deformation, and the object itself is obscene in its deformed state when its being in that state is so brought about. Finally, we behave obscenely when in our behaviour we deliberately bring about such a state in some such object, or in an instance of some properly attaching good. Now the comments.

(i) In the first place the suggestion implies that the natural world, taken in itself, contains no obscenity. As described it can be brought to exist only as a result of men's intentional behaviour. Thus, because nature itself has no intention in the production of men suffering from deforming diseases, disease itself, however horrible, is no obscenity. So when we say that naturally occurring disease is obscene we are either guilty of blasphemy—imputing to God an evil intention—or else we speak metaphorically, falsely but with an illuminating purpose.

(ii) By contrast we can see that many of the obscenities there are do involve natural objects, for it is natural objects—ourselves included—that make up the richest stock of things to love and revere. Given that it is the natural world to which we primarily attach ourselves, that is what we will degrade in this particular kind of obscene thought and behaviour. The selection of natural objects as internal to our concept of obscenity will also explain why so many of the things with which we surround ourselves are immune to obscene treatment—our houses, the stores in the larder, our cars and bicycles, the paper in the desk, and so on. Even though we may differ about which objects are commonly recognized as proper objects of reverence, these things, it is certain, are not among them. More likely candidates are, for instance, particularly loved landscapes, health, animal life, human love, the sacred, and maybe even death itself. To someone who takes these things as a good sample of what in our culture are thought to be natural objects of reverence it will come as no shock to hear described as obscene the occasional disfigurement of the landscape (vandalism), the production of a deformed body (through torture), the mutilation of animals, the defiling of holy monuments, and the degradation of the dead (as in Evelyn Waugh's *The Loved One*) as well as the more common cases that involve the mockery of human love and sexuality. In the absence of any special reason to restrict the idea to the last of these I should recommend treating each as equally central, providing of course that they are backed with the right kind of motive, that of unfitting them for our attachment. By contrast we should see as metaphorical application of the concept to cases where what distresses us is indeed some intentionally produced state of something to which we are attached, but where the intention in question is not so to degrade it. Thus we sometimes speak of travesties of justice, the horrors of war, or grinding poverty, as obscene, without having any good reason to think that they have resulted from any desire to degrade what we naturally love or revere. There we are using metaphor. Occasionally we may feel quite uncertain whether we are dealing with a case of literal obscenity or one that is metaphorical. And this uncertainty is easily understandable, perhaps because we then find it hard to see how the offensive result could have been intentionally produced except out of a deep-seated and maybe unconscious desire to do dirt on the object of our attachment.[14]

(iii) It is common to associate obscenity with aggression. In the sorts of case I am concerned with it is plain why. The production of obscenity aims to make something that is picked out as an object of reverence or love unfit for it. Now since we attach ourselves primarily to things we think of as sources of goodness, the desire to destroy or deform them can be understood not just as an attack on the object itself but through the object on those whom we think enriched by it. Very often it seems that the source of goodness that comes under attack is a source precisely for him who is gratified by his own obscene treatment of it. And this fact will explain why we sometimes easily think of obscenity as pathologically tinged. For if we recognize something as a source of good for ourselves then it would be natural for us to protect it from harm. There will be something internally amiss if, recognizing it as a good, I feel compelled to degrade, defile, or deform it. That I might do so out of envy or as a defence against the bad parts of myself is a thought not alien to modern psychology, and we see the pathological colour of such cases when we realize that they are peculiarly self-defeating, they destroy the very source of goodness outside the self whose integrity must be preserved if a stable and firmly structured ego is to be achieved.

(iv) It is notable that as I have presented it, obscenity is what Kant would have called a subjective concept—it cannot be elucidated without bringing in the subject's response. But no more than in the case of beauty is the response that of pleasure or pain. It is, I have suggested, the response of self-abandon. And just as with beauty, the importance of response detracts not at all from the objectivity—the assessability as true or false—of judgements that an object or event is an obscene one. No more does it detract from the objectivity of these judgements that they can be assessed only in relation to what the society in which the objects or events arise regards as a proper object of reverence, what it takes to be a degradation of them, and what forms of deformation it experiences as inviting self-abandon.

(v) Apart from being almost universally found in some measure alluring, the obscene is also universally feared. The reason why this is so is continuous with what I said at (iii). We savour it at the cost of damage to those sources of goodness on which we depend for healthy psychological development. It is also inviting to see a commonly made connection—though not, as English law has it, a constitutive one—between the obscene and that which tends to deprave and corrupt. A man who, deliberately or not, takes into himself attractive, though debased and forbidden images of proper objects of attachment is liable to develop a corrupted view of what he sees, a view which inevitably tends to thwart the formation of sound attachment to the deformed objects. More than this though, because of the natural tendency of the mind to spread itself over objects it sees to be alike, obscene views of particular objects may come to infect the way in which we conceive of other similar objects too. It is not simply that our ability to attach ourselves to those objects which are presented as deformed is lessened; more seriously, our capacity to form attachments is itself progressively undermined. If we have no way to isolate the contamination, the ego itself is at risk.

Pulling these things together, then, we have a proposal about a kind of obscenity that offers fairly determinate expectations about what objects can be obscenely treated and under what conditions; it shows us where to look for an explanation of why we fear and deplore the obscene, and suggests why it is reasonable to find a connection between it and the depraving and corrupting. It has the merit of fitting our suspicion that obscenity is at root aggressive and sometimes pathologically tinged. Finally it shows a way of detecting a move from a literal application of the term to metaphorical uses. On its basis we may again approach the question for the sake of which the subject has here been introduced.

One writer certain that obscenity could pose no threat to generalization of the earlier argument is Adrian Stokes, who in *Painting and the Inner World* broaches the topic of 'bad objects, of aggression, of envy, of all that is negative'. There he writes:

These drives, and the objects imbued with them, could not figure in art—and they figure prominently—except under the sign of coordination, of the form in art that stems from the presence of good objects. Tragic art, to be so, must bear nobility. But many appreciators today seem to find it more exciting if formal elements can be observed barely to survive a monstrous expression of say, greed. What is entirely negative or chaotic, or merely unfeeling, can never be art, and what is near it is never great art.[15]

Now it would evidently be too cursory a way with obscene art to insist with no further ado that its negative nature precludes it from entering art altogether. Too swift, not because it is evident that the bawdy and the lascivious have a long acknowledged place in the arts—on my account neither characteristic makes the work that carries it obscene[16]—but simply because nothing is achieved by defining this possibility away. By whose definition, we must ask, does art exclude these matters? And is that definition correct? Happily, this is not a mistake that Stokes makes, for it is only when shorn from context that the passage sounds unduly stipulative. In its setting it arises out of an argument with which the reader who has come with me so far will probably have some sympathy. Stokes's psychoanalytically inspired position is—the similarity with the Hegelian thesis earlier discussed in Chapter 5 is striking—that the aesthetic impulse from which art springs is rooted in the need to repair and constitute the inner world by co-ordinating projections of it in the outer. Since art is the creative form this impulse takes in its social aspect, it too must aim at reparation. The purely negative and non-reparative image cannot express this impulse at all. Hence art and negativity must live at odds.

Although it certainly does not lay itself open to the charge of proceeding by stipulation, it remains a way of settling our problem that moves too quickly. The most we might say is that the standard or paradigm cases of art we come across stem from the reparative impulse; or that what the finest art appeals to is an impulse that has a reparative root and that unless this were so we would be unable to explain the generation of art within our social practices at all. This more guarded and more nearly acceptable claim, however, does little to rule out wholly negative art except as a paradigm. Its existence remains a serious possibility. In the quoted passage there is even a suggestion that Stokes himself recognizes this, for his reference to the enthusiasm of modern collectors for forms that scarcely survive the expression of greed is surely a reference to art of just this kind. And if it is a serious possibility, how are we to resist the thought that the widespread appeal that the negative appears to exercise gives it an even chance of establishing itself in the canon in due course, just as that art does which we admit without hesitation to be of stature.

A reply that goes well both with the earlier sections of this chapter and with the weakening that has to be imposed on our understanding of Stokes's claims is this. We could not on a large scale seek those reparative things we do from the arts —joy and pleasure in order, integration, understanding —and *knowingly* embrace something the appeal of which we recognized to be wholly negative. While we may individually find aggressive consolation in the negative in art either as artist or as spectator, we do so as victims of our own psychology. By contrast, the embedding that the obscene has to achieve to be a serious counter-example to the wider argument I am prosecuting is not individual but social. Its being properly embedded would *ipso facto* be a reflection of the place the obscene work has come to hold in the culture as a whole. And as a whole, despite our occasional doubts, our culture is not so grossly deformed. Recognizing the obscene for what it is, and granting ourselves a shrewd enough grasp of the idea, it is hard to see it as more than a logical possibility that we should both endorse the central appeal of the arts as integrating or reparative, and also admit into the centre the obscenity that we recognize to strike against the whole and the healthy. Indeed, as has been sharply observed by Ruby Meager, there is a very special difficulty in supposing that we might do so in this particular case. As she puts it, 'in the obscene we adopt or are given a double sense of ourselves . . . able deliberately to think humiliatingly of persons through their bodies as inescapably corrupt, dirty and diseased, *by standards to which we are ourselves committed*'.[17] Put in my terms, we cannot explain obscenity except as an attack on what we prize. Consequently it is only if our attachment to the values that are attacked is tenacious that the obscene can get any grip. Were that attachment weaker, the obscene would lack all motivation. But once we allow the hold of the attacked values on us to be firm, the predictable recognition of the obscene *as* obscene—provided by the now standard application of the *Principle of Transparent Understanding*—effectively precludes its embedding. This is the consequence we want; for it shows that no more than sentimentality or vulgarity does obscenity stand in the way of broadening the over-all argument.

Chapter 12

The Test of Time in the Theory of Art

On ne vit dans le mémoire du monde que par des travaux pour le monde.

Chateaubriand: Notice for Joubert (1824).

The interest of the preceding chapters will be increased if it can be shown difficult or even impossible to envisage situations to which their argument does not apply. To do that would be to come as near as may be to establishing time's test as inelimin-able from art theory, and to showing that despite having recently attracted much invective it makes up one stable strut in a proper conception of art. To say this is to say that we abandon that test at the cost of abandoning significant concern with art itself. In defending this claim now I come to the second of the two obligations incurred in the Introduction, that which concerns not so much the soundness of this critical device as its over-all theoretical standing.

I

Historicism and Minimal Art

The main sources of the desire to minimize the test's impor-tance have already been discussed. They stem, it will be remembered, largely from the fact that over time the perspec-tive we have on earlier art changes, a fact that an age addicted to relativism in all its various forms has regarded as licensing an untenable ontological doctrine about much of the art we know. In the case of literature, we have seen how Eliot and critics whom he influenced took such a step; and it is not only Anglo-Saxon thinkers who have been so tempted; nor has the argu-ment been directed solely to the literary arts.

Writing some twenty years after Eliot, Ortega proposes just such a move in relation to the visual arts as well, in a passage towards the end of *La desumanización del arte*:

If all that were meant by talking of the timelessness of art were that its creation and appreciation involve the hope that its value should not fade, no harm would be done. The fact of the matter though is that the aesthetic value of works of art ages and decays even quicker than their material base. It is the same here as it is with love. All love, at a given moment, vows its own eternity. But that moment, with its yearned for eternity, passes. We watch it fall into the stream of time, wave its arms for help, and then drown in the past. In the case or art the explanation of the wreck and the drowning is very simply that the painter or writer does not—can not even—set down upon his canvas or on his paper everything that goes into the work's production. The fundamental things—the ideas, preferences, aesthetic and cosmic convictions in which the uniqueness of the canvas is rooted—are all left out. The brush points up only those things that the contemporary viewer does not take for granted.[1]

Here we see him striving for a conclusion that repudiates the timelessness of art and puts in its place something like its evanescence. But this is not a position that his elucidation of the simile of decaying love supports. For Ortega, it should not be art, the analogue of love, that wanes, so much as our capacity to retrieve its value from a position on the river bank from which our view of the object is progressively obscured as it floats downstream. That this is what he really has in mind—despite an unguarded assertion that our appreciation of the art of the past is *ironic*, and requires the invention of a factitious contemporary self through which to see it—is attested by his also saying that only a man of unrefined sensibility would expect to be able to enter fully into earlier art without making an especial effort. This clearly carries the implication that if the effort is made the book of the past need not remain closed. Yet that thought is not one that the quoted lines present.

The same lackadaisical conflation of epistemology and ontology is displayed in the writing of another critic, André Malraux. When speaking in *La Voie royale* of the status of succeeding generations' appraisal of an artist's work, he says that 'what interests me personally is the gradual change that comes over such work. . . . Every work of art, in fact, tends to develop into myth.'[2] And scanning the most recent literature for a writer who outspokenly and in full theoretical consciousness writes the same illicit move into his aesthetics, we see Theodor Adorno explicitly deriving a conception of art as being processlike from an eroticized version of the very simile from which Ortega sets out. In Adorno's view, art has a life span of its own which gradually unfolds, and when the process of exfoliation is complete, so is the work's decay. 'Am Ende ist ihre Entfaltung eins mit ihrem Zerfall.'[3]

To point out the illegitimacy of these moves is to do no more than to repeat what was discovered in Chapters 3 and 6, in which I also argued that the justifiability of time's test depended on adopting instead the conception of art I have called 'historicist'. However, such an array of thinkers all lined up in the opposing camp makes it urgent now to ask a question I have so far deliberately left unanswered. That is, whether we have to extend the historicist conception of the matter beyond the art with which we are most familiar and for which it is already established, and resign ourselves to applying it right across the board; or whether for some segment of the art we know— or for some as yet unknown, though coherently imaginable, future art— we might not quite properly adopt the more relaxed view earlier discussed under the heading of art's autonomy. If there really is no compulsion to extend the boundaries of historically considered art further than we already know it to range, then despite anything said so far these notable authorities may yet be right— at least for this possibly increasingly important segment of art. And that would indeed upset my claim about the over-all significance of time's test. For to such a segment the test could not apply.

The thought that we must not project over the whole range of art what is appropriate only to some of it is neither surprising nor novel. In the present context it is certainly relied on in a well-known passage of Valéry's 'La conquête de l'ubiquité' where he discusses our age's increased ability to reproduce particular works of art:

Il y a dans tous les arts une partie physique qui ne peut plus être regardée ni traitée comme naguère, qui ne peut pas être soustraite aux entreprises de la connaissance et de la pensée moderne. Ni la matière, ni l'espace, ni le temps ne sont depuis vingt ans ce qu'ils étaient depuis toujours. Il faut s'attendre que de si grandes nouveautés transforment toute la technique des arts, agissent par là sur l'invention elle-même, *aillent peut-être jusqu'à modifier merveilleusement la notion même de l'art.*[4]

The issue is interesting enough in its own right. But here it is especially pressing; for if Valéry is right, then as time goes by, the relaxed conception of art may be expected to become progressively more firmly entrenched. Then because the test of time cannot operate under that condition it will fade as a tool of critical practice; and, contrary to what I have asserted, the stability of its place in the theory of art cannot be assured.

If Valéry is right: and one condition of his being so is that it should be possible to relieve the arts of those very elements that forced on us the historical view for such areas of art for which it is already known to be correct, and yet still rightly call the resulting product 'art'. Should this demand fail, historicism will not just rank as one conception of art among others; it will be written into the very concept of art itself and of necessity leave its imprint on all its instances. Its contrary, the autonomous conception, would then, despite the pervasive support it enjoys, not be a conception of art at all; or rather only be one that necessarily misrepresents it.

We saw in Chapter 4 that the features of art that give rise to historicism are those deriving from identification of works of art by reference to their authors' minds, whether or not the specific features so referred to are in fact independently articulable by the artist himself. It is this that we depend on in thinking of art as something to be understood, or as assessable in terms of the artistry that it displays, or as evidencing particular expressive capacities; and one might easily enough be forgiven for thinking that these three things are so very much to the fore in our reflection on the subject that of necessity any art whatever will comply with at least one of them, if not with all. But such a claim would be too swift; for we cannot assume without argument that this putative necessity applies to art *simpliciter* rather than just to those types of art with which we are familiar. Of less familiar art it is not to be determined by fiat in advance that its works are, or will be, similar in this respect. Or so my opponent may say. And he could certainly be expected to emphasize his claim by drawing attention to the fact that in recent decades artists have striven harder than ever before to retreat from their work, and so have opted to leave more and more to the spectator; that they have insistently abdicated from their traditional role of mastery and control, and have willingly left more and more to chance. At the limit, he will say, we have already come to recognize works of aleatory art which we can identify without any historicity-enforcing reference to the mind; and here, if nowhere else, we are at liberty to adopt the autonomous conception.

But would it still be art? In making art as mindless as this has he not reduced it to nature, or, less question-beggingly, made it indistinguishable from what is not art at all? If so, my critic has of course made a mistake. But it is quite unclear that this accusation can be made good just by pointing out how closely art and nature might, on his view, come to approach each other. After all, maybe some natural objects are or could be works of art anyway, and we should not just rely on this not being so to make our point against him. Anyway, he may say, whatever the relation between art and nature may be, a distinction between art and non-art will be well enough preserved if we note that it pertains to art that it be intended for display and be normally produced by the artist for public view.[5] What is displayed may be natural or artificial, but what constitutes the object art is the way it is publicly used. How right this is, he may say, can be judged from the fact that only if we accept it do we begin to find interesting such remarks as de Goncourt's: 'A woman, when she is a masterpiece, is indeed the first of all works of art.'[6] Otherwise it and its like would simply be unintelligible.

However, this way of casting the distinction cannot be right. It is far too generous and lets in as art a host of things it would be mistaken to recognize as such: a show of precious stones at the Natural History Museum, for instance, or the flower arrangement on the sideboard, or even the carefully chosen view across the ha-ha through the embrasure of my study window. Against this objection the anti-historicist is not without defence. All he needs to say is that what flaws these cases is that the display for which they are chosen is not display under the concept *art*. They are simply presented as interesting and beautiful things to look at, and nothing more. If they were displayed under that concept, and if we did take ourselves to be invited to assimilate them to what we already understand as art, that is what they would be. As it is, they are not; and that is what makes the difference. Furthermore, it is open to him to say that when the required distinction is drawn in this way, because the resulting presentation of the natural world under the concept *art* introduces no specific way of taking the object that is determined through the artist's mind, the extent of historicism's rule remains a matter for dispute. After all, the various arguments in favour of its extension depend on the artist being presumed to make a specific contribution to his work, and that supposition is here deliberately avoided.

This last strategem may, however, look defective in appearing to salvage one important distinction at the expense of obscuring another. Just as we wish to distinguish between what is art and what is not, so too we want to keep apart that which is genuinely art from what is only fraudulently so. In speaking of what is only fraudulently art, I allude not to forgeries or fakes—objects that hold themselves out as particular works they are not, or as being by a hand other than that which is truly theirs—but to objects that are presented as art by way of practical joke or hoax, while not in fact being art at all. If, as is proposed, it were enough for something to be a genuine work of art to be held out as such, then what is held out as art while not being so would cease to be a possibility. Not the hoaxer, but his intended dupe would then have the last laugh; and if the objection is correct, what his hilarity would show would be that my opponent could not have drawn the other distinction, that between art and non-art, in the right way.

Yet this objection is not a good one. The only place at which the possibility of a hoax has genuinely to be preserved is where it has a point, and on the borderlands now under investigation it is unclear that it does. After all, what makes a hoax effective is its capacity to embarrass; either to embarrass the pretensions of the mediocre artist, or those of the would-be connoisseur. It does this by offering as work of skill and labour what has demonstrably required no effort and no talent for its production; and embarrassment arises with the demonstration. But when we consider those cases of minimal art that purportedly distinguish themselves from non-art simply by being presented under the concept *art*, we need not take ourselves to be thinking of objects of which the production or appreciation is assumed by the artist or the viewer to endow them with any notable aesthetic virtue. And where such endowment is disclaimed, there is nothing that a hoax could show up as fraudulent. Then it would have no point. Hence the impossibility of its perpetration in these narrowly delimited circumstances tells us nothing whatever about the correctness of extending the concept *art* into this twilight area by means of the recursive device. Once again, it will be felt, the universal pretensions of historicism have been foiled.

Not for long. For this last reflection gives rise to another that does ultimately thwart the anti-historicist's hopes. It is that in the last resort, where all specific elements of mind are excluded, the recursive machinery is operating idly. When we look back over the history of art's development, we see that wherever we have wanted to extend the concept beyond an area to which it had previously reached, we have in retrospect recognized something in the new forms that warranted their assimilation to the older paradigms. Our doing so was what was needed for the extension of the concept's scope to establish itself. However, when we now come to consider this extension being effected by presentation of an object under the concept *art*, and by nothing else, there is no available answer to the question: What licenses the application of the recursion? Then the proposed extension is arbitrary and without adequately rich point.

We may suppose the proponent of the extension trying to counter this argument in either of two ways. He may insist that there still is indeed a point, but one that has so far gone unrecognized; or he may say that the absence of point may be admitted but that it is harmless to his case. Neither reply is satisfactory. The latter, throw-away, option can be rejected very quickly. If there really is no point in making the assimilation, there is no point for anyone *as artist* to propose that it be made. More perspicuously, there is no point for the would-be artist to select an object for admiration *except* one that we interpret by reference to its function in his own psyche. What has to be accounted for, though, is not just the construction of some particular putative work of art or some particular man's motives in making what he does, but the stable existence of *a whole genre*. To account for that we must be able to appeal to something more than the vagaries and disturbances of individual psychology.

Following the other path, let us suppose that a point is claimed for the assimilation. It will be one that preserves the distinction between art and non-art, and at the same time satisfies the demand that the motivation for the production of the work be suitably public. Now the only thing I can imagine anyone offering as meeting these two requirements is something whose point is located in features of the chosen objects which, unless displayed within the context of art, would all too easily escape us. The 'artist' will thus see himself as drawing attention to their worth by presenting them as art where otherwise we should ignore them. As a result the motivation that drives him is suitably non-private and the distinction between art and non-art remains one with a difference because it is grounded in the valuable aesthetic features of the object chosen. But this notwithstanding, the appearance of securing everything he wants in this way is just illusion, and because it is, the motivation that is purportedly satisfied is itself ultimately thwarted

What makes it an illusion is the assumption that is surreptitiously imported that the natural objects selected for display as art should receive the public's attention on the basis of which they are offered, failing which they will not count as properly viewed and appreciated and not satisfy the supposed point of the exercise. This assumption cannot be given up. For if it is, there remains no more community between artist and spectator than that they agree to scan selected objects for features of interest about which they might legitimately differ. In that case no more would be achieved by displaying the objects under the concept art than is done by the man who sets out his curios upon the what-not. This challenge to the reality of point in the residual use of the recursive device can only be met by effecting the required publicity of what the artist does through letting him determine which *particular* features of the objects underlie their proper appreciation. But in doing this he holds up the object to us *as something to be understood*; and again imports his mentality into the work in a quite specific way. Thereby he immediately hands it over to the demands of historicism. True, his motivation is coherent, and he does retain the desired distinction between what is art and what is not; but only in a way that goes against the tenor of the thesis that his case is meant to support. What results, I think, is a pleasingly determinate reading of an observation of Romain Rolland's about the artist: 'pour répandre le soleil sur les autres, il faut l'avoir d'abord en soi.'[7]

My conclusion now is further-reaching than it could be before. It is no longer simply that we have to view art through the historicist conception if we are to use time's test in criticism. Art, I now say, is of its essence so viewed. This being so it is not open to anyone to cut down the ambit of the test by saying that it will at best apply only to that segment of art that is historically taken. For *pace* Valéry *et alii*, there neither is nor could be other segments, waiting so to speak to usurp the rightful king. So if the place of the test in art theory is genuinely to be minimized, that result must be achieved in some other way.

II

The Scope of Aggression

Setting aside attacks on historicism, there are two other fronts on which the critical inferences may be brought under pressure; directly, by way of strong and systematic counter-examples to a move from survival to stature other than of a kind discussed and set aside in Chapter 11; or obliquely, by way of attack on the converse relation. In this section and the next I shall concentrate on the latter approach.

Up to now I have disclaimed concern with inferences running in the direction from stature to survival. Since no one has any concern for survival as an end in itself, they could scarcely have any practical utility for criticism. But supposing that we have succeeded in establishing the legitimacy of the move the othe way round, where there are no special reasons not to do so it should be reasonable to expect that great art will hold public attention over time. Consequently, if this expectation were to be regularly frustrated we might believe the proffered defeasible support for time's test to be of only restricted application—restricted, that is, to just those kinds or art on the centrality of which the preceding argument has been erected, and not further extendible. So, by demonstrating the possibility of detaching ourselves from these traditional kinds of art, an opponent could unsettle our willingness to affirm the inferences' unfettered use. That would naturally reflect on the over-all place they hold in art theory. So it might be argued; and argued strongly by one who thought he could see a real prospect of this kind of breakdown occurring. Against such a person my own strategy must be either to dispute the plausibility of the cases he adduces to support his contention or to deny their significance. Of these, two in particular deserve some detailed comment.

The first is provided by art that is of its nature only short-lived and therefore apparently incapable of survival. History is replete with examples. One thinks of firework displays or of agonistic combat, of musical improvisation, or of extempore dance, and more recently of the art of Happening—all of which, at one time or another, have been thought of as fully fledged art. Moreover, all of them yield non-repeatable, non-surviving particular works quite unlike such universals as the musical set piece, the choreographed dance, or even the floral festival float. While members of the last group are approached through their instances or performances, the former are the works themselves, 'as individual as a motor accident', so one writer puts it,[8] needing no intermediary for their appreciation, and lasting no longer than their own performance.

As things are, only the rarest of such works approximate to greatness. In general they are not considerable and belong only to arts that are indisputably minor, to arts, that is, where stature is not easily achieved—if achievable at all. But this thought should not deter us from wondering whether such short-lived art might not provide examples of great art that does not survive, since the fact that we rarely find stature in these genres is unconnected with the short span of life of their instances, but depends on something else. So we cannot say in advance that the future may not turn some up. Nor, secondly, is there any patent absurdity in supposing that such genres might one day come to supplant those other kinds of art with which we are more familiar from the centre of our consciousness. Should that befall, then, with the passage of time, we could find the converse relation—that from stature to survival—holding with less and less reliability; and confidence in the obverse would then be correspondingly diminished.

However, the case is far from straightforward. Even when stress is laid on the advent since the late fifties of new kinds of would-be art, only with the help of a false assumption could they be relied on to make a breach in my most ambitious claim. This assumption is that the shortness of their life span in the individual case is properly connectable with the failure of such works to survive. But right at the start of Chapter 1 I was at pains to deny this. What I there asserted was that as long as it is possible to preserve a record of art in the appropriate medium, there will be no contradiction in speaking of its survival even though the work in question is no longer extant. Only by neglecting this possibility has it been made to sound plausible in the last couple of paragraphs that essentially short-lived art could ever come to challenge the over-all thesis that is here maintained. And this neglected possibility is surely one we should expect to be actual; for if we are to suppose that there may be great instances of novel kinds of short-lived art, we should have every reason to think that some survival-effecting record of their occurrence would be kept. True enough, in the past there have been technical obstacles to this being done. The Ruggieri brothers' *feux d'artifice* for the Peace of Aix in 1748 and those of the Crystal Palace shows of the late 1860s are lost to us for this very reason; and it was only by good fortune that the phonograph was invented in time to preserve some of the greatest jazz. But of course it is not with the past that we are now concerned; it is with the future. And for it the technical obstacles are already overcome.

This thought does not, however, fully rebut this kind of counter-example. What it does is to show how much more specific the case must be made before it can be successful; and against all seeming probability there is certainly one way in which such specificity may be achieved. It is notable that most genres of art that enforce short span of life upon their instances connect it only contingently with considerations about the way in which their quality is assessed. In matters of evaluation, the fact that the work itself ceases to exist as its materials are spent is generally neither here nor there. Maybe this is less true of the bullfight or the gladiatorial combat than of most other sorts of entertainment, but even there events might not strike the *aficionado* so very differently if bull and torero were each regularly blessed with more lives than one. By contrast, there is at least one specific sort of modern art where matters are very different, namely, that kind called 'auto-destructive' and exemplified most notably by Tinguely's *explosifs* and, more wildly, in the Futurists' eyes at least, by large-scale wars.[9] Here whatever excellence the 'work' possesses is intimately connected with the destruction of its constiuent materials and with the particular way in which this destruction is achieved. This being so, the prospective recording through which it might survive could be thought to weaken our experience of it and make the record counter-effective, subverting whatever might be found particularly glorious about the case. Then it could be a condition of our experiencing such works properly that even their indirect survival should be resisted.[10]

However, once the example is concentrated to this degree we see immediately that it is unable to undermine the converse relation. For in this case it is for a very special reason that we expect that relation not to hold— the reason being that just set out. And, as I said before, where there is a special reason for the breakdown it can be contained. Yet it is only if the breakdown cannot be contained that it has any impressive power. In the case of these idiosyncratic, short-lived things we do not expect time's test to apply either, since that supposes what is here rigourously ruled out—namely that the antecedent of the relevant conditional (survival) should be satisfied. So however ready we may be here to acknowledge that there may be cases where the relations do not hold, that will not weaken the use we want to make of them elsewhere.

Nevertheless, in putting it like this I may have seemed to overlook my opponent's second hypothesis, the hypothesis that this short-lived art might at some future date come entirely to displace the rest from the centre of the cultural stage. Perhaps he will say that that is how the artist will ultimately escape the tyranny of the market, by making his work utterly unsaleable, or saleable only at a price that reflects the use-value that is consumed in the destruction that makes up its very point. And then, he wants to suggest, we can see how the theory of art might dispense altogether with time's test and not just abandon it over a narrowly restricted area.[11] The place it holds in art theory is therefore far less secure than I have asserted it to be. That, he will say, is all he wants to show.

I do not propose to argue that there is anything inconceivable about this supposition. Perhaps it is even a real and not just a logical possibility. However, that would still not be enough to carry the day, for what has to be shown is that in the envisaged circumstances the arts could still be taken seriously and might still have a significant and autonomous role to play in our culture. This is quite a different matter; and as the case has been described, it looks very much as though art lingers on only as a withered residue from the past. Its life has departed and all that is left is the sloughed off skin.

How should we be convinced that this last comment contains more than pious rhetoric? In part, I think, by noticing how underdescribed the imagined situation is. Once it is filled in, the prospect for defending its compatibility with a serious concern for art is slim indeed. For one thing, in adopting this futuristic tale we have committed ourselves to abandoning any deep and persisting interest in literature and music, for in these arts, notwithstanding Adorno's eulogy of Stockhausen (see this chapter, n. 10), there is, and can be, no analogue with the self-destructive work. Secondly, to make the case convincing we shall have to dispense with the element of magic I have relied on in assuming that, for unstated reasons, present attachment to traditional art might wane. Unless that process were fully and acceptably explained, its very occurrence, posited to set up the threatening example, would count heavily against the suggestion that our interest in art could remain a deep one even through this putative change in its objects.

Most serious of all, the salient point of the category of art that is imagined to bear the weight of the argument has had to be located in *destruction*. And I do not see how one could avoid thinking that the pleasure and satisfaction that this genre provides is either purely infantile, or if not infantile, at the very least untoward. In either case its potential for stature is unacceptably reduced, and once this is acknowledged it will be correspondingly difficult to make out a claim for the importance to us of such art.

We have seen before that art of stature takes to a limit something that both sustains the institution of art and satisfies one or more of the major demands we make of it. It sustains the institution by satisfying such demands. In the present case maybe the first of these two requirements can be met. But the

second cannot. As for the first, it is easy enough to see how the aggressive satisfaction of destruction might sustain the kind of art that embodies it; for we tend to think that the fulfilment of aggressive desire fuels that very desire. Attachment that fixes on what is destroyed and broken inhibits the introjection of whole objects and prepares the way for further aggression.[12]
So satisfaction founded in destructive art could well breed more of it. But by contrast such work, even if sustained, would not make a contribution to the satisfaction of those desires which I have argued in Chapter 5 give art its point. Whatever satisfaction is provided by the *explosif* and its like must, if art is to remain something that we prize, be a satisfaction that we can self-consciously embrace. But here there is no scope for that. So, in general, while art can certainly tame the aggressive instinct, if it set out to foster and encourage it we could not welcome it among us because to do so would be to welcome our own diminution; yet auto-destructive art can offer nothing else.

This important truth is nowhere better stated than in the extract from Adrian Stokes's *Painting and the Inner World* I cited in the last chapter. The negative feelings he pointed out figure prominently in art, but under the sign of co-ordination. 'Tragic art, to be so, must bear nobility.' Where we make great art of conflict, as we do in the tragic case, or out of the disjected and fragmented, what enables us to treat it as sustaining the institution is nothing like the vicious spiral of aggression, but its ability to bring these things together in healing unity and to give a home to the broken that we feel enjoys an ultimate serenity. But that is as far removed from the infantile and diminishing as could be. And this is what ensures that the attack on time's test from the side of non-reproducible, short-lived art must ultimately fail, even when the example is (omnipotently) filled out through the kind of thought-experiment just explored.

III

The Neo-Marxist Attack

A stronger and more familiar attack on the converse relation is ubiquitously encountered in a certain sort of neo-Marxist writing on aesthetics. What makes great art great is one thing—vulgarly, its relevance to the social situation of its time—but, so the line goes, this has no connection at all with its tendency to hold our attention at other times. Indeed, the correlation may even be a negative one, for survival of earlier art can testify to a reactionary attachment to obsolete values. Is it not evident that what is vital and relevant at one period may, at another, be quite dead? Once the myth of absolute value is unmasked, it will be plain that the relation does not hold. 'When Shakespeare's texts cease to make us think, when we get nothing out of them, they will cease to have value.'[13]

In justice to the classic authors of the tradition, to Marx himself, to Lenin and to Trotsky, it should be said that they at least had no time for this sort of argument. In an eventually deleted but much discussed passage from the 1857 draft of the *Grundrisse*, Marx acknowledges it to be a problem why we should still find enjoyment in Greek epic art, given that is sprang from a primitive form of social development; and while the precise way in which he thought to resolve the question was wildly wrong—by reference to our desire to hark back to childhood—the general form of his answer fits the pattern of my thesis well enough. The desire to return to childhood is something that Marx takes us all to find of urgency, and one that is capable of satisfaction through the arts. It is nice to think that there is no dissonance at all between this thought of his and the very un-Marxian Walter Pater's claim that in all great art resides something of humanity's soul.[14] Similar observations can be made of Trotsky's account of Dante's hold upon us and of Lenin's enthusiastic appreciation of Tolstoy.[15]

Later authors have discerned in such appeals to what is socially transcendent a sad inconsistency with the rest of orthodox Marxist theory and a deplorable manifestation of 'bourgeois subjectivism'.[16] What grounds the accusation is the thought that only unjustifiable special pleading could suppose the arts to escape the false consciousness that the exploitative base of a non-socialist economy forces onto the superstructure of society. It is, they think, an illusion to exclude art from the superstructure, and once its place there is acknowledged there is no temptation to think that the values it embodies are conditioned by other than temporally local factors.

To meet this argument I shall not discuss particular sociological accounts of the arts.[17] It should be enough to point out how unattractive are the assumptions that have to be accepted by anyone who is convinced that, even in broad outline, such an argument must hold. And this is best done by focusing on the mechanism by which it is supposed the artist's product is determined: a mechanism that either operates through crudely described economic considerations, or else works less visibly, through those pressures that form the artist's and his patron's over-all pattern of values.

The direct way in which the economic system might determine artistic output is through the market. The artist has to find his buyer, the writer to sell his books. True, in doing this each is freer than the wage slave; for no one forces him to produce at a word of command. Moreover, as things are today, the patron tends modestly to stand back from the work and not to interfere.[18] Nevertheless, the artist's choice of theme and his expressive range have to satisfy those whose economic power enables them to strengthen their domination over others by the possession and display of the art they buy. So the artist's output is quite directly formed through ideology.

It is hard to find this argument appealing. It relies too heavily on three premises that few will want to accept. First, it assumes that within the frame-work of what the buyer will accept, the artist has no expressive freedom to exploit. Then it presumes that the patron can only conceive of the art he commissions as serving indulgent self-gratification or as promoting his personal or public glory; and finally, it supposes that if the arts do not have some better end than this they must be frivolous, and open to all the moralistic objections that fall down upon the abused doctrine of art for art's sake. On these three premises it comes as no surprise that even the best of earlier art has a worth only for those whose local values it endorses, and that to one who stands at any distance from those preoccupations it can only speak by chance and by association. But lack of surprise here stands poles apart from conviction.

The first of these suppositions need not detain us. As an empirical claim it has no warrant, and a priori reflection points quite the other way. Whenever the patron specifies how he wants his canvas to be, he cannot so describe it that nothing is left to the artistic imagination in satisfying the commission. If there were truly nothing that the artist could add, then the patron himself would *be* the artist. But assuming that they are two and not one, the question must always arise, for the artist, of how to execute his task, and the 'how' is the locus of his expressive freedom. It can never be entirely abolished.

The second supposition has a life in aesthetics only because its appearance there is so unexpected as to pass without challenge—off on a holiday abroad, one might say, from a home in philosophical psychology where anyway it lives in disrepute. What is surmised is that the motivation the patron has for interesting himself in the arts, like his motivation for any other choice, could only be provided by the prospect of thereby satisfying some antecedent desire he has. Anything else strikes this theorist as incomprehensible. Among the other things he finds so is the idea that under capitalism a man might descend into the market not as a means to some further end he already has, but as giving him access to a good that is, and is seen as, being quite independent of any concern he has for status or dominance over others. Most people only have to have this pointed out to see the deficiency that is thus introduced into the argument. In the case of many Marxists, however, there is a peculiar difficulty in stepping aside from this quite general thought in its application to aesthetics. It is that as far as they are concerned—and this has certainly been true of those who dictate the place of the arts in communist states—it is indeed a proper end of art that it should function in the attainment of some dearly held, extraneous end, in particular the achievement and maintenance of a Utopian social order won through the efforts and the sufferings of the proletariat. But while art can of course be so used, that would not be its proper, internal, end. For if it were, its criteria of excellence would be governed by considerations of its propagandistic success. Yet propaganda that achieves success through artistic means relies on doing so by achieving what are represented as *artistic* standards—which shows the idea to be absurd.

What buttresses the retention of this view of art as a means to some end is the third assumption—that which presumes that if art is not so viewed it must be trivial. Few slogans have come in for more abuse than that of *l'art pour l'art*, and it is notable how rare it is for Marxist thinkers to try to give it a content that extends its scope much beyond the mindless inanities reviewed in the last section. However, once we are clear that there is no dichotomy between seeing art as a means to satisfying an external end and the adoption of the most trivial sort of aestheticism, and clear also that without embracing either extreme we can see the arts as autonomously enlarging vision and extending the power of feeling, the last hope for this crude form of aesthetic determinism must be abandoned. If there is a sociological account of art to be had that casts inferences from stature to survival in doubt, it must take a more sophisticated form.

Not surprisingly, there is a more subtle version to hand where both artist and patron are blinder to the forces that work on them than is assumed by this lumbering machinery. More realistically than before, it is now supposed that the values both share as members of the society from which they spring are the product of social forces of which it is difficult to be aware.[19] While both artist and amateur act as if they are free agents, in fact the art that is produced and sought, in a belief in its perennial value, will much more likely function in a non-socialist society to maintain oppressing inequalities and to force alienation upon its members. As before, the values it embodies are local. They have little power to extend beyond the moment.

Is this thought any more attractive than the cruder version just dismissed? The trouble with it is that we have no reason at all to think that there is any regular and sufficiently law-like connection between the forms of social life and the values espoused in its art. Yet this is what we would have to be assured of to be justified in thinking that such a form of social determinism were true.[20] Indeed there are strong grounds for thinking that such connections could not be had;[21] and if that were right the prospect would be even darker. Putting it at its strongest, we might say that certain forms of social life tend to favour certain interests and the appearance of certain themes in art. But this is as far as we could go. Yet to serve its purpose, the version of determinism to which appeal is here being made has to sustain a stronger claim. It has to say that what the artist makes he makes *because of* the social factors that impinge on his mind, and that the criteria of merit by which we judge his productions are intimately linked with the desires these forces promote. This, however, there is no reason to think is true. Even if certain values are favoured at certain times, that does not place any limit on what can be found of sustenance at those times; and when matters are cast in this less rigid form, everything that supports the supposedly temporary interest of particular works of art has disappeared.

Let us suppose that these various criticisms could be set aside. As Marx saw, the determinist still owes an explanation of what we find to be a fact—of the present experienced value of earlier art. Consistently with his thesis about the local interest of even the greatest art, he might say that the work's value is exhausted in its ability to bring satisfaction to those for whom it was conceived, and given that the interests of later times are usually different from the interests of art's intended audience, the work does *not* really survive—it just *appears* to do so as it is reinterpreted to fit new and anachronistic concerns. This is a view that enjoys persistent popularity with those professionally involved with the performing arts and one against which we should by now be well protected. Quite apart from the contempt it shows for proper interpretation, what goes wrong with it is the superb condescension it displays towards the audience of later date.[22] True, we do often 'update' the relics of the past. But all too frequently in doing so we merely indulge our laziness and ignorance. In no way do we honour men's capacity for understanding or do justice to their imaginative powers. When ignorance is permitted and actively encouraged to yield to knowledge, experience itself gives this easy, temporizing device the lie.

Alternatively, it is sometimes suggested, as for instance by Adorno and Eagleton, that art's value to the later viewer is seated in its capacity to show by its very silence the fault-lines in the society it represents.[23] This is what Eagleton has in mind in writing, obscurely, that 'ideology so produces and constructs the real as to cast the shadow of its absence over the perception of its presence',[24] and thus the greatest art is that which gives us the sharpest insight into the real nature of the society to whose values it gives expression. 'It is not that Jane Austen's fiction presents us merely with ideological delusion; on the contrary, it also offers us a contemporary version of history which is considerably more revealing than much historiography'.[25] What is crucial about this explanation is that the perceptions it depends on were very likely not perceptions that could have guided the writer in the construction of what she wrote. That knowledge is formulable only in terms of a theory (Marx's) of whose truth she was not even dimly aware. 'The real', says Eagleton, 'is by necessity empirically imperceptible, concealing itself in the phenomenal categories it offers spontaneously to inspection.'[26]

To us this cannot but be objectionable. For precisely what explains the value of earlier art is made unavailable (or potentially so, and that is enough) to the artist himself. While this is no obstacle to our finding the work of historical interest, we know now that it is not an explanation that makes the aesthetic appeal of the work of any importance in coming to understand it. That is regarded as somehow extraneous to the matter's heart. Instead, archaeology and literature are seen as one. Yet in truth they are two; and the value to us of the second is not to be accounted for in terms of the limited and different charms of the first.

Standing back from these arguments, what jumps to the eye is their extreme myopia—a myopia of a twofold nature. In the first place they are myopic in insisting on the social and the variable at the expense of the individual and the stable. But why, one wonders, should both not have their place? The reason is, I believe, because the Marxist has assumed it to be a consequence of abandoning an absolutist conception of value, while none the less retaining something he still can recognize as non-subjective.[27] But that inference is overhasty. We still abandon absolutism if we insist that the values we hold are fixed in relation to common and persisting human interests and needs. Without intellectual sacrifice we can allow that these often constant and general demands may find their satisfaction and fulfilment in many different social forms.[28]

Secondly, the view is myopic in presuming that the only way in which we could find art of moment would be if it offered us solutions or advice about our own pressing practical problems —all else being quietly dropped overboard. Witness Arnold Hauser, writing of the artist's deliberation whether to follow an existing style or to abandon inherited tradition, asserting that 'one is always faced by the same question: is the received style still serviceable as a guide to life in a changed world? Can it still impress, convince and spur to action? Is it still a suitable weapon in the struggle for life? Does it reveal what should be revealed and veil what should be veiled?'[29] But this kind of view entirely neglects the interest and support we find in seeing how the world appears from stand points that are different from our own and how other visions, other modes of feeling, and other ways of finding order than those which we adopt may all compel. In cultivating these interests we learn to see beyond our own horizons and come to share in the rest of humanity in the only way we can—by understanding and imagination. If the denial that this is a present concern of ours is taken as saying no more than that it is not an immediate practical concern, it may be true enough. Only we should not think that all the concerns we have are practical and pressing. Eloquent testimony to this, and a far more generous conception of relevance than sociological accounts of art can deliver—one eminently compliant with adherence to the critical inferences—is again provided by Adrian Stokes: 'It is remarkable surely that though cultural situations alter, no considerable achievement in art ceases to have relevance. The urgency of bringing together, of making one out of what is diverse, remains unique just because the material varies, yet continues to give echo, to make itself felt and thereby to encourage us, even in those instances where we have reason to deplore the emotional ingredients on display.'[30]

IV

A failure of the inferences when challenged directly would naturally be far more impressive than a failure of the converse relation, and from our inability to shake the latter nothing whatever follows about the chances of success by more direct means. The literature contains two attempts of this kind about which I have said nothing so far. To maintain my own contention it should by now be enough to show why both must fail.

Arguments from Veneration

Over the past two and a half centuries one worry that has regularly exercised critics has been the prospect of ossification over-taking the lively and direct appreciation of the writing and painting, music and sculpture that we meet. It is remarkable that in the *Preface to Shakespeare* itself, from which I set out at the start, and where Johnson so forthrightly sets out the claims of time's test, the spectre of unwarranted survival walks lively.

Antiquity, like every other quality that attracts the notice of mankind has undoubtedly votaries that reverence it, not from reason but from prejudice. Some seem to admire indiscriminately whatever has been long preserved, without considering that time has cooperated some-times with chance; all perhaps are more willing to honour past than present excellence; and the mind contemplates genius through the shades of age, as the eye surveys the sun through artificial opacity.[31]

Likewise, more than a hundred years later, in 'The Study of Poetry' Matthew Arnold comments on the fallacy in poetic judgement caused by an estimate he calls 'historic' and which attaches to what 'claims not study, but veneration'. In our own time lesser critics recur with regularity to the theme.

It would be silly to deny that ossification of response does sometimes occur. But unless the phenomenon is more perva-sive than either Johnson or Arnold take it to be, it presents little challenge. In the first place, and quite generally, having rep-resented the main inference with which I am concerned as defeasible, it would be quite proper to allow that on occa-sion the antecedent of the relevant conditionals (i.e. survival) could well enough be satisfied even though the consequent were not. More to the point is the fact that the survival as contem-plated under the condition of veneration is survival of the wrong sort. As we saw in Chapter 1 it was crucial that the survival which is of critical interest be rooted in considerations that are suitably aesthetic; and even when that idea is glossed as loosely as it was there— that is, as attention of a kind we need to rely on in the correct understanding, perception, and evaluation of art— it is plain that veneration-based survival is ruled out. The reason for this must be that the age of a work, that quality from which veneration is usually assumed to flow, is not something that could possibly lie within the artist's control.[32] Because of this it could have no place within his theory of his own activity, and since we have to use that theory in coming to understand what he does, in coming to interpret his work as it must be interpreted, mere age is excluded as a quality in which attention could properly take root.[33]

This granted, one may happily adopt Arnold's own specific for dealing with the halo that the established and respected author so easily acquires: 'If he is a dubious classic, let us sift him; if he is a false classic, let us explode him. But if he is a real classic, if his work belongs to the class of the very best, then the right thing is to feel and enjoy his work as deeply as ever we can and to appreciate the difference between it and all work which has not the same high character.'[34] Whatever reservations we harbour about Arnold's own 'touchstone' method of sifting, exploding, and appreciating, what he stresses here is undoubtedly correct. We have the ability to tell whether the classic holds its place merely on account of its constant presence among us or whether it does so for a better reason; and it is an ability we must exercise in deciding whether it is proper to draw any inferences from art's survival. So too must we judge that the place the established work has enjoyed in the past is one it has there held on a properly aesthetic footing. Otherwise the evidential power of continuity of appreciation will be weakened. But here too while it is an admitted possibility that we should make a mistake, if we do, that is something that is rarely beyond our wit to discover. Hence no theoretical difficulty is raised by allowing that the prospect of veneration touches on the issue of survival both in the present and in the past. In neither case is the challenge it poses crippling.

These matters would scarcely be worth mention were it not that in recent years the aura of veneration, which Johnson and Arnold both accurately describe, has been argued to be more closely connected with our appreciation of much traditional art than either of them supposed. This contention is made in one way by Walter Benjamin in *The Work of Art in the Age of its Technical Reproducibility* (1931), and in another by Roger Taylor's *Art, an Enemy of the People* (1979). If the almost a priori twist that these authors lend to the connection between established appreciation and veneration were correct, matters would be more serious than either Johnson or Arnold supposed, for then properly aesthetic survival would itself be a suspect idea, and the inferences we seek to base upon it quite empty. I should not leave this topic without making plain that this supposition deserves no credence.

On Benjamin's account what gives rise to veneration and provides the work with a falsifying air of mystery is not its age, but what he calls its authenticity. This he rapidly identifies with its spatio-temporal uniqueness and the property relations that the work thereby acquires. Thus literature and music are exempt from the danger but traditional painting and carved statuary are not. And the danger he perceives in fitting out that art with reverence is not simply that we then make our critical judgements askew, but that we transfer the veneration from the work to the possessor. Because non-spatio-temporally identified art cannot be uniquely possessed, it is exempt from the prospect of spreading corruption, while its physically unique counterparts are, by reason of their authenticity, sure prisoners of political reaction and easily manipulable tools of fascism.

Certainly it is a perverse use of art so to handle it that those should be oppressed by it who do not have the power to withstand the suggestions that are put to them in the display of the individual work by its owner. And it may indeed be true that some are so affected, either on account of their unfamiliarity with the cultural institutions of their society or for other reasons that make them unduly impressionable. Yet this is not to admit that what secures this possibility is the physical uniqueness of the art of certain kinds; nor is it to allow that such uniqueness guarantees this perversion. The untoward phenomenon ranges wider than Benjamin appears to think, and because it does his diagnosis of it can only be partial at best.

The thrust of Taylor's book is to relieve the idea of physical particularity of any special responsibility in the abuse of art. In contrast to Benjamin, the concept through which he argues *oppression* is exercised is not so much *uniqueness* or *authenticity* as that of *art* itself. And this thesis is put forward on the basis of considerations about the way in which our perception of popular music—in particular of jazz—is corrupted by our coming to think of it as art and thereby removed from the possession of those to whom it properly belongs. Here the oppression is effected without the mediation of the idea of property at all. This result is not so much to correct what Benjamin says, as to broaden the target of his critique in a way that my opponent cannot but find congenial. For once the threat of veneration is detached from considerations of antiquity or of physical particularity it is no longer restricted to some arts among others or to some of art's objects among others, but ranges absolutely everywhere. Consequently the very idea of aesthetic survival is itself at risk.

But while Taylor shows us how the thesis may be widened, the nature of his claim needs only to be accurately stated for us to see how it should be met. In the last paragraph I said that it was the concept of art that Taylor presents as being potentially corrupting. But what he should have said was that our view of art may be corrupted not by the concept *art*, but by a certain *conception* of it. It is not art as such that oppresses those who venerate it; rather it is a false *view* of art or a use to which it may be put that gives rise to the depressing effects that Taylor deprecates. Then the thesis he offers is less philosophical than sociological— that in our society to come to appreciate something as falling within the category of art is as a matter of fact unwittingly and almost inevitably to endow it with a corrupting reverence. And this claim is surely overstated.

First, the arts only attract abuse of the kind described if they are recognized by those who abuse them as having a value of their own. The oppressive way in which the conception of art functions is possible only if the objects falling under it genuinely have a worth. (If we try to deny this, we shall be owed an explanation of how the oppression can be successfully maintained.) And by the account of art that I have everywhere relied on, the only way in which this value could be something real is ultimately dependent on our having a correct perception of what embodies it. The deformation of art at which Taylor and Benjamin protest is therefore only genuinely possible on the assumption that a proper appreciation and perception of it lies at the centre of the culture. And if *this* is a reality, it is a reality from which even those who feel themselves oppressed or overawed are not in principle excluded. The right response of theory to the fact of oppression in art is thus not to say: let art be buried; it is, let art not be misunderstood.

That would be the right response to Taylor. But Benjamin might now well object that it is one that too glibly overlooks the force of property as it applies to those arts whose objects make particularly prized possessions. Before the power of property such a theoretical liberty as that just mentioned is surely no more than an illusion or a sham. To this it should be said that, in the hands of those who really do understand why particular works of art are beneficient, they are not oppressive tools at all. We need to recognize among collectors and connoisseurs a distinction between those who love their possessions and those who hate them. We need also to see that neither part of the field is empty, and that there is no reason to think that property is everywhere equally corrupting.

Secondly, it is worth remembering that as the finest particular works pass into public collections so they depart from the market. What once enters the National Gallery or the Louvre rarely leaves again. The particular force of property is then extinct. And that is a further point that tells against Benjamin's diagnosis. This, of course, is not to deny that art may be less easily at home in the museum than it is elsewhere. There even more than anywhere else the public is falsely encouraged to feel itself entering on hallowed land. In our day, museum and hospital are more like church than church itself, and this is something on which the official guardians of our culture often trade with deadening effect. But is this inevitably so? Surely not. To the extent that the individual comes to be aware that this is how he feels, it lies within his power to strip off the bandage that is tied around his eyes. As before, the fact that we can easily come to see the individual work as having a place in our esteem for reasons that are unsound does absolutely nothing to establish that we cannot get things right. Where ossification looms, whether for reasons connected with age, or property, or simply fear, we have the power to ward it off.

Lastly, as far as this putative extension of the theme that Johnson and Arnold introduce bears upon the workability of time's test, we must beware of being over-impressed by the appeal that Benjamin and Taylor make to the sad effects the oppressive conception of art has upon the people. For by 'the people' what is meant is the industrial proletariat. When we come to look in detail at particular examples of the test's application, we shall have to recall that the outcome can only be reliable to the extent that the work of which it speaks is well-embedded in the culture. In society as we know it such embedding has occurred for the most part outside the proletariat, whose members are for obvious reasons (however deplorable they may be) largely strangers to the arts. Whatever future our society manages to hold out for them, it will only be when they become better able to determine the embeddedness of fine art than they have been to date that their responses will play an important role in determining whether any of the future's art is judged to have survived the pressures that passing time will come to exert upon it.

V

The other direct challenge I propose to deal with is also one associated with writers of the Frankfurt school. In abstract form it is espoused by Theodor Adorno; more concretely, by their doyen, Max Horkheimer. In Adorno's work the greatest art, at least since the middle of the nineteenth century, is presented as that which takes a stand against the prevailing ideology, against the false consciousness of the world that capitalism produces, and against the resulting deformations that characterize men's personal interrelationships. Typically it achieves this through rejection of accepted forms and by turning its back on the received artistic tradition, received, Adorno thinks, in a way that allows that tradition to be identified with passive acquiescence in the going order. He further believes that where we find art surviving it will do so either because we find in it unchallenging and docile political assumptions with which we feel at ease, or else because we have imposed upon the more critical forms through which it speaks an order by which we defuse its negative force. In either case, the surviving work has no capacity to stand out against ideology. It persist only through its own corruption or through our connivance in its corruption.

That such a fate should be thought liable to overtake even greatly innovative and self-consciously critical art might surprise us until we recall Adorno's illegitimate conception of art as processlike. For in accordance with that view, the familiarity that survival of these works brings with it cocoons us from the impact with which they may once have resisted and stood firm against their time. Seen through historicist eyes, however, this argument does not work. When we understand and experience the innovative work as it demands we do not abandon the recognition of its novelty, and familiarity with it need not obscure the breach with tradition against the background of which the work allegedly achieves its negative thrust. If this is so, truly negative art—whatever that should be agreed to be—cannot be said a priori to be less capable of survival than is its supposedly affirmative counterpart. Schoenberg and Stravinsky, Adorno's paradigms of negativity and affirmation, stand in this regard on equal footing.

So the claim that persistence and stature live at odds has broken down. All that really follows is that survival is quite indifferent between them. But as long as the associations on which Adorno insists—between the negative and the admirable, and the affirmative and the corrupt—are allowed to pass unchallenged, the outcome for the thesis I have sought to advance remains bleak. If survival really is indifferent between negative and affirmative, and if the reputed associations to value and disvalue hold, then time's test would fail reliably to filter out the worse, and in consequence the inferences' appearance of utility would indeed be counterfeit. However, there is no good reason to accept Adorno's evaluative associations, not just because it is so easy to produce counter-examples, but because there is evidently no hope of finding a valid argument that might support them.

I envisage two ways, and two ways alone, in which a man might seek to establish such correlations. One lies in positing a connection between the *representation* of corrupt states and a consequential limitation on the stature of the works that undertake this task. Then, in addition, it would be surmised that representative art pursuing its goal through traditional forms chooses for its content the representation of corrupt state. However, Adorno does not proceed like this; and that is just as well. For everything that could be wrong about this thought is wrong. It is at odds with history; it is false that the representation of the untoward must itself be untoward; and false also that the choice of traditional forms determines the content that is represented within them in the way supposed. This tack is one that must be abandoned straight away.

Alternatively, and not quite so obviously falsely, it might be said that traditional forms are expressively, not representationally, corrupt; and that we cannot in the long run repeatedly take within ourselves what is expressive of the bad and not succumb to corruption itself. The second of these two claims I shall leave alone. It is not one from which I would dissent—though in a minute we shall see that it is not one which Adorno could consistently endorse. Even so the argument still does not go through, for its other half, that which correlates the adoption of and attachment to traditional forms with what is expressive of the bad, is quite unwarranted. Expectation indeed leads quite the other way.

What a work of art expresses, it expresses by reliance on a correspondence that the artist and his audience find peculiarly natural between expressive form and what it is that form is found expressive of. This association is one that expression depends on in order even to get off the ground. Now, where traditional forms have succeeded in establishing themselves and are also recognized as being traditional, they will have established their place in our minds by offering within them things to which we have become affectively attached; and quite regularly we find this attachment extending beyond the content of these forms—where we can identify a content—to the form itself that makes the attachment possible. So traditional forms are particularly ill-suited as expressive vehicles of states we flee, and particularly ill-suited to express the subversion of integrity that Adorno thinks they do express. Since a general argument to support the evaluative association that he relies on depends on some version of one or other of these arguments—and since they both must fail—the correlation is not one we should adopt.

Furthermore, in an entirely *ad hominem* way let us note that there is a very special reason why even Adorno should not welcome the less implausible of these two arguments. Earlier on in the chapter I said that he is one of those thinkers who believe the ideal of human wholeness in not one that the artist today can honestly accept. As he prescriptively puts it, it is the task of modern art not to bring serenity, but to introduce chaos where order reigns. 'Aufgabe der Kunst heute ist es, Chaos in die Ordnung zu bringen.'[35] Lest we lose our soul in the amenities that socially corrupt wholeness holds out, we have in

music, painting, and literature to face a view of the world that is
expressed through the artistic equivalent of Raphael de Valentin's microscopic lorgnon—a view that is fragmented and
broken, and which strips the world of all familiar enchant-
ment.[36] If this harsh doctrine is applied within the framework of
the second argument, I do not see how to avoid the inference
that we should welcome living with the consequences of taking
within us what is expressively broken and chaotic—the consequence that we accept disorder within us. Now, whatever
attitude Adorno takes to the corrupting force of acquiescence in
the order that present-day social forms hold out, he certainly
does not view personal disorder as something to be put in its
stead. Chaos within the self is a danger he knows we must
withstand. Since we could not admit chaos into art if that was
where it led, he is further prohibited from making out the
evaluative correlations that he wants. For if it were true that the
finest art did bring chaos within the self, the institution of art is
not one that we should desire to uphold.

A less theoretically encumbered and initially more plausible
version of the same dismal pessimism is found in Horkheimer's
'Art and Mass Culture':

The opposition of individual and society, and of private and social
existence, which gave seriousness to the pastime of art, has become
obsolete. The so-called entertainments, which have taken over the
heritage of art, are today nothing but popular tonics, like swimming
or football. Popularity no longer has anything to do with the specific
content or the truth of artistic productions. In the democratic countries, the final decision no longer rests with the educated but with the
amusement industry. Popularity consists of the unrestricted accommodation of the people to what the amusement industry thinks they
like. For the totalitarian countries, the final decision rests with the
managers of direct and indirect propaganda which is by its nature
indifferent to truth.[37]

Obviously there is something true in this, as well as a large dose
of unjustified contempt for the supposition of a fruitful mass
culture. My concern, though, is not for the *present* warrant for
these remarks; it is for the idea they suggest that we may here
have identified forces which could be envisaged so to develop *in
future* as to generate art of longevity which is none the less
damagingly impoverished, and hence to constitute a genuinely

forceful counter-example to my main contention. But I doubt whether this really does lie within its power.

One objection not to pursue against the idea is that under such a regime, where culture is dominated by show-business or by propaganda, we could not be speaking of art at all, but only of a surrogate. People are inclined to say as much for two different, though equally bad, reasons. The first—of which we see an instance in the first passage of Stokes' *Painting and the Inner World* quoted above—is that bad art is not art at all. And that there is no reason to accept. Then, too, it is sometimes said that because art is of necessity autonomous, it could not coherently be used as a means to the satisfaction of other goals. So its use as mere entertainment or as propaganda subverts its nature and makes it art no more. But this argument rests on a conflation of internal function and external purpose. Just as the internal function of a chair as a seat in no way protects it against being used in extremity for firewood, so a painting's artistic function (of the kind described in Chapter 5) cannot safeguard it against acquiring a propaganda use.

A better, though by no means compelling, objection to the mooted development of Horkheimer's thought is to point out how inimical to the ends of either the entertainment industry or propaganda it would be that the art they commission should survive. In the former case, it is important for the industry's profit and for its long-term future that its customers should feel a need for new delights. So if no measure of obsolescence were built into its products the industry's own interests would be ill-served. And if we are also to assume that the artistic quality of the examples in view is no more than mediocre, then the supposed longevity the case relies on is doubly jeopardized.

As for propaganda, the same is true, if for a different reason. It is that propaganda has to fit itself to a world of unstable political exigencies. If the art it turns to its own purposes has such a hold on us as to become deeply entrenched in our culture, the assumptions and beliefs it encourages risk becoming dangerously fixed—dangerously, because they would be unamenable to future and unforeseeable political needs. One important truth about propaganda must be that the attitudes it cultivates should themselves be controllable when need arises;

so again the supposition of long-lived propaganda art would unfit it for the very purpose it is envisaged to meet.

It might seem to be another and further-reaching reason not to fear the prospect that Horkheimer holds out that even if one or other of these two forces should, against all expectation, give rise to long-lived art of insignificant worth, that art would not be central in the culture, but live far out on the periphery. In terms of the argument at stake, it would then be insufficiently well-entrenched. At least as Horkheimer himself talks, that is how it looks. For on his view, it is plain that the arts of entertainment and propaganda exist against a dominating background of higher culture that embodies values that mass art does not admit. But as it stands this objection results at best from a reflection of how things are, or how Horkheimer saw them at the beginning of the 'forties. It does nothing to allay the fear that in times to come we may not enjoy such assurance. Why, it will be asked, should what lies on the periphery and what lies at the centre not come one day to change their places— slowly and by degrees maybe, but in the end with total revolution? Or if matters cannot be taken as far as this, why should we think that the centre–periphery model of the culture has to hold at all? Might the time not come when we should instead think of there being independent streams that, like the legendary Alpheus and Arethusa, flow side by side without any commingling of their waters? In either case resistance to developed pessimism would not be fully justified, and in either case the application to the arts of old established critical practice would be unwarranted. Can we really be so sure that these suppositions are empty?

These challenges can both be met. For once again we have not to show that what they propose is an impossibility— to ask that would be too much— but to make out that if these changes come about we could not take the art that is produced under their regime as anything to care about. And if our interest in the arts is itself a trivial interest, it could not matter for our present understanding of our subject that the critical practices on which we rely should come to fail us.

The supposition that what lies on the periphery of our culture and what is sited at the centre might change place is one that has often been described, and not only as a fate that might befall the arts. In one of his sour diatribes against academic philosophy, Schopenhauer instructively depicts a parallel occurrence where.

there now result those productions as deplorable as they are numerous, wherein commonplace minds, and indeed such as are not even
commonplace, deal with those problems on whose solutions the
greatest efforts of the rarest minds equipped with extraordinary
abilities, have been directed for thousands of years ... The real
philosophers, the instructors of hundreds and even thousands of years
are left unread as being obsolete and refuted, but their works solemnly
wait in silence on the shelves of bookcases for those who desire to read
them.[38]

What this passage strikingly brings out is that when centre and periphery change places the value of the peripheral as it moves to the centre remains the same. Its worth changes not at all. And for present purposes—for those of the counter-example—we can not assume otherwise, since if we did, the art that by this process becomes well-embedded would not be clearly insignificant. But if such art is thought to hold its place while none the less being of minimal significance, the very fact that it continues to hold its place speaks for the triviality of the interest with which it is regarded. To a more demanding interest it would wilt, yielding precisely to those pressures of time with which I have been so concerned. For the corrupted interest, those aims of art that I have represented as so central to it are not in play. It is then seen as something that merely subserves amusement. In that case even if we recognize that time's test may not apply, we should not have abandoned it while retaining a serious interest in art itself.

The other alternative is no more inviting. A pluralistic conception of the artistic culture we live in, where each stream is isolated from the others, supposes that the concerns around which the separate channels are formed are independent of one another. Now I dare say that this is at least a logical possibility. But it is not a possibility that is consistent with any of our deep-seated, human preoccupations having their place in the different streams. For if it were, the different prospects of handling them that each offered would extend their appeal to those of inquiring mind far beyond the particular channels in which culture's discrete streams were now thought of as flowing. Once again, the very thing on which we depend to make our occupation with art a serious one is missing: the expression that is gives of our common humanity. The consequence is just what it was before: the abandonment of the centre–periphery model could indeed lead to breakdown of time's test; but then it is not a model of our society in which a developed institution of art would have much part to play.

VI

Picking our way over these stony tracks we see that the place the test holds in the theory of art is one from which it could be dislodged only with the greatest difficulty. The inferences are bound to be available when we care sufficiently about their subject-matter to want to use them. But it would be ill-advised of me to end without a note of warning. The thesis I have upheld is not one that either does, or is intended to, license every plausible-seeming application of time's test. I have repeatedly stressed how hard it may be to be sure that the premiss from which it sets out is truly fulfilled. We need to be confident of the interpretation under which we seek to apply it; we need to be similarly confident in the correctness of the interpretation under which the tested works come down to us; and we need to be confident that our judgement concerning their embeddedness is not badly wrong. These are daunting requirements. When we face them we may be in some measure reassured to find one of the most distinguished art-historians of our time writing that

the answer of common sense is that we can understand some works of art better, some worse and some only after a lot of work. That we can improve our understanding by trying to restore the context, cultural, artistic and psychological, in which any given work sprang to life, but that we must resign ourselves to a certain residue of ignorance. In art, as in life, on certain elemental levels men of different civilisations have understood each other even though they were ignorant of each other's language. On others only an acute awareness of the context in which an action stands may prevent misunderstanding.[39]

This, observes the writer, is a philosophy that is commonplace.

Notes

Introduction

1. Proponents of the practice other than Johnson have been Longinus (*On the Sublime*), Horace (*Ars Poetica*), Lord Kames (*Elements of Criticism*, esp. Ch. xxv), Hume (*Essay on the Standard of Taste*), Burke (*Essay on the Sublime and the Beautiful*), Pope (*Essay on Criticism*), and Joseph Warton (*Essay on the Writings and Genius of Pope*). See aslo R. Hurd (*Discourse on Poetical Imitation* (1751)), *Wordsworth's Literary Criticism*, ed. N. C. Smith (London, 1905), 194, 200–1, and Wordsworth's letter to C. North in 1802. Less enthusiastic have been Novalis, E. Young (*Conjectures on Original Composition* (1759)), J. Moir (*Gleanings* (1785)), and Shaw (Preface to *Plays for Puritans* (1900)). More recent opponents have been J. Ortega y Gasset, A. Malraux, P. Valéry, W. Benjamin, and T. Adorno in works discussed in Chapter 12.
2. N. Goodman, 'Merit as Means' in *Art and Philosophy*, ed. S. Hook (New York, 1968), 57.

Chapter One

1. M. Rostovtzeff, *Rome* (New York, 1960), 289.
2. As is proposed by R. A. Wollheim in *Art and Its Objects* (New York, 1968), §§ 60–1. The greatest difficulty would be to free the recursive account from any particular base, for we would not want to say that in the absence of those basal exemplars art could not have arisen.
3. E. Auerbach, *Mimesis* (New York, 1953), 174.
4. A. Schönberg, *Berliner Tagebuch* (Berlin, 1975).
5. Autographic and allographic art may here be treated on a par. We only need to remember that whereas standardly the direct object of our attention in the former case is the material object the constitutes the work, in allographic art our attention is given to the work via attention given to a range of other things (a series of performances, or readings, etc.). The formulation can remain the same in either case, only the ways in which it is satisfied will differ from art to art.
6. Hume, 'Of the Rise and Progress of the Arts and Sciences,' in *Essays Literary, Political and Moral*, (George Routledge, London, n.d.), 63.
7. Cit. E. Wind, *Art and Anarchy* (London, 1963), 86.
8. See n. 5 above.

Chapter Two

1. See e.g. J. Hirsch, *Der Genesis des Ruhms* (Leipzig, 1914), 239–47, or I. A. Richards, *Principles of Literary Criticism* (London, 1931), Ch. xxix, or O. K. Werkmeister, 'Marx on Ideology and Art', *New Literary History* (1973), 510–19: 'Marx, who ascribed the continuing fascination of Greek art beyond the period of its origin to its intrinsic significance, does not seem to have reflected on the possibility that it might be this later fascination alone which accounts for the exceptional appearance of an art which transcends its historical conditions from the very start'.
2. *Architectural Review*, Dec. 1968.
3. See P. Lavedan, *French Architecture* (Harmondsworth, 1944), 150.
4. M. Podro, *Times Literary Supplement*, 27 Feb. 1976.
5. The best-known opponents of progress in the arts are perhaps Hazlitt, 'On Why

the Arts do not Progress' (1814); the Nazarenes, the Pre-Raphaelites, and A. Riegl (replacing *Können* by *Kunstwollen*); and Croceans who stress the uniqueness of each work of art. Proponents of progress have been Pliny the Younger, Vasari, Burke, and Shaw.

6. Vasari, *Lives of the Painters, Sculptors and Architects*, Everyman edn. (London, 1963), II, 151.

7. See Cennino Cennini, *Il libro dell'arte*, ed. D. W. Thompson jun. (New Haven, 1933).

8. Burke, *Of the Origin of our Ideas of the Beautiful and the Sublime* (London, 1911), 81.

9. Pliny, *Natural History*, XXXV, Loeb edn. 65, 66.

10. Vasari, I, 203.

11. Unforgettable not because of the image conjured up of some classical Miss Magna Graecia contest, but because of the story's importance in the development of Renaissance and post-Renaissance art theory. See E. Panofsky, *Idea* (New York, 1968), esp. Ch. 2.

12. Pliny, XXXV, 64.

13. A. Riegl, *Die Historische Grammatik der Bildenden Künste* (Graz, 1966), 216.

14. Lord Kames, *Elements of Criticism* 11th edn. (London, 1839), 450. He continues without a blush: 'We are so constituted as to conceive this common nature to be not only invariable but also perfect or right; and consequently that individuals ought to be made to conform to it.'

15. Hume, *Essays Literary Political and Moral*, ed. cit., 138.

16. Johnson, *Preface to Shakespeare*, in *Selected Writings*, Penguin edn. (Harmondsworth, 1968), 261.

17. Among these other difficulties would be that the suggestion would not exclude a thing's being both a large and a small F, or a beautiful and an ugly one; nor would it know how to resist the suggestion that all men are beautiful or all mountains sublime. The natural suggestion that it is comparison with *most* possible members of the class that settles the issue could not help, for when we are concerned with possibles, how are judgements of most to be understood, let alone made?

18. F. N. Sibley, 'Objectivity in Aesthetics', *Aristotelian Society, Supplementary Volume* (1968), esp. 49–51.

Chapter Three

1. T. S. Eliot, 'Tradition and the Individual Talent' (1919), in *Selected Essay*, (London, 1951), 15.

2. See e.g. R. Wellek and A. Warren, *Theory of Literature* (Harmondsworth, 1963), esp. Ch. 18, G. Boas, *A Primer for Critics* (Baltimore, 1937) and *Wingless Pegasus* (Baltimore, 1950), Dame Helen Gardner, 'The Waste Land 1922–1972' (pamphlet, Manchester, 1972). The same view is well established in Continental thought too. See for example the works of P. Valéry, J. Ortega y Gasset, W. Benjamin, and T. Adorno discussed in Chapter 12.

3. See R. Scruton, *Art and Imagination* (London, 1974), esp. 109–10. For a contrary view compare A. Fowler: 'Let us admit at once that the fullness and spontaneity of the original are inaccessible', *New Literary History*, VIII (1975), 48; or J. Dewey, *Art as Experience* (New York, 1958), 109.

4. See D. Davidson: 'In our need to make him make sense, we will try for a theory that finds him consistent, a believer of truths, and a lover of the good (all by our lights, it goes without saying)', 'Mental Events', in *Experience and Theory*, eds. L. Foster and J. Swanson (London, 1970), 97. Again: 'Since charity is not an option but a condition of having a workable theory it is meaningless to suggest that we might fall into massive error by endorsing it', 'The Very Idea of a Conceptual Scheme', *American Philosophical Association, Presidential Address, 1973*.

5. Of course this does not mean that there are no undecidable cases and genuine uncertainties. But what we are looking for is an argument to show that such distortions are theortically necessary, and uncertainties do nothing to establish that.

6. These arguments are suggested by passages in R. A. Wollheim's *Art and its Objects*, esp. §§ 38, 39, 52. Wollheim however does not endorse the autonomous conception I am here using them to support, as is plain from his 'Are the Criteria of Identity that hold for a Work of Art in the Different Arts Aesthetically Relevant?' *Ratio*, 20, (1978), 29–48.

7. Hume, ed. cit. 146.

8. Wollheim, *Art and Its Objects*, § 38.

9. Cit. *Times Literary Supplement*, 12 Dec. 1975.

10. That Eliot himself would acknowledge this freedom is plain from remarks he makes in his 1945 essay, 'The Social Function of Poetry'. He writes: 'What Lucretius and Dante teach you, in fact, is *what it feels like* to hold certain beliefs; what Virgil teaches you is to feel yourself inside the agrarian life.' The feelings of which he talks are ours, yet they are not natural to us; they are evoked in us through the poets' and our own exercise of free imagination.

11. Keats, *Lamia*, II, 227–30.

12. See Nietzsche, *The Birth of Tragedy*, xii; Burckhardt, *Griechische Kulturgeschichte* (1900), 251–60; Wind, fn. 92. This old canard is well exposed by C. Brooks's 'The Poet as Organism', *English Institute Annual* (1940).

13. Wind, 66.

14. Eliot himself remarks 'Some can absorb knowledge, the more tardy must sweat for it', and we must beware of letting the undeniable fact that sometimes knowledge is inaccessible become a general excuse for idleness.

15. M. Shapiro, 'On Perfection, Coherence and Unity of Form', in *Art and Philosophy*, ed. S. Hook; R. Wellek and A. Warren, loc. cit.; S. C. Pepper, *The Basis of Criticism* (1948); G. Boas, *Wingless Pegasus*, Ch. III; N. Hartmann, *Aesthetik* (Berlin, 1953), Ch. 42, 467–70.

16. Shapiro, 6.

17. Stendhal, *De l'amour*, I. vi 'De la naissance de l'amour'.

18. There is of course no objection to its being *difficult*, but that supposition is quite compatible with historicism.

19. It could be rescued from vacuity only if we saw the work of art as a natural kind of thing like a vegetable or a fruit whose point of ripeness can be clearly described. Many of the metaphors used in talking about the arts under the thesis of autonomy are indeed vegetable metaphors, but rarely do their users see that they are only metaphors.

20. Wellek and Warren, 155–6.

21. Pepper, 68.

22. G. Boas, 'The *Mona Lisa* in the History of Taste', *Journal of the History of Ideas* (1940). Cf. Hartmann, 468.

23. Boas, 'The *Mona Lisa*'.

Chapter Four

1. A deeper question is how contemporaries could rationally have preferred one reading to another. And how does their system of choice *not* show up in statement of the canon?

2. Sir Walter Scott, 'Essay on the Drama' (1819), *The Prose Works* (Edinburgh and London, 1834–6), vi, 310.

3. Cf. Kant, *Critique of Judgement*, § 43 (Frans. J. H. Bernard, New York, 1951): 'It is not inexpedient to recall that in all free art there is yet requisite something

compulsory or, as it is called, mechanism—without which it would have no body and would evaporate altogether . . . It is not inexpedient to recall this for many modern educators believe that the best way to produce a free art is to remove it from all constraints, and thus to change it from work into mere play.'

4. Wollheim, 'Are the Criteria' . . . Discussing the same issue A. Harrison instances Capability Brown's landscapes, *Making and Thinking* (Hassocks, 1978), 111.

5. Vasari, 'Lionardo da Vinci', ed. cit., II, 164.

6. The restoration of the West Window at Chartres provides an instructive example. *The Times'* report of 20 Apr. 1976 runs: 'The peculiar brilliance of the blues in the mediaeval stained glass of Chartres Cathedral was in fact due to the accretions of the ages, restorers have discovered. The mediaeval glass suffers from a kind of disease such as that affecting old stone. But in addition, the blues at Chartres have, for a chemical reason not yet established, resisted better than the reds, greens, purples and yellows. The specialists at the research laboratory have, in the past year, first cleaned the windows and then applied a protective layer of a translucent synthetic resin to each piece of glass. Now, the restorers say, what one sees of the "Stem of Jesse" corresponds approximately to its creators' intent. The variety of colours inevitably lessens the impact of the blue which itself has also subtly altered. The restoration has upset two contemporary French painters who use glass themselves, Jean Bazaine and Alfred Manessier. "The dispute runs deep" the chief architect responsible for Chartres said, "because abstract painters like Bazaine and Manessier carry with them a vision of the Chartres windows which corresponds to their own personal aesthetic. But the men of the Twelfth century would have been equally shocked by the windows as they were before the cleaning."'

7. e.g. A. Furtwangler, 'The Venus de Milo' in *Masterpieces of Greek Sculpture*, II, (London, 1895).

8. When it comes to the practical issue of restoration this may be the better plan. For as Wind points out (75–6) we are all too prone to impose *our* theories onto *their* works. Admission of the work's physical mortality can be the best policy.

9. Cf. Rolland, *Jean Christophe* (29th ed., Paris, n.d.), IV, 52: 'Le cas est fréquent de braves gens, incapable d'aimer une œuvre neuve, qui l'aiment sincèrement quand elle a vingt ans de date. La vie nouvelle a une odeur trop forte pour leur tête débile. Il faut que l'odeur s'évapore au souffle du temps. L' œuvre d'art ne commence à leur être intelligible que quand elle est recouverte de la crasse des ans.'

10. For a musical case see R. Scruton's discussion of a passage in Beethoven's *Diabelli Variations*, op. 135. (Op. cit. 178–9).

11. See Q. Skinner, 'Hermeneutics and the Role of History', *New Literary History*, 7 (1975).

12. And only in this case. I am concerned here with non-exploitable indeterminacy in the work, not with indeterminacy between theories that seek to understand it.

13. See K. L. Walton, 'Categories of Art', *Philosophical Review*, 79 (1970), on this point. Croceans, impressed by works of art's uniqueness, would of course contest this, but wrongly.

14. Gautier, *Émaux et Camées*, 'L'art'.

15. Hegel, *Werke*, (*Jubiläumsausgabe* (Stuttgart, 1953)) XIII, 36–7, my translation.

16. A. W. Schlegel, 'Uber den Geist ächter Kritik' (1805), *Werke* (Leipzig, 1846) V, 5.

17. J. Shearman, *Mannerism* (Harmondsworth, 1967), 15.

Chapter Five

1. S. N. Hampshire, *Thought and Action* (London, 1959), 246.

2. Witness for example the aesthetics of the French Symbolists. See A. G. Lehman, *The Symbolist Aesthetic in France 1885–1895* (Oxford, 1950) Ch. 3. The immediate object of their contempt was Taine, but Taine himself wrote firmly in this sup-

posedly Aristotelian tradition. The funniest comment on the subject is Hegel's: 'By mere imitation art cannot stand in competition with Nature and if it tries it looks like a worm attempting to crawl after an elephant.' (73.)

3. I stress that this is a non-solipsistic reading. It purposely ignores *Tractatus*, 5.641: 'The world is my world,' and 5.621: 'The world and life are one.' My comments are offered not as criticisms of the *Tractatus* itself but of a conception of the world that one reading of that work invites.

4. Cf. Homer, *Iliad*, 2. 851; 16. 554; Plato, *Theaetetus*, 191–5, *Philebus*, 38–40, Timaeus, 71–2; Aristotle, *De anima*, 424a; Aquinas, *De veritate*, Q8 a9; Bacon, *De argumentis*, V. 4; and Locke, *Essay concerning Human Understanding*, II. i. 25, II. xi. 17.

5. It is an important and rarely appreciated fact that the eighteenth-century willingness to regard the secondary qualities as fundamentally subjective provided one of the most important struts of all in the foundations of much formalist aesthetics. Kant, for instance, accepted a Berkeleian interpretation of Locke on this subject, assigned the secondary qualities to the content of material aesthetic judgements, and could not then see his way to acknowledge them as the proper subjects of communicable knowledge. (See *Critique of Judgement*, § 14.) Since Kant takes aesthetic judgements to approach objectivity (despite saying that they have 'only subjective validity') he concludes that they must be based on considerations of form.

6. I draw heavily here on D. Wiggins's 'Truth, Invention and the Meaning of Life', *Proceedings of the British Academy* (1976), 331–78.

7. Cf. W. Dilthey: 'Every square planted out with trees is comprehensible to us because each object is assigned its place by human purposes.' 'Everything that surrounds man he understands in terms of life and mind which he has objectified therein.' Cit. O. F. Bollnow, *Dilthey* (Stuttgart, 1955), 36. See also Heidegger, *Sein und Zeit*, § 31: 'Dasein als Verstehen'.

8. For Kant necessity and universality are marks of judgements of experience in contrast with judgements of perception (see *Prolegomena to any Future Metaphysics* § 18). Aesthetic judgements are objective to the extent that we can come to agree with others about them, and exemplary in that we have something like an obligation to do so. (See *Critique of Judgement*, § 40).

9. See G. Watson, 'Free Agency', *Journal of Philosophy*, 72 (1975), 205–20.

10. Hazlitt, *Works*, ed. P. P. Howe (London, 1931), IV, 68.

11. See M. H. Abrams, *The Mirror and the Lamp* (New York, 1953), esp. Ch. III.

12. Cf. Husserl's distinction between *Welt* and *Lebenswelt*, and Heidegger's insistence on distinguishing between *Welt* and *Erde* in 'Der Ursprung des Kunstwerkes', in *Holzwege* (Frankfurt am Main, 1957).

13. Hegel, XIII, 57–8 (my translation). It is an interesting question just how much of this passage Hegel might have derived from Schiller's *Letters on the Aesthetic Education of Mankind*. See esp. Letters XXIII–XXV.

14. See K. Friedemann, 'Die Romantische Kunstanschauung', *Zeitschrift fur Aesthetik und allgemeine Kunstwissenschaft*, xviii (1925), 487–525.

15. Schelling, *Philosophie der Kunst*, III, § 36.

16. K. W. F. Solger, *Erwin* (Berlin, 1907), 220.

17. Schiller, *Letters on the Aesthetic Education of Mankind*, trans. E. M. Wilkinson and L. A. Willoughby (Oxford, 1962), Letter XIII, fn., 91–3.

18. Ibid.

19. Ibid., Letter IV.

20. Much the same has been said of opium and other drugs. Baudelaire for instance observes this, and immediately makes the connection with the arts in his essay on Delacroix: 'E. Poe dit que le résultat de l'opium pour les sens est de revêtir la nature entière d'un interêt surnaturel qui donne à chaque objet un sens plus profond, plus

volontaire, plus despotique. Sans avoir recours à l'opium, qui n'a connu ces admirables heures, véritables fêtes de cerveau, où les sens plus attentifs perçoivent des sensations plus retentissantes, où le ciel d'un azur plus transparent s'enfonce comme un abîme plus infini, où les sons tintent musicalement, où les couleurs parlent, où les parfums racontent le monde des idées. Eh bien, la peinture de Delacroix me parait la traduction de ces beaux jours de l'esprit. Elle est revêtue d'intensité et sa splendeur est privilégiée.' *Curiosités esthétiques* (Paris, 1922), 251.

21. Hazlitt, IV, 73.

22. See also R. Fry's 'An Essay in Aesthetics' in *Vision and Design* (London, 1957), 18: 'If in a cinematograph we see a runaway horse and cart the appropriate resultant action is cut off; we do not have to think either of getting out of the way or heroically interposing ourselves. The result is we *see* the event much more clearly; see a number of quite interesting but irrelevant things which in real life would not struggle into our consciousness, bent as it would be entirely on the production of the appropriate reaction.'

23. Think how a patriotic Russian may in the light of party propaganda view the end of the Kurile chain as part of Russia rather than of Japan.

24. Cf. Baudelaire: 'Nous savons que les symboles ne sont obscurs que d'une manière relative, c'est-à-dire selon la pureté, la bonne volonté ou la clairvoyance native des âmes. Or, qu'est-ce qu'un pòete si ce n'est un traducteur, un déchiffreur?' *L'Art romantique* (Paris, 1925), 305.

25. Maybe the credit for seeing this is due to Kant. It was he who said (*Critique of Judgement*, § 42) that 'the beautiful prepares us to love something disinterestedly, even Nature herself', and his analysis of the beautiful is, as we have seen, one that is conducted in terms of our ability to find *pleasure* in orderings that we are able to project on to the world. These are surely experiences which enlarge our ability to attach ourselves to the objects of this pleasure, and thus to feel ourselves in harmony with them.

26. E. Muir; *An Autobiography*, (London, 1954), 91.

27. Hume, *Treatise of Human Nature*, II. i. viii, ed. L. A. Selby-Bigge, (Oxford, 1967) 299.

28. See R. Scruton 'Architectural Taste', *British Journal of Aesthetics*, 15 (1975), especially Sec. IV: 'Certain forms look right, and in looking right reassure us of the values that seem implicit in them.' See also 'Architectural Aesthetics', *British Journal of Aesthetics*, 13 (1973). Both articles are substantially reprinted in his *The Aesthetics of Architecture* (London, 1979).

Chapter Six

1. Not that it never happens. Perhaps Old and Middle Kingdom funerary art provides one example, *within* the dominance of that dynasty and for its duration. If the Russian Empire is long lived, within that empire's confines the art of social realism may come to present another.

2. There is no inconsistency between (ii) and (iii). Another artist could have got to Donatello's workshop before Donatello and produced his *St. Michael* from that very block of stone, carving away those same pieces of marble that Donatello in fact carved away (setting aside for the sake of simplicity all problems about the emblematic shield). Nor does this idea threaten us with saying that Donatello's statue must therefore display an indeterminacy, for identification of the statue of my fantasy as being of St. Michael could be explained by reference to some suitable convention about location which may be imagined to have determined the reading that the work would best have received.

3. Homer, *Odyssey*, I, 325.

4. Wilde, *Intentions* (London, 1949), 46.

5. S. N. Hampshire, 'A Ruinous Conflict', *New Statesman*, 4 May 1962.
6. Cit. B. Croce, *Estetica* (Bari, 1912), 428f.
7. Wilde, 'The Critic as Artist', *Complete Works* (London, 1966), 127.
8. C. Rosen, *The Classical Style* (London, 1971), 9.
9. Dante, *Purgatorio*, XI, 95–7.
10. E. H. Gombrich, 'The Renaissance Concept of Artistic Progress and its Consequences', in *Norm and Form* (London, 1966), 1–10.
11. J. Shearman, *Mannerism* (Harmondsworth, 1967), 46.
12. E. H. Gombrich, *Ideas of Progress and their Impact on Art*, Mary Duke Biddle Lectures (New York, 1971), Lecture I.
13. We have to read them in different ways because Dante is being warned by Oderisi against pride, and it is plain that pride is only a serious temptation where the merit that is its object is taken to be genuine and not factitious. Oderisi indicates clearly enough how Dante's merits stand in the lines:

> così ha tolto l'un all'altro Guido
> la gloria della lingua, e forse è nato
> chi l'uno e l'altro caccerà del nido (96–9)

and *immediately* afterwards speaks of the capricious wind. This cannot be more than a stratagem to ensure that Dante is not overcome by pride's 'gran tumore'. Having made his point Oderisi can go on (115–17) with the more accurate image of artistic change which we may take to express Dante's own view and which makes its occurrence a predictable, non-arbitrary matter.
14. J. Dewey, *Art as Experience* (New York, 1955), 109.
15. As late as 1812 Byron, accoutred with opera glasses, attended a Roman execution. 'Quite hot and thirsty' it left him. (See P. Quennell, *Byron in Italy* (London, 1941), 83.)

Chapter Seven

1. Nietzsche, 'Von den Ersten und Letzten Dingen' § 15, in *Menschliches, Allzumenschliches*, I (my translation).
2. Hazlitt, 'On Depth and Superficiality', in *Selected Essays*, ed. G. Keynes (London, 1946), 271–90. It is rarely noticed that we are concerned with the elucidation of a metaphor here. But see M. Tournier, *Vendredi ou les Limbes du Pacifique* (Paris, 1967), 57–8: On his island Crusoe finds he can only speak literally: 'Je ne puis parler qu' *à la lettre*. La métaphore, la litote et l'hyperbole me demandent un effort d'attention démesuré dont l'effet inattendu est de faire ressortir tout ce qu'il y a d'absurde et de convenu dans ces figures de rhétorique. . . . Telle par exemple, cette notion de *profondeur* dont je n'avais jamais songé à scruter l'usage qu'on en fait dans des expressions comme "un esprit profond", "un amour profond" . . . Étrange parti pris cependant qui valorise aveuglément la profondeur aux dépens de la superficie et qui veut que "superficiel" signifie non pas "de vaste dimension", mais de "peu de profondeur", tandis que "profond" signifie au contraire "de grand profondeur" et non "de faible superficie". Et pourtant un sentiment comme l'amour se mesure bien mieux il me semble—si tant est qu'il se mesure—à l'importance de sa superficie qu'au degré de profondeur. Car je mesure mon amour pour une femme au fait que j'aime également ses mains, ses yeux, sa démarche, ses vêtements habituels, ses objets familiers, ceux qu'elle n'a fait que toucher, les paysages où je l'ai vue évoluer, la mer ou elle s'est baignée . . . Tout cela, c'est bien de la superficie, il me semble! Au lieu qu'un sentiment médiocre vise directement—*en profondeur*—le sexe même et laisse tout le reste dans une pénombre indifferente.' Crusoe's reflections here remind us just what a successful elucidation of the metaphor must do; make as much sense as possible of what he sees as absurd and conventional.
3. Examples taken from J. Searle, letter in *Times Literary Supplement*, 22 Oct. 1976.

4. Schopenhauer, *Die Welt als Wille und Vorstellung*, Bk. III, § 52.
5. Proust, *Contre Sainte-Beuve*, Préface (Paris, 1954), 55. 'Chaque jour j'attache moins de prix à l'intelligence. Chacque jour je me rends compte que ce n'est en dehors d'elle que l'écrivain peut resaissir quelquechose de nos impressions, c'est-à-dire atteindre quelquechose de lui même et la seule matière de l'art.'
6. Goethe, *Wilhelm Meisters Lehrjahre*, Bk. III, Ch. xi (my translation).
7. Coleridge, *Biographia Literaria* (Oxford, 1907), II, Ch. xxii, 121.
8. Joyce, *Ulysses* (London, 1949), 335.
9. C. Brooks, 'The Uses of Literature', in *A Shaping Joy* (London, 1971), 12–13.
10. Coleridge, I, Ch. iv, 60.
11. Ibid.
12. Hazlitt, 'Of the Ignorance of the Learned', *Table Talk*, Essay VIII.
13. Pope, *Essay on Criticism*, II. 297–300.
14. Proust, 'Gérard de Nerval', in *Contre Sainte-Beuve* (Paris, 1954), 181.

Chapter Eight

1. 'We desire it because it seems good to us: it does not seem good to us because we desire it.' Aristotle, *Metaphysics*, 1072^a 20.
2. Aquinas, *In divinis nominibus*, 398–9.
3. *Pace* Moore, who saw aesthetics as being as fraught with the naturalistic fallacy as ethics. See *Principia Ethica*, § 121.
4. Alberti, *De re aedificatoria*, Bk. VI, Ch. 2.
5. See Kant, *Critique of Judgement*, § 7.
6. F. Hutcheson, *An Inquiry concerning Beauty, Order, Harmony, Design* (a republication of Treatise I of *An Inquiry into the Original of our Ideas of Beauty and Virtue* (1725)), ed. P. Kivy (The Hague, 1973), 34.
7. Moore, § 121, The last phrase will be true only if we understand him to mean that very beauty the object does have, since organized in a different way the same object might well display a different beauty.
8. R. P. Knight, *An Analytical Inquiry into the Principles of Taste* (London, 1805), 9.
9. R. Scruton, *Art and Imagination*, 134. See also H. N. Lee, *Perception and Aesthetic Value* (New York, 1938), 98.
10. These other properties might be physical properties or aesthetic properties supervenient on physical properties. Hume's own choice of constitution of parts points to the latter.
11. The predicate letter ψ here stands in for the mental set that Hume characterizes disjunctively. The quantifier $\exists o$ ranges over orderings of parts, an ordering being a universal instantiated by individual things.
12. See D. Wiggins's comment of Aristotle's *Metaphysics* 1072^a 20 in 'Deliberation and Practical Reason', *Proceedings of the Aristotelian Society*, (1975/6), 29–52, fn. 5.
13. The recurring phrase 'tends to be such that' serves to weaken the universality of the succeeding conditional to allow occasional failure. This is essential if the elucidation is to be plausible. Dispositional properties are scarcely ever fail-safe.
14. See D. Davidson, 'Causal Relations', *Journal of Philosophy*, 64 (1967), 691–703 and 'The Logical Form of Action Sentences', in *The Logic of Decision and Action*, ed. N. Rescher (Pittsburgh, 1966). Both are reprinted in his *Action and Event*, (Oxford, 1981).
15. Kant actually speaks of harmony between imagination and understanding, but this can only be understood in reference to the object. Hence my way of introducing the object. In a certain way of looking at it, i.e. when imagination and understanding are in free play, we feel ourselves in harmony with it. I do not think this amounts to a travesty of Kant's thought.
16. It may be wondered what this has to do with necessity. The answer is that Kant

calls a judgement necessary if its appropriate assertion by one person entails the appropriateness of its assertion by anybody. See my 'Kant, Truth and Affinity', *Proceedings of the Fourth International Kant Congress* 1974 II.1, 336–45.

17. See P. Ziff, 'Reasons in Art Criticism', *Philosophical Turnings* (Cornell, 1966), 71. Also M. Cohen, 'Aesthetic Essence', in *Philosophy in America*, ed. M. Black (London, 1965), 115–33.

18. Cf. Goethe's *Epigrammatisches*, 'Natur und Kunst':
> In der Beschränkung zeigt sich erst der Meister
> Und das Gesetz nur kann uns Freiheit schaffen.

19. Wittgenstein, *Lectures on Aesthetics*, ed. C. Barrett (Oxford, 1966), 19. Admirers of Kant may find some pre-echo of this thought in his discussion of dependent beauty in *Critique of Judgement*, § 16. Here the beautiful object has to fit a concept and there is a satisfaction in the recognition that it does so. What else could this satisfaction be except a thought that the object is just right 'in reference to the internal purpose that determines its possibility'? It is fortunate that Kant should have given his most serious attention to free beauty, a beauty that he thinks is predicative in contrast with the attributive notion that he tends to regard as impure and of secondary importance.

20. e.g. along the line: (w) (Beautiful work of art w to extent E iff. . . . f causes e & Measure (e) = E), where the measure of e is one of pleasurability.

21. It is of course also compatible with the fact that many beautiful works of art may leave us cold.

22. *Ausgewählte Philosophische Schriften* (Berlin, 1954), 477, in criticism of T. Vischer's *Kritische Gänge* (Stuttgart, 1860–6) V, 25, and VI, 131. Cited by G. Lukács, *Die Eigenart des Aesthetischen* (Berlin, 1963), 2, 525.

23. E. H. Gombrich, *Art and Illusion* (London, 1962), 134.

24. Wilde, 'The Decay of Lying', in *Intentions* (London, 1934), 53 ff.

25. See *Critique of Judgement*, § 45. Earlier than Kant we find a hint of the same idea in Vasari's Preface to Part I of the *Lives*: '. . . art owes its origin to Nature,' he says, and immediately goes on: 'In our own time it has been shown that simple children, roughly brought up in the wilds, have begun to draw by themselves, impelled by their natural genius instructed solely by the example of these beautiful *paintings* and *sculptures* of Nature.' (I, 5. my italics).

26. The response clause may be read as 'y recognized x as a just answer to P and in S'. Similarly in later formulations.

27. Recall that a problem was introduced as no more than a description to which something is made to fit, and a style as no more than a set of aesthetic constraints that determine correctness or incorrectness. Both of these minimal descriptions of the two notions demand further elaboration.

28. Of course he may make a boring choice, or an imaginative one; only it is not criticizable as mistaken or incorrect.

29. Though it is notable that at the end of the century one writer did explicitly ask why we find this pleasure. In a letter to Schiller in February 1793, Körner wrote: 'The pleasure we take in beauty stems from our sympathy with other life. Hence the enthusiasm it awakes—and our endeavour to widen our horizons.' What use may be made of his idea of sympathy emerges in section viii of this chapter.

30. To be interested in the normal case is, I take it, to be interested in what Schiller thought of as 'the pure rational concept of beauty', an a priori notion that has provoked some commentators to derision (e.g. V. Basch, *La Poétique de Schiller* (Paris, 1911), 48). Unlike Schiller (Letter XVI) I presume that the normal or ideal case must be pretty frequently realized.

31. Why we find benign precisely what we do, and why benignity should have motive power for formation of attachment, are perhaps matters for psychology rather than

aesthetics. And unless it enters into the artist's own theory of his own activity and via the mechanism of Chapter 4 into our understanding of his art, this will not be the benignity about which I am talking. Whatever it is that gets into the represented world and determines our judgement of fit must do so by a route to which both artist and spectator have access. It should show up in descriptions that they could both give of the work's world.

32. See n. 2 to Chapter 5.

Chapter Nine

1. See N. Frye, 'On Value Judgements' in *The Stubborn Structure* (London, 1970), 66–73, and *Anatomy of Criticism* (New York, 1966), 20–9.

2. N. Frye, 'Criticism, Visible and Invisible', in *The Stubborn Structure*, 35.

3. N. Frye, *Anatomy of Criticism*, 27.

4. Y. Winters, 'Robert Frost or The Spiritual Drifter as Poet', in *On Modern Poets* (Elnora, New York, 1959), 193.

5. See M. McCarthy, 'The Fact in Fiction' in *On the Contrary* (London, 1962), 252.

6. In the eighteenth century it was quite common to speak of categories of art as though they were rigorously defined by certain rules, and the inability of anyone to produce acceptable definitions across the board has sometimes seemed an objection to my proposal. But the sting of this criticism is removed by our not demanding that the conventions in play should be other than vague, and by not insisting on our ability to articulate them sharply. This was quite clearly perceived by Sir Joshua Reynolds in his *Sixth Discourse*: 'Unsubstantial, however, as these rules may seem, and difficult as it may be to convey them in writing, they are still seen and felt in the mind of the artist; and he works from them with as much certainty as if they were embodied, as I may say, upon paper.' *Works* (ed. E. Malone, 1801), I, 155.

7. Kant's arguments are the first *systematic* ones to make this point, though somewhat similar observations were made a little earlier by his English contemporary James Harris (see *Philosophical Inquiries, Works* IV, 228–9, 234–5). Perhaps we can also detect such a thought in Giordano Bruno's saying a couple of centuries before: 'Conchiudi bene che la poesia non nasce de le regole se non per legerissimo accidente; ma le regole derivano de la poesia; e pero tanti son geni e specie de vere regole, quanti son geni e specie di veri poeti,' *Opere* (ed. A. Wagner, Leipzig, 1830), II, 315.

8. A development of this argument might well be used to controvert any purely formalist aesthetic. An indication that this is so is provided by the incapacity of authors like C. Bell and R. Fry to explain just what it is that is significant about significant form.

9. I once heard Harold Macmillan call the late Sir Robert Menzies 'a great Australian'. Clearly Menzies was not being judged to be as Australian as a man can be. Here there must have been an ellipsis whose understanding the context provides: a great man (or a statesman), and an Australian to boot.

10. The example is not entirely fanciful. For thirty years or more now a Polish mega-sculptor, Korczak Ziolkowski, has been shaping in the rock of the Black Hills of Dakota a granite statue some 560 feet high to commemorate the Sioux chief Crazy Horse, who defeated Custer at Little Bighorn in 1876 and was subsequently killed in United States Army custody (see *The Times*, 20 May 1978). If the Indians come to recognize this monument as one their hero deserves, and think that the statue's size contributes to its being that, why should they not tell strangers that it is a great one with all the evaluative force we are accustomed to hear in the words?

11. Of course these figures may well be admirable in respects other than their outstanding sexual heartlessness, their simony, or their treachery.

12. See Nietzsche, *The Uses and Disadvantages of History for Life*, § 2. Nietzsche explains

the interest we have in monumental history—the history of great men and their deeds—by saying that it reminds us that feats we consider great have actually been achieved. This is proof that they are still possibilities for us.

13. Reynolds, I, 152.

14. Ibid. I, 152–3.

15. It is of crucial importance to realize that this is not inconsistent with our wanting to say that the great achievements of the past are even today of interest to us when estimated against the modes of thought of the past. So too should it be apparent that there is plenty of scope for us to say that, judged against earlier modes of thought, a given work may be better appreciated by us to whom these are strange modes than it was by those to whom they were second nature. Just as for them the good contemporary critic could detect poor judgement, so without any anachronism may we too.

16. Vasari, I, 203 (my italics).

17. C. Rosen, *The Classical Style* (London, 1971), 445. He goes on: 'Beethoven is perhaps the first composer for whom this exploratory function of music took precedence over every other: pleasure, instruction and, even, at times, expression. A work like the *Diabelli* Variations is above all a discovery of the nature of the simplest musical elements, an investigation of the language of classical tonality with all its implications for rhythm and texture as well as melody and harmony.'

18. C. G. Argan, *Brunelleschi* (Mondadori, 1955), 54 (my translation, my italics). Argan is probably quoting from the life of Brunelleschi usually attributed to Antonio Manetti.

19. E. Panofsky, *Problems in Titian, Mostly Iconographic* (London, 1969), Introduction. I have drawn closely here on sentences on pp. 16, 18, and 22.

20. Interestingly enough the same seems to be true of 'perfection'. If I am right in thinking of this as a defeasible notion too it has the provoking consequence that a perfect F may not be one which we are bound to esteem most highly. Perhaps in the case of God this need not worry us because of the specific demands we make of divinities. It is a flaw in a divinity to have any virtues less than maximally developed. Hence a perfect God would of necessity be a great God too.

21. Cf. P. Fuller, *Art and Psychoanalysis* (London, 1980), 21. 'I am tempted to conclude that a very important part of what gives a work of art enduring value concerns the nature of its relationship to elements of experience which do not change, or rather which change at a very slow rate indeed and, for our purposes, may effectively be regarded as constants.'

Chapter Ten

1. Lest the argument here offered should appear vacuous the reader should note that nothing I have yet said in the elucidation of beauty or depth entitles me yet to assume that they make for stature in the art that displays them. This is something whose truth has to be established.

2. Of course this does not imply that if a man *does* believe p and q rationally he will actually believe r. For he may not see that p and q entail r, and therefore not come to believe r at all. It is simply that if the principle is correct it could not be true that (9) and (10) and false that (12)—whatever he in fact believes. *PDC* is not offered here as a rule of acceptance, only as a principle that might elucidate the notion of rational belief.

3. Where this is understood not to exclude the acceptance of p and the acceptance of $\sim p$, but as excluding the conjunctive acceptance of p and $\sim p$. This is a reflection of the fact that rational belief is not closed under deduction.

4. See G. Harman, *Thought* (Princeton, 1971), esp. Ch. 7.

5. Although in the previous pages I have attempted to demonstrate the truth of (17)

as following from that of (15) and (16), (17) would have relied on inductive support in as much as that was what we needed to give us confidence in (15) and (16).

6. It is a matter of considerable interest what the right measure for the best explanation is. Adding explanatory power to our whole set of beliefs in a way that minimizes change, and is maximally coherent, simple, and intuitively plausible while still remaining refutable, would be the sort of thing I have in mind. See Harman, 168, and W. v. O. Quine and J. S. Ullian, *The Web of Belief* (New York, 1970), Ch. IV.

Chapter Eleven

1. Cf. Freud, *Totem and Taboo*, Ch. III, 2: 'Our psychoanalytic work will begin at a different point. It must not be assumed that mankind came to create its first world system through a purely speculative thirst for knowledge. The practical need of mastering the world must have contributed to this effort.' And Freud was no stranger to the idea that one way of mastering the world was to make it up.

2. The example comes from M. Tanner 'Sentimentality', *Proceedings of the Aristotelian Society* (1976/7), 127–47.

3. Ruskin, *The Crown of Wild Olives*, § 118.

4. Not that great art cannot be sentimental. It can, but its greatness cannot have its source in sentimentality as it can in beauty or depth.

5. Consequential because while we may well learn from art that we misperceive, in doing so we shall not learn from it what it has to show—except of course by fluke.

6. My assertion what we use the word 'sentimental' only metaphorically in application to the abstract arts forces me to offer a slightly different argument about them. This can be done by applying the *Principle of Transparency* to the metaphorical base—in the musical case to the recognition that the gratifying emotion is not fully grounded in the music itself. This perception I suggest cannot coexist with the deep embeddedness of the music (if that is what its appeal is supposed to rely on).

7. Cf. Ortega's remark that 'mass' signifies not so much number as inert stuff, not active but merely reactive, in *La rebelión de las masas* (32nd edn., Madrid, 1958), 112.

8. It would be wrong to think that no diversity of thought is allowed here. Rolland gets this right when he speaks of 'le système de bascule, qui est un des lois du goût artistique en France'. He goes on: 'Pour savoir ce qu'il pense, un Français a besoin de savoir ce que pense son voisin, afin de penser de même, *ou de penser le contraire.*' (V, 150. My italics.)

9. This is not to deny that to lead a properly human life I am dependent on my fellows' approval and company: life is naturally social. But within a satisfactory social life we want our views to be genuinely our own.

10. J. Bayley, 'Vulgarity', *British Journal of Aesthetics*, 4 (1964), 298–304.

11. It should not be objected that we do not need to make this allowance on the grounds that vulgarity is always deplorable and that these buildings are so because the entertainment they accommodate is low. That would not only be wrongheaded and priggish but, worse, would be based on the mistake of thinking that the vulgar mind is essentially *flawed*. What is true is that the vulgar mind is *limited*, and that is quite a different matter. Admittedly seaside entertainment will not provide nourishment for everyone, but then it is not meant to. For those to whom it caters it provides vital entertainment and good fun. We have every reason to think well of the uninhibited and boisterous architecture that emphasizes these values.

12. By association because very often there is nothing in certain choices or forms of behaviour that by themselves reveal a vulgar cast of mind. Think, say, of having printed rather than engraved visiting cards, of ignoring the conventions about not tipping club servants, or of wearing a ring on the wrong finger.

13. As (say) does Mrs Brookenham in James's *The Awkward Age*, Bk. II, Ch. vii.

Comparing herself to Lord Petherton she sees herself afflicted with a vulgarity that she takes to be beyond her power to change. But we may think that if only she had a full understanding of what she recognizes in herself it would be far harder than it is to explain how she acts in accordance with the traits that she so deprecates.

14. The phrase 'do dirt on' comes from D. H. Lawrence's 'Pornography and Obscentiy', *Phoenix* (London, 1966), 675: 'Pornography is the attempt to insult sex and do dirt on it.' That does not seem to me to be a good account of pornography, which is quite a different concept from obscenity, but it does I think well describe one form that obscenity can take. It would come nearer to the mark for Lawrence to say that pornography consists in the sexually stimulating representation of sexual activity, and on my account that may well not be obscene. Nor are pleas for the social utility of pornography pleas in defence of obscenity.

15. A. Stokes, *The Critical Writings*, III (London, 1978), 213.

16. No matter how ribald and outrageous are the writings of Boccaccio, Chaucer, Rabelais, *et al.*, which give 'dangerous matter an airing' (Stokes's phrase) they are surely not obscene.

17. R. Meager, 'The Obscene—A new danger in Literature', *Proceedings of the 5th International Congress of Aesthetics* (Amsterdam, 1964), 11 (my italics).

Chapter Twelve

1. J. Ortega y Gasset, *Obras* (Bilbao, 1932), 953 (my translation).

2. Cit. E. H. Gombrich in 'André Malraux and the Crisis of Expressionism', reprinted in *Meditations on a Hobby Horse* (London, 1963), 80.

3. T. Adorno, *Aesthetische Theorie* (Frankfurt am Main, 1970), 262 ff.

4. P. Valéry, *Pièces sur l'art* (Paris, 1934), 103–4 (my italics). What has made the passage so well known is its use by W. Benjamin as an epigraph to the essay discussed in Sec. IV above.

5. 'Normally' is important here. Otherwise we should be forced to exclude as art works such as Donatello's out-of-view statuary in S. Maria del Fiore, which we only understand as art through their oblique reference to the normalcy condition.

6. *Journal*, April 1868. It is interesting to see how P. H. Johnson introduces this remark in her *Six Proust Reconstructions* (London, 1959), 38: 'Goncourt: April 7, 1868. Dinner ... with the Princess [de Guermantes-Bavière] and Sainte-Beuve, the Princess vivacious in a gown of china crêpe, the delicious colour of lime trees in the early sunlight of spring, amethysts about her renaissance brow and on her full and creamy bosom. A woman . . .' The element of self-conscious display is, we suppose, not absent from the Princess's mind.

7. Rolland, IX, 14. 'Determinate', in that we may take 'le soleil' as picking out not just a fixed character or a stable temperament that the artist may transmit to his public through his work, but also a particular thought that is only expressible in the work if it engages with the artist's mind.

8. H. Osborne, 'An Intellectual Crisis in Aesthetics', *Proceedings of the International Conference on Aesthetics* (Cracow, 1979), 218. The stress laid on the individuality of the motor accident might be misleading. Universals are no less individual than particulars. What is essential is that any replication of the same set of properties is not an instance of the same motor accident or Happening. I shall not pursue the uninteresting objection that the examples are miscast as particulars. That would only count against my opponent and would obscure more important matters.

9. Cf. Marinetti's obscene panegyric of the Abyssinian invasion: 'War is beautiful in symphonicly uniting the machine guns, the mortars, the silent intermissions of fire and the odours of putrescence.' That example, even if correct, could not serve here for its very obscenity, which we have already seen is stature-excluding. The *explosif* is not hampered in the same way.

10. Lest it be thought that the example is too silly to be taken seriously it is worth noting Adorno's praise for Stockhausen's conception of electronic music as music not scored in the usual way but ' "realized" through its material', and destroyed in performance. It is, Adorno says, a great conception in that it envisages an art that makes emphatic claims on us, but is at the same time ready to jettison itself, to throw itself away (265). Clearly he thinks that a record of such work would ruin the point. More paradoxical yet would be for the rise of such art to displace other kinds. The whole tenor of modern aesthetics has insisted more and more strenuously on the very reproducibility of art. Witness the work of Valéry, Malraux, and Benjamin for example.

11. The suggestion also makes the false assumption that such imagined art could be understood apart from its actual history. And the history it would have would be constituted by the art that is and has been ours. For it time's test does apply, as has been shown already. So even under the secondary hypothesis my critic's claim is exaggerated. This fact need not be turned against him, though, unless the argument of the remainder of this section fails.

12. See H. Segal, *Introduction to the Work of Melanie Klein* (London, 1973), 42.

13. T. Eagleton, 'Marxism and Aesthetic Value', in *Criticism and Ideology* (London, 1969) 169. The sentence is offered as a gloss on Brecht's 'Anything that was worn out, trivial or so commonplace that it no longer made one think, they did not like. If one needed an aesthetic, one could find it here.' ('Brecht against Lukács', *New Left Review* (March/April 1974).)

14. Pater, 'Style', in *Appreciations* (London, 1898), 32.

15. See Trotsky, *Class and Art, Problems of Culture under the Dictatorship of the Proletariat* (London, 1974). See also Lenin's articles on Tolstoy. Eagleton is inclined to scoff at these writers' insistence on the 'Romantic category of greatness' (op. cit., 174). He speaks of the inability of 'idealism' to render more than subjectivist accounts of criteria of value. 'What is meant by the claim that Yeats is a great poet? Bourgeois criticism has characteristically no convincing answer beyond intuitionist rhetoric.' (179.) For polemical purposes absence of analysis and its impossibility are equated, a contrivance that should deceive no one.

16. e.g. O. K. Werkmeister in 'Marx on Ideology and Art' *New Literary History* (1972/3), 500–18; R. L. Taylor, *Art, an Enemy of the People* (Hassocks, 1978) Ch. 3, and T. Adorno, *Dialektik der Aufklärung* (Amsterdam, 1947).

17. See R. A. Wollheim, 'Sociological Explanation of the Arts', *Atti del 3° Congresso di Estetica* (Turin, 1963), 404–10.

18. But one should not too readily presume that patronly interference may not be beneficial to the work. See Wind, Ch. VI.

19. See A. Hauser, *The Philosophy of Art History* (London, 1951), 27–8: 'The artist never puts these questions to himself in so many words. Seldom does he answer them consciously or directly; nor are they put to him by any particular agents of society.'

20. See Wollheim, 'Sociological Explanation . . .', esp. 405.

21. See Davidson, 'Mental Events', and C. McGinn, 'Natural Kinds and Psycho-Physical Laws', *Aristotelian Society, Supplementary Volume* (1978), 195–220.

22. Cf. Hauser, 38: 'Each generation judges the artistic endeavours of previous ages more or less in the light of its own artistic aims; it regards them with renewed interest and a fresh eye only when they are in line with its own objectives.'

23. Cf. T. Adorno, *Notes on Literature III*: 'The greatness of art consists solely in this, that it brings to view what ideology conceals.'

24. Eagleton, 'Towards a Science of the Text', op. cit, 69.

25. Ibid., 70.

26. Ibid., 69.

27. Eagleton supplements what he says elsewhere by allowing that 'even an histori-

cally alien world may "speak" to us in the present, for human animals share a biological structure even where they do not share a direct cultural heritage. Birth, nourishment, labour, kinship, and sexuality and death are common to all social formations and to all literature.' (Op. cit., 178.) Yet on the very same page he writes: 'Literary works "transcend" their contemporary history, not by rising to the "universal" but by virtue of the character of their concrete relations to it—relations themselves determined by the nature of their historical conditions into which the work is inserted.'

28. Contrast Hauser, 34: 'In art, especially in art, the setting up or postulating of supertemporal values has something about it of "fetishism", which Marx held was the essence of "reification".'
29. Ibid., 27.
30. Stokes, III, 234. See also J.-M. Guyau, *L'Art au point de vue sociologique* (Paris, 1889), 22: 'Art is concerned with what is possible, and constructs a new world which by means of imagination it sets beside the world in which we really live.' (My translation.)
31. Johnson, *Selected Writings*, Penguin edn., (Harmondsworth, 1968), 261.
32. This is quite consistent with allowing that it may be of aesthetic significance that the artist chooses to make what he does of materials that have such-and-such an age. Nor does it exclude the possibility of his aiming at an effect that only comes with age. These are things that we can properly take into account when we judge the work. In the latter case we might even think it proper to modify our usual dating practice to take the ageing into account, so that when the work has acquired the desired patina we could speak of it as in its first youth.
33. The same argument also rules out veneration rooted in the admiration the work has enjoyed from venerated men.
34. Arnold, *Essays in Criticism, Second Series* (London, 1913), 10.
35. T. Adorno, *Minimal Moralia* (Frankfurt am Main, 1951), § 143 'In nuce'.
36. Balzac, *La Peau de chagrin*, Ch. III. The lorgnon is a device de Valentin ingeniously commissions to help him avoid entertaining desires which once conceived are magically realized and thereby shorten his life.
37. M. Horkheimer, *Studies in Philosophy and Social Science*, IX (1941), 304.
38. Schopenhauer, *Paraerga and Paralipomena*, I, 'On Philosophy in the Universities' trans. E. Payne (Oxford, 1974), 158, 180.
39. E. H. Gombrich, *Meditations on a Hobby Horse*, 80. Cf. also Ortega's remark 'La ardua faena del historiador, del filologo, consiste justemente en reconstruir el sistema latente de supuestos y convicciónes de que emanaron los obras de otros tempos.' (995.) For an example in a restricted domain of the difficulties one faces see Paul and Eva Badura-Skoda on the tonal quality of Mozart's piano writing in *L'Art de jouer Mozart au piano* (Paris, 1974), Chapter I.

Index of Names